Elusive Security

NEW MILLENNIUM BOOKS
IN INTERNATIONAL STUDIES
Series Editors
Deborah J. Gerner, University of Kansas
Eric Selbin, Southwestern University

NEW MILLENNIUM BOOKS issue out of the unique position of the global system at the beginning of a new millennium in which our understandings about war, peace, terrorism, identity, sovereignty, security, and sustainability—whether economic, environmental, or ethical—are likely to be challenged. In the new millennium of international relations, new theories, new actors, and new policies and processes are all bound to be engaged. Books in the series are of three types: compact core texts, supplementary texts, and readers.

Editorial Board

Titles in the Series

Global Backlash
Edited by Robin Broad

Globalization and Belonging
Sheila Croucher

The Global New Deal
William F. Felice

Sword & Salve
Peter J. Hoffman and Thomas G. Weiss

International Law in the 21st Century
Christopher C. Joyner

Elusive Security
Laura Neack

The New Foreign Policy
Laura Neack

Negotiating a Complex World, Second Edition
Brigid Starkey, Mark A. Boyer, and Jonathan Wilkenfeld

Global Politics as if People Mattered
Mary Ann Tétreault and Ronnie D. Lipschutz

Military-Civilian Interactions, Second Edition
Thomas G. Weiss

Elusive Security

States First, People Last

Laura Neack

ROWMAN & LITTLEFIELD PUBLISHERS, INC.
Lanham • Boulder • New York • Toronto • Plymouth, UK

ROWMAN & LITTLEFIELD PUBLISHERS, INC.

Published in the United States of America
by Rowman & Littlefield Publishers, Inc.
A wholly owned subsidiary of The Rowman & Littlefield Publishing Group, Inc.
4501 Forbes Boulevard, Suite 200, Lanham, Maryland 20706
www.rowmanlittlefield.com

Estover Road, Plymouth PL6 7PY, United Kingdom

British Library Cataloguing in Publication Information Available

Library of Congress Cataloging-in-Publication Data
Neack, Laura
  Elusive security : states first, people last / Laura Neack.
    p. cm.—(New millennium books in international studies)
  Includes bibliographical references and index.
  ISBN-13: 978-0-7425-2865-9 (cloth : alk. paper)
  ISBN-10: 0-7425-2865-0 (cloth : alk. paper)
  ISBN-13: 978-0-7425-2866-6 (pbk. : alk paper)
  ISBN-10: 0-7425-2866-9 (pbk. : alk. paper)
  1. National security. 2. Security, International. 3. Respect for persons. 4. Human
rights. I. Title. II. Series.

  UA10.5.N435 2006
  355'.033—dc22

                                                                    2006017355

Printed in the United States of America

♾™ The paper used in this publication meets the minimum requirements of
American National Standard for Information Sciences—Permanence of Paper
for Printed Library Materials, ANSI/NISO Z39.48-1992.

This book is dedicated to all parents around the world who struggle in trying times to provide security for their children and their children's children.

Contents

Acknowledgments

My gratitude goes to Mustafa (Paul) Rejai for his generous endowment of the Rejai Professorship and to Miami University for bestowing this honor on me these past several years. Thanks, too, to my department chair, Ryan Barilleaux, for protecting me from a few extra committees while I was working on this project. My colleague Patrick Haney deserves a "shout out," too, for reading and commenting on an earlier draft.

I am appreciative as well for the editorial advice of Susan McEachern, editorial director for New Millennium Books at Rowman & Littlefield, who inherited this project without blinking an eye. Thanks also to Alden Perkins, production editor, especially for her patient replies to my e-mail messages; Bruce Owens, copyeditor; and M. Kent Bolton for his review. My gratitude also goes to NMB series editors Deborah Gerner and Eric Selbin for their enduring encouragement and good cheer. New Millennium Books is one of many outstanding legacies of Misty Gerner, and I am proud to have been associated with her in this endeavor.

Special thanks go to my son Harry Neack for his research assistance and student perspective on earlier chapters. And, of course, any mistakes of fact or judgment herein are entirely my own. My deepest gratitude goes to my husband, Roger Knudson, for reading and rereading multiple drafts of this book nearly on demand after putting in his own long days at the academy. His "outsider" perspective and renaissance insight helped me beyond measure.

1

Elusive Security

This is a book about the elusive nature of security. Security is elusive because we remain in the grasp of a centuries-old ethic that ultimately is self-defeating. That ethic insists that states are the primary and most important international actors, can rely ultimately only on themselves for protection, and must keep all options on the table toward the goal of achieving security.

This book is about the idea of security and the ideas embedded in security policies. In the modern era, the sovereign state has been seen as the primary and generally exclusive referent of security discussions; international and human security have been understood as derivative of state security. In order to understand why states have such difficulty achieving security individually and collectively, we must dissect this idea of state primacy. If there ever was a time when states could pursue their security without regard for and without the help of others, that time has long passed. The security threats of today require cooperative action, but the leaders of states are disinclined to work together because they cling to this centuries-old ethic.

Security is a concept that can be widened to include almost any facet of state, international, and human existence. My focus here is limited to a discussion of security from violence. First and foremost, I explore how states act unilaterally to secure themselves against violent attack. Following this, I consider twentieth-century efforts to protect states through the construction of an international security system. Finally, I explore how the security of human beings has mattered only in terms of servicing the state's security needs.

This journey begins by asking questions taken from the headlines. What does it mean to be secure in a world in which a suicide bomber might at any moment walk into a restaurant in Israel and detonate explosives strapped to her waist, murdering innocent civilians in order to publicize the brutal reoccupation of Palestinian territories by the Israeli army? What does it mean to be secure in a world in which young children in Sierra Leone and Liberia have their hands or arms hacked off in order to demonstrate how weak the government is and how strong the opposition? What does it mean to be secure in a world in which commercial aircraft are turned into weapons of mass destruction by hijackers who steer them into the sides of skyscrapers in New York City? Is there such a thing as security in such a world?

What is security? When the Israeli government demolishes the family home of a suicide bomber or launches a retaliatory air strike against alleged terrorist training camps in other countries, will Israeli citizens gain more security from the threat of suicide bombings? The suicide bomber who killed nineteen people in Haifa, Israel, in early October 2003 did not attend a foreign-based terrorist training camp. Instead, Hanadi Jaradat was a twenty-eight-year-old woman from Jenin in the West Bank who attended law school and was about to qualify as a lawyer.[1] Her sister believed that Hanadi Jaradat was motivated by revenge. A few months earlier, her brother and cousin had been killed by Israeli forces. What did security mean to Jaradat? What did it mean to her surviving family members who expressed pride in her suicide attack?[2]

What did security mean to the Jewish and Arab families who jointly owned and operated the restaurant where Jaradat killed herself and nineteen others? What was security to lunch patron Bruriya Zer-Aviv, her son, daughter-in-law, and two grandchildren, none of whom survived Jaradat's act of revenge?[3] Were the lives of any Israelis or Palestinians or anyone living in the wider Middle East region made more secure when Israel, acting in the name of national security, retaliated for the Haifa bombing by launching air strikes against a location in neighboring Syria *and* demolishing the Jaradat home in the West Bank?

What is security? This book attempts to sort out the many definitions and referents of security in this post–Cold War, post-9/11 world. The International Commission on Intervention and State Sovereignty has called this a time marked by "a convulsive process of state fragmentation and state formation that is transforming the international order itself."[4] The international order is being transformed by pervasive violence and insecurity as well as unilateral and multilateral efforts to curb this violence and restore security.

This book is offered as a way to understand what governments and security analysts mean when they make claims in defense of *national security*, what internationalists mean when they seek to protect and strengthen *international security*, and what international organizations, nongovernmental organizations (NGOs), individuals, and even some governments mean when they assert that the best way to ensure state and international security is first to ensure *human security*. I make no pretense of balancing these three referents of security by giving equal time to each. The international order as we know it privileges states over all others and national security over all else. Issues of international and human security come up in any discussion of national security, to be sure, but current-day notions of international and human security can be understood only in terms of their relationship to state security. To understand these related terms, we must begin and remain for a while with the state and its search for elusive security.

Defining Security

Defining security is no easy task. The *Penguin Dictionary of International Relations* says that security is a "term which denotes the absence of threats to scarce values. In principle security can be absolute, that is to say freedom from all threat is the equivalent of complete security."[5] This definition is as good or as bad as any other. "Freedom from *all* threat" sounds like an impossible objective. Can we even begin to name all the threats that might endanger our values? Are there some we might overlook or not understand as threats until too late? If freedom from *all* threat is unimaginable because we cannot imagine all possible threats that might arise, is there some degree of freedom from threat that will make us feel secure? If we cannot feel 100 percent secure, can we feel 90 percent secure? If we can agree on the degree to which we want to feel secure, what methods should we take to best achieve that security? Can we or should we attempt to secure all values to the same degree, or are some more important to us than others? What do we mean by "values" and "threats"? Unfortunately, the dominant understanding of national security has done little to answer these questions in a way that might lead to a more "secure" state or world.

One of the most widely quoted academic definitions of security was offered by Arnold Wolfers in 1962:

> Security points to some degree of protection of values previously acquired. . . . [A] nation is secure to the extent to which it is not in danger of having to sacrifice core values, if it wishes to avoid war, and is able, if challenged, to

maintain them by victory in such a war. This definition implies that security rises and falls with the ability of a nation to deter an attack, or to defeat it. This is in accord with the common usage of the term.

   Security is a value, then, of which a nation can have more or less and which it can aspire to have in greater or lesser measure. . . . [S]ecurity, in an objective sense, measures the absence of fear that such values will be attacked.[6]

David Baldwin, another widely quoted security scholar, suggests rephrasing Wolfers's definition because of the ambiguity in the phrase "absence of threats." Baldwin's rephrasing is that security entails "a low probability of damage to acquired values."[7] Even with this rephrasing, the definition is troublesome because of the things left unspecified in it: values, threats, and damage.

Defining security will remain a persistent problem throughout this book. The definitional problem drives an operational problem: without a clear understanding of what we are securing and what we are securing against, how do we know when we have found the right policy, doctrine, weapon, or alliance that will in fact secure us? Definitional and operational problems ultimately are political problems. Political problems turn on value judgments, and the ultimate value judgment is determining what must be secured at what expense.

As confusing as this might seem, I seek to explore security and its attendant ideas on a practical level in this book. Much of the definitional work has been done for us. Although we might have heated arguments about the proper ways to defend against, say, invasion or terrorism, the starting point for our arguments was established long before any of us were here. The international system of the present day is constructed on very old, very well-entrenched assumptions and definitions.

To say that the starting point for our discussion is long established is not to imply that this starting point is "right" or "correct" or inevitable. Those of us who might wish to construct a less violent and more human-friendly world need to work with what is and has been. This book attempts to set forth what is and has been and to expose the flaws and self-defeating assumptions that cause states (and their people and the world) to remain insecure. The current international system has had a long time to develop in the way it has; it cannot easily be dismantled short of a major catastrophic event that would serve no good purpose! However, this present order could be made more humane and thus more secure at multiple levels. In these pages, I will examine the rules of the security game that are well entrenched and the ways in which these rules do not help to make the world or the people in it more secure. In this, perhaps, will be suggestions for how we might revise the rules to obtain security.

Organization of This Book

Chapter 2 starts by defining national security. As we will explore, security has both internal and external dimensions; the state (or, more precisely, the ruling regime) seeks to secure itself from all those who seek to replace it from within or without. In chapter 2, I also examine the concept of sovereignty in its internal and external dimensions and how protecting sovereignty became the primary purpose of states since the mid-seventeenth century. The struggle for national security in a world of sovereign (and technically equal) states may come down to a violent struggle to maintain one's sovereignty against the claims of other sovereign states. I look at contemporary examples to see how, even today, ruling state authorities guard against potential limitations on their sovereignty. I also consider what is meant by the concept of the state and how this differs from the concept of the nation. This difference is critical in determining who gets protected by the state's use of violence as well as who gets targeted by state violence. I conclude this chapter by reviewing how the use of violence has been integral to the process of building internally and externally secure states.

A fundamental feature of the post-9/11 world is the recognition that even the most stable states are not fully secure from terrorism. Chapter 3 examines how terrorism has been and is politically defined. I take up here the idea that one person's terrorist is another person's freedom fighter. I also examine the internationalization and increasing lethality of terrorism and consider how states defend the homeland against this threat.

Chapter 4 takes up the larger issue of threats and how states perceive and respond to them. I consider the bedrock notion of international anarchy—the idea that there is no overarching international political authority to protect states from one another. We see that because of the predominant value placed on state sovereignty in international politics, no overarching international political authority *could* be created to protect states. Thus, to survive in a world so imagined, states must see threats in every other actor's behaviors. What do states do in such a system when they perceive ubiquitous threats to their interests? I conclude this chapter by examining strategies aimed at balancing against threats or accommodating and bandwagoning with the source of threats. Alliances and coalitions are part of this discussion.

In chapter 5, I examine defensive national security policies aimed at protecting against the possibility of an enemy using force or violence to cause unacceptable damage to one's territory, population, or critical infrastructure. The first topic here is the odd notion of using military force to protect against the use of military force. Next, I take up the defense dilemma or the inevitable and problematic trade-offs that states make when they decide to secure some national values rather than others. The defense dilemma is evident in deterrence policies, especially those involving nuclear weapons and what is called "stable nuclear deterrence." I also consider here the value of containment policies over deterrence. Finally, I look briefly at an idea that seems somewhat alien to this violent, state-centric system: I examine how states might pursue national security through what is called defensive or nonprovocative defense.

States sometimes go on the offensive rather than wait for security threats to materialize. Chapter 6 explores going on the offensive by first exploring historical discussions on the positive value of war. Then I move to discuss particular offensive policy formulations starting with the Bush doctrine elaborated by the Bush administration in its war on terror. I compare the Bush doctrine to the concepts of preemptive and preventive war and attempt to distinguish one from the other. This leads to a consideration of when and why states engage in military intervention. Finally, I consider offensive strategies in light of so-called new wars involving nonstate actors, such as insurgencies and international terrorist groups.

With this foundation in place, chapter 7 discusses twentieth-century efforts to construct an international security system. The twentieth century saw the beginning of universal institutionalized agreements among great and small powers. Twentieth-century great powers were like great powers of previous times in that they used their military might to construct a world order that kept them privileged and protected. But in the twentieth century, great powers also conceded to building institutions that appeared to constrain them as well. Early in the century, national leaders agreed on the need to curb the use of armed force by states because armed force threatened globalization and because global threats required cooperative rather than unilateral responses. Yet states would not leave behind their fundamental belief that international security must be premised on state sovereignty, creating a tension that put strains on the most famous twentieth-century international security system, the United Nations.

Chapter 8 makes the discussion in chapter 7 more tangible by looking specifically at the UN international security system. I explore the ideas that drove the founding of the UN system and how the winners of World War II ensured that the UN Security Council would be a rigid, unchanging great power system. A primary argument in this chapter is that the UN Charter established an international security system that openly supported a great power spoils-of-war system *and* promoted a more idealistic commitment to establishing universal rules governing the use of force. This contradiction limits effective UN intervention to promote international peace and security. Part of the discussion here involves examining collective security within the United Nations from the 1950–1953 Korean War to the post–Cold War era and the 1991 Gulf War.

The contradictions contained in the UN system are in a delicate balance, a balance that was nearly upset by a crisis in the early years of the United

Nations. In response to this, some visionaries interpreted the UN Charter to allow neutral peacekeeping and later not-so-neutral peace enforcement. Chapter 9 explores how the United Nations has attempted to restore and keep the peace through peacekeeping and peace enforcement using key cases from the 1990s. I examine the problems and failures of the United Nations as well as proposals for improving the way the United Nations might help keep the peace.

Many of the UN interventions in the 1990s were prompted by massive humanitarian disasters. These interventions often did little to stop large-scale violence that claimed many lives. Because the international system privileges states over all other entities, human beings have been seen as assets of or liabilities to states. National efforts to secure the state often lead to acute human insecurity. Debates over security still stumble over questions of who should be protected from violence and how as well as whether there exists an obligation or responsibility to protect others—states, neighborhoods of states, and regular people—from the harmful externalities of one's own pursuit of security. Chapter 10 explores efforts by individuals, NGOs, and states to promote a human security agenda that would move the human person to the forefront of national security discussions. We examine how the land-mine ban treaty and the International Criminal Court are efforts to link human and national security. I also consider proposals that assert an international responsibility to protect human beings from large-scale violence when states cannot or will not and how these proposals fared in the recent 2005 World Summit of national leaders. Efforts to promote a responsibility to protect human beings from violence have yet to make headway in this state-dominated world.

The reader will find that each chapter explores key concepts and debates, blending old arguments with more contemporary illustrations and case applications. Boxed material provides extra cases and information in some chapters. Case studies offer helpful entries into more difficult conceptual material and help us understand the real-world consequences of arguments over ideas. To start our discussion of elusive national, international, and human security, let's consider a first case study under the simple question "Whose security?" This case study will be taken up from time to time throughout this book.

Whose Security? Or, "What We Seek to Protect Reflects What We Value"[8]

Two weeks before the massive 9/11 terrorist attacks on the United States, a humanitarian crisis was brewing in the South Pacific. Although the crisis would fall off the radar screens of most of the world on 9/11, one

country in particular claimed that 9/11 and the crisis combined to illumi-
nate a major national security threat. The story of that crisis in the Pacific
can help us begin to delineate national, international, and human security
concerns and take us firmly into the exploration of our first major topic:
national security.

On August 26, 2001, an Indonesian ferry packed with people began to
sink about halfway between the Indonesian island of Java and Australia's
Christmas Island. Acting in reply to the ferry's distress call, the Norwegian
freighter *Tampa* rescued 438 people. These people were mostly Afghan and
mostly men (there were twenty-six women and forty-three children as
well). The rescued people asked to be taken to Christmas Island, but on
August 27, Australia refused to grant permission to the *Tampa* to offload
the people on its territory. According to the Australian government, all the
people were unauthorized migrants—that is, people attempting to enter
Australia without visas or other proper documentation.

The Australian government did not want the migrants to set foot on
Australian national territory. The government's position was that the
Afghans should be taken to the nearest port of call, which would be in
Indonesia. Indonesia refused to take the rescued people and warned that
it would take blocking action to prevent the *Tampa* from entering its
waters. The captain of the *Tampa*, the government of Norway, and the UN
High Commissioner for Refugees (UNHCR) insisted that Australia had a
moral and legal obligation to assist the rescued people by letting them
land on Christmas Island. Although the migrants were no longer on a
sinking ship, the *Tampa* did not have adequate facilities or enough food
and water for so many people. The living conditions on board deterio-
rated with each passing day.

Three days into the crisis, the captain of the *Tampa* steered the freighter
into Australian waters off Christmas Island. In response, Australian navy
commandos boarded the freighter and took control of it and its crew. The
situation remained in this tense stalemate for several more days as
regional and international diplomats attempted to find a mutually acceptable solution. Ultimately, New Zealand and Nauru offered to take the
Afghans until their claims for asylum were processed. On September 3,
the Afghans were transferred to an Australian troopship for transport to
New Zealand and Nauru. In a controversial move, Australia agreed to
give some U.S.$10 million to Nauru for taking in the migrants.

Why was the Australian government so adamant about not letting the
Afghans land on Australian territory? The simplest answer is that the
government did not wish to incur responsibility for these people. But a
simple answer may not do justice to the concerns of the Australian government.

The Afghans were not typical, legal migrants to Australia or even
tourists, students, or people doing business. They had left behind a coun-

try that was mostly under the domination of the repressive Taliban regime; thus, one might safely assume that they were fleeing persecution. If this were the case, the 1951 Convention on the Status of Refugees would apply, and the Afghans could be properly labeled "refugees." By the 1951 Convention, a refugee is

> Any person who owing to a well founded fear of being persecuted for reasons of race, religion, nationality, membership of a particular social group or political opinion, is outside the country of his nationality and is unable, or owing to such fear, is unwilling to avail himself of the protection of that country; or who, not having a nationality and being outside the country of his former habitual residence, is unable, or owing to such fear, is unwilling to return to it.

If the Afghans themselves had not been subject to persecution, they may have been fleeing the ongoing violence of Afghanistan's unresolved civil war. By various regional agreements starting with a 1969 policy adopted by the Organization of African Unity and reinforced by a 1984 declaration by the Organization of American States, the global standard on refugees also includes "persons who have fled their country because their lives, safety or freedom have been threatened by generalized violence, foreign aggression, internal conflicts, massive violation of human rights or other circumstances which have seriously disturbed the public order."[9]

By the 1951 Convention and in line with ongoing international custom, refugees have a right to remain in the country of first asylum, that is, a right to remain in the first country to which they flee. Also by the 1951 Convention and subsequent practice, host countries agree not to forcibly return the refugees to their home countries (this is known as the principle of *nonrefoulement*).[10] Once a refugee enters a country and claims asylum, the host country is obligated to conduct an inquiry into whether the person has a proper claim to asylum or safe haven. The UNHCR was established in the post–World War II period to assist refugees and states in the logistics of processing asylum claims and caring for the short-term basic needs of refugees.

Despite international agreements, customs, and expected behaviors, whether and how states grant asylum to claimants is ultimately left to the prerogative of states. A state may decide a claimant was not, in fact, fleeing persecution based on his or her ethnic, religious, or political affiliation or fleeing to avoid clear threats of violence. As Laura Barnett explains, "Although [the 1951] Convention guarantees refugees the right to seek asylum it cannot grant the right to obtain asylum, as this is strictly a national prerogative. In fact, UNHCR has no formal supervisory mechanism with a mandate to review state performance."[11] States decide whether and how they will assist refugees and whether and how they will process and allow asylum claims. Some states are more generous in this regard, some far less so. The decision to allow in "unauthorized migrants" is left to states because the modern international system privileges the rights of states above all other entities. As Barnett puts it, the concept of refugees has been entrenched firmly "within the territorial notion of boundaries"—of *state* boundaries.[12]

Why would states accept refugees and assist in processing their claims to asylum? All kinds of humanitarian reasons come to mind. A basic belief in the dignity and worth of every human being might lead a country to want to help people fleeing from repressive governments or violent places. Humanitarian concerns might also combine with political reasons for giving sanctuaries to refugees. During the Cold War, persons fleeing communist countries were given all possible assistance by the United States when requesting safe haven. The cause of political prisoners sitting in Soviet jails often preoccupied Western governments and NGOs. Countries might also act on the moral imperative that there is a basic obligation to help people in need.

Why would states refuse to allow in refugees? There are many specific and immediate reasons that could be given. The refugees could put economic strains on the host country, diverting resources from the care and protection of its citizens. The refugees, if admitted and settled into the host country, might create social tensions between different peoples, especially in regard to the availability of jobs and the distribution of finite government resources. The host country may be inundated with refugees while other just-as-capable countries are left free of the problem. All these reasons were given at various times by Australian government officials, editorial writers, and everyday citizens to justify "pushing off" the Afghan migrants to other countries.

There is an additional reason why Australia might wish to push off these migrants: they might have included "sleepers" or members of terrorist groups who sought to enter Australia in order to live quietly among its citizens while studying how to attack it. This is a problem cast in an especially sharp light by the magnitude of the subsequent 9/11 attacks on the United States and the 2002 Bali bombings in Indonesia that specifically targeted Australians. The threat of "sleeper cells" had to be taken seriously by Australian authorities.

When states take in boat people or other kinds of refugees, they make a clear statement in support of the rights and security of the individual person. When states take in refugees, they also signal their participation in and responsibility to international order. When states refuse to take in refugees, they assert a "higher" obligation than the protection of stateless individuals or the protection of international order: that obligation is to defend the state and its interests above all else. This right is firmly supported by the organizing ideas that form the foundation of the international system dating back to the mid-seventeenth century.

The international system since the mid-seventeenth century is what we call *state-centric*, that is, the primary and most important unit in the system is the state. All the "rules" of international behavior as well as the "rules" of domestic politics flow from the primacy of the state. Contemporary discussions of national security, international security, and human security must begin with an understanding of how the state came to be primary. I turn to this discussion in the next chapter.

2

National Security

The State . . . must create for itself its own imaginary right and necessity for existence, because no other authority can create this on its behalf; and because there does not exist any directive and arbitrative State-authority over all States.

—Friedrich Meinecke, 1924[1]

The state—or the government that speaks for the state—acts preemptively, marshaling all its power to meet the enemy and answering to no one but itself. The chapter-opening quote from a historian writing early in the twentieth century speaks to these ultimate operating principles of the state. There is a fundamental agreement among states about the essential national security doctrine: states must protect themselves and have a right to protect themselves against threats. At the same time, however, there is considerable disagreement about the national security method; from country to country and even within countries and particular governments, there is wide disagreement about what steps are necessary to ensure some degree of protection against threats.

Internal versus External Security

As discussed in the previous chapter, when the Australian government set up a naval quarantine line to stop boats of unauthorized migrants coming from Indonesia, the government was protecting Australia from what it deemed a threat. The threat posed by unauthorized migrants before 9/11 might not be characterized as a *national security* threat. Instead, the boat people represented more mouths to feed, more jobs to supply, more different people to accommodate in the societal mix, and so on. The threat posed by boat people *after* 9/11 was portrayed by Australian authorities as a matter of national security, with loud worries about the real intention of the undocumented migrants and the possibility that they might form terrorist "sleeper cells" inside Australia. Keeping would-be terrorists *out* of Australia is an issue of external security. Identifying and detaining would-be terrorists *inside* Australia is an issue of internal security.

For most countries, security as a function of the government is divided for practical (and conceptual) reasons into external concerns and internal concerns. External security in traditional terms—that is, security against a military attack launched from the outside—is handled primarily by defense ministries or departments of defense. Defense ministries are frequently assisted in their duties by other government agencies with a strong external face; for example, the U.S. Department of Defense often works with the Department of State to provide an external security net.

Internal security is not typically maintained by defense ministries using the national military. The exception to this would be in countries in which civil war or some active and sustained insurgency necessitates the use of the national army to fight a war against an internal enemy. Contemporary Colombia is the site of a long-standing, multiparty civil war in which the government uses the national army and military assistance from its ally the United States in its efforts against multiple armed opponents.

In countries not beset by civil war or insurgency where national power has been firmly consolidated in the hands of a central, civilian government, national militaries are generally not used to provide for and maintain internal security. Instead, the central government makes use primarily of interior police, such as the Gendarmerie in Turkey, the National Police Force in South Africa, or the Federal Bureau of Investigation in the United States. Governments generally treat disturbances to internal security as criminal matters that must be met with law enforcement efforts. Law enforcement agencies are often assisted by internal intelligence-gathering agencies. Thus, uncovering the whereabouts of suspected terrorist sleeper cells among refugees or other immigrant communities in Australia would be the task of the Australian Security Intelligence Organization, whose actionable information would be tasked to the Australian Federal Police, perhaps with the help of local police.[2] Even domestically based groups who may harbor plans—realistic or overly ambitious—to disrupt or overthrow a country's government typically are treated as law enforcement problems. This is the case whether the group is homegrown or comes from abroad. (See extended discussion box 2.1 for the example of the U.S. Department of Justice versus the millennialist cult the Branch Davidians.) Later I discuss how states respond internally and externally to terrorist threats specifically. For now, I'll stay with the more general theme.

Governments treat external and internal security threats as different matters to be handled by different agencies or departments. The threat posed to the United States by al-Qaeda operatives outside the United States is handled primarily by the Department of Defense along with the assistance of the Central Intelligence Agency, the Department of State, and other agencies. The activities of these government agencies are aimed outward and take place on foreign soil and international waters. The threat posed by al-Qaeda sleeper cells within the United States is handled primarily by the Department of Homeland Security and some of its many subsidiary agencies. The activities of Homeland Security take place on U.S. soil.

Within security studies, analysts often make a similar distinction between external and internal threats. In some tangible ways, this division makes the subject matter easier to handle. The division also derives from a Western world versus Third World distinction left over from Cold War days. In the West during the Cold War, security threats were defined as primarily external in nature and required primarily a military response. In the developing world, by contrast, and "despite the rhetoric of many Third World leaders, the sense of insecurity from which these states suffer[ed] emanate[d] largely from within their boundaries rather than from outside."[3] Internal security threats have external ramifications because, as Mohammed Ayoob points out, "these internal conflicts are frequently transformed into interstate conflicts because of their spillover effect into neighboring, often similarly domestically insecure states."[4]

These spillover effects can have enormous consequences for both neighboring and faraway states. Internally weak or failing states become the training camps and launching pads for international terrorism and transnational criminal organizations. The internal-external security divide is becoming more blurred over time, although most states still respond to internal threats differently than they do external threats and most security analysts will focus on one or the other side of security issues.

Protecting the State's Core Values

With the understanding that national security has both internal and external components and that these are generally addressed using different policies and government agencies, let's explore what is meant by the term "national security." An important qualification is in order: the following

national
security
threatened
by external
sources

discussion starts with the assumption that national security is threatened by *external* sources. In time, we'll see how the concepts discussed can be used to describe both external and internal threats.

One of the most widely used definitions of security is credited to Arnold Wolfers writing in 1962:

Security points to some degree of protection of values previously acquired. . . . [A] nation is secure to the extent to which it is not in danger of having to sacrifice core values, if it wishes to avoid war, and is able, if challenged, to maintain them by victory in such a war. This definition implies that security rises and falls with the ability of a nation to deter an attack, or to defeat it. This is in accord with the common usage of the term.

Security is a value, then, of which a nation can have more or less and which it can aspire to have in greater or lesser measure. . . . [S]ecurity, in an objective sense, measures the absence of fear that such values will be attacked.[5]

Many scholars have tried to refine Wolfers's definition, especially after the Cold War ended and Western scholars began to broaden their focus beyond military security against Soviet-based threats.[6] The essential elegance of Wolfers's definition is that it accommodates such alterations in the political environment that would in turn alter the types of values to be secured.

Wolfers suggests a definition that allows room for divergent policies aimed at protecting core values. Even core values are open to variations on theme. To some degree, this variance, in Wolfers's words, makes national security an "ambiguous symbol." This is not to say that national security cannot be pinned down or that "national security" is an endlessly expanding term. Instead, Wolfers asserts that national security has an established discourse:

We know roughly what people have in mind if they complain that their government is neglecting national security or demanding excessive sacrifices for the sake of enhancing it. Usually those who raise the cry for a policy oriented exclusively toward this interest are afraid that their country underestimates the external dangers facing it or is being diverted into idealistic channels unmindful of these dangers. Moreover, the symbol suggests protection through power and therefore figures more frequently in the speech of those who believe in reliance on national power than of those who place their confidence in model behavior, international co-operation, or the United Nations to carry their country safely through the tempests of international conflict.[7]

Wolfers uses the word "security" interchangeably with "national security." To Wolfers, national security connotes measures taken to protect the "national self" as distinguished from the protection of some narrow group (such as the ruling regime or officeholders) or some more expansive, international interests. The national self is embodied in the state. Protection of the national self—national security—is privileged over protection of the international community or protection of individual human beings in both academic and practitioner accounts of security. R. B. J. Walker explains that this is because

the meaning of security is tied to historically specific forms of political community. . . . In the modern world, states have managed to more or less monopolize our understanding of what political life is and where it occurs . . .

The security of states dominates our understanding of what security can be, and who it can be for, not because conflict between states is inevitable, but because other forms of political community have been rendered almost unthinkable.[8]

This is not to suggest that national security has no connection to international or human security. As we will see in chapter 7, international security traditionally is defined in terms of securing the international order for states. When states define their national security in terms of connections to the broader community (as most do in some manner), it is because they perceive that their security cannot be ensured without the assistance and cooperation of others. I will discuss this in due time. But the important point remains that in the hierarchy of security referents, national security historically and presently dominates.

What about the national unit must be secured? Earlier I quoted from Wolfers, who said that states seek to ensure the security of their core values. Essentially, all states seek to protect three core values: territorial integrity and protection of citizens, political independence and autonomy, and economic well-being. These three values often come into conflict with one another. For example, to become more economically well off, a government may choose to deepen interdependence with a common market or economic trade bloc. Entrance into that group, however, requires coordination of policies such that some autonomy in economic decision making is lost. Or a country may choose to be economically less well-off in order to put maximum emphasis on political autonomy. This might be done by severing trade ties to a former colonial power, although cutting such ties may seriously undermine economic wealth in the short term. Protecting and enhancing one core value may come at the expense of another. This is particularly the case when the security of one value is pursued as if to achieve "ultimate security" or the removal of all threats of damage to that value. For example, attempting to ensure the absolute protection of the territorial integrity of a state may require so many troops, military hardware, and missile defense systems that the national economy may become seriously endangered or even bankrupt. Wolfers suggests that the best any state can do is to balance the pursuit of security against its other national objectives. This balance requires the constant reexamination of perceived threats and perceived remedies.

Barry Buzan tells us that the bottom line for any state is survival and that security policy must be directed at protecting those conditions necessary for the continued existence of the state, keeping in mind the constant trade-offs required and the absolute inability to achieve absolute security.[9] Buzan boils the issue of security down to its essentials: security is aimed at maintaining the independent identity and functional integrity of states and their societies. To distill this even more, we can say that national security is about protecting a state's sovereignty.

Sovereignty

If national security is about preserving the sovereignty of the state, what is sovereignty? (Shortly I will also ask the important question, What is the state?) The *Penguin Dictionary of International Relations* explains, in part, that sovereignty is the "enabling concept of international relations."[10] Sovereignty, like security, has external and internal components.

External sovereignty refers to the situation in which states act as autonomous political units, as "free agents in foreign affairs, negotiating commercial treaties, forming military alliances, and entering into other types of agreements without the supervision of another state."[11] External sovereignty also signifies that states are equal in terms of possessing the "same privileges and responsibilities" as all other states and in claiming the right to use "the same rules of conduct [as all other states] when defending themselves and seeking to exercise influence over others."[12]

Assumptions of equality are not always borne out by reality. Some states possess more power than others in the international system. More powerful states often exert their influence and authority over less powerful states. The 2003 invasion of Iraq by the United States (along with its primary coalition-of-the-willing partner, the United Kingdom) demonstrates that respect for sovereign equality only goes so far. If Iraq's sovereign rights were equal to those of the United States, the United States would not have invaded Iraq. Sovereign equality did not form a protective shield or "force field" around Iraq. Further, when the U.S. occupation authorities—the Coalition Provisional Authority (CPA)—handpicked the interim Iraqi government as well as wrote the legal framework under which "sovereignty" would be restored to this interim Iraqi government and *then* wrote the rules that the "sovereign" Iraq would function under after "sovereignty" was restored, Iraq's sovereignty was shown to be at the behest of the United States/CPA. Yet sovereignty as an ideal envisions no right of other states to determine the internal political structure, leadership, and laws of another sovereign state. Sovereignty as an ideal envisions no right of other states to take away and give back one's sovereignty.

The struggle for national security in a world of sovereign (and techni-cally equal) states may come down to a violent struggle to maintain one's sovereignty against the claims of other sovereign states. Charles Kegley and Gregory Raymond write that the "first right" of sovereignty is "the right to continued national existence, which really [means] the preroga-tive to use force in self-defense for the acclaimed higher good of self-preservation."[13] Sovereign states retain the absolute right to use violence in the name of preserving their sovereignty. This is true for external sov-ereignty as well as internal sovereignty, as I discuss next. The use of vio-lence against other states to make them conform to one's own sense of one's own security needs is a clear demonstration of the fiction, so to speak, of sovereign equality.

Internal sovereignty refers to the "supreme decision-making and enforcement authority with regard to a particular territory and popula-tion."[14] Just as there is no higher authority than the state in the interna-tional system, sovereignty within the state's borders means there is a cen-tralization of power and authority within a single, dominant government.[15] Achieving this centralization of power and authority is no easy process. For example, years after the U.S. war against the Taliban in Afghanistan, the U.S.-endorsed president, Hamid Karzai, and his govern-ment could not exert full authority over all Afghan territory. Former gov-ernment ministers and various "warlords" or militia leaders (some asso-ciated with the Taliban) competed with and sometimes bested the Karzai government in some areas of the country. Karzai himself relied for a time on American military subcontractors for personal security rather than trust his life to Afghan security personnel.

While external sovereignty denotes fragmentation of authority and internal sovereignty denotes centralization of authority,[16] the two are inseparable. We can continue the example of Afghanistan to demonstrate this point. A significant weakness of the pre-Karzai government, the Tal-iban, was its questionable internal sovereignty. The Taliban never con-trolled all the territory of Afghanistan. The so-called Northern Alliance occupied and exercised authority over about 10 percent of Afghan terri-tory. This alternative authority was a coalition of anti-Taliban forces, many of whom had been members of the *previous* central Afghan govern-ment, which *also* had failed to exercise full power and authority over the country. Indeed, under the pre-Taliban government, lawlessness was so rampant and the spillover problems for neighbor Pakistan were so numerous that in 1996 Pakistan helped the Taliban overthrow the Afghan government. The Taliban exerted a severe grip on most of Afghanistan, yet its inability to consolidate total territorial control left the Taliban in need of additional external help. To some extent, the Taliban counted on Osama bin Laden and al-Qaeda for this additional help. Bin Laden supplied the Taliban with money and fighters to continue the war with the Northern Alliance. However, this external help turned out to be not as fortunate as Pakistan's earlier help since bin Laden used Afghanistan to plan and launch attacks against the United States, particularly the 9/11 attack. Afghanistan's lack of effective sovereignty left its various governments vulnerable to both external and internal security challenges.

Origins of the Sovereign State

The notion of the sovereign state (which, although much contested, is still controlling in the early twenty-first-century international system) is said to derive from the Treaty of Westphalia signed in 1648 at the conclusion of the Thirty Years' War (1618–1648) in Europe. The treaty divorced the authority of the small states of Central Europe from the Holy Roman Empire. Sovereignty in its two aspects no longer resided in the emperor and pope but became the prerogative of states. That is, sovereignty— absolute decision-making and decision-enforcing authority—moved conceptually and practically from the Holy Roman Empire to territorial states. Westphalia did not mark the beginning of *popular* sovereignty, or rule by the people through some form of representative government. Indeed, Westphalia enshrined absolutist states that could and would claim the right to take whatever measures they deemed necessary to protect their national interests and national security.

Kegley and Raymond have turned a constructivist eye on the Thirty Years' War and the Treaty of Westphalia. To understand Westphalia, they suggest, we need to understand the nature of the times that were cemented into the Treaty and turned into the "reality" of international politics. The Thirty Years' War was a time of unrelenting brutality originally fought over religious differences. The religious divisions that characterized the early years soon broke down as the war took on its own momentum and became all that was known and knowable by Central Europeans. The war was marked by the decimation of thousands of villages and the deaths of untold hundreds of thousands people.[17]

The factors that kept the war going for so long became foundational elements of the modern international system. Kegley and Raymond conclude that four factors kept the war going. First, the "belligerents became callous in the pursuit of state power."[18] Second, "opportunistic pursuers of personal wealth . . . saw in the role of military entrepreneur a means of achieving social stature and financial gain. Such men had few incentives for a negotiated truce that would end their acquisition of territory and titles as spoils of war."[19] Third, "[w]arfare rationalized the rise of absolute monarchs for desperate people who began to value order over freedom" and saw absolutist states as their only hope for safety. Further, war put back the cause of peace by concentrating "military might in the throne, making state power unassailable for those religious and humanitarian groups that otherwise could make a moral argument for peacemaking."[20] In short order, the rise of the absolutist state meant that democracy and human rights would be put on hold for a hundred or more years.[21] Fourth, Kegley and Raymond conclude that intolerance and mutual disdain locked people into a self-enforcing cycle of mistrust.[22]

In Kegley and Raymond's view, while the Treaty of Westphalia ended the war, it did not construct a world beyond that in which the signatories lived. The signatories locked into place the brutal "rules" that had developed through much bloodshed and plundering. The sovereign absolutist state arose and was reified. This reified state claimed the right and the need "to use war to increase [its] power and advance national interests."[23] "Europeans began to think of warfare as a naturally occurring and appropriate institution."[24] The doctrine of *raison d'état* (by reason of the state or by the need of the state) ensured that international politics became separated from issues of morality and ethics since no sovereign state dwelling in such a brutal world should be denied any means to protect itself and its interests, nor should it subject its security to the veto of others. Leaders began declaring their own wars just and the wars of others unjust as "[t]he legality of state conduct was now reserved for the state itself to judge."[25] In short, the "reality" asserted by political realists was written onto international and domestic affairs.

Kegley and Raymond's central thesis is worth repeating at length here, as we see in it the claims made by states today in the name of national security and the ways in which these claims undermine the pursuit of a more comprehensive international security that provides for human security. Their thesis is as follows:

> After evaluating the peace treaties . . . that brought the Thirty Years' War to a close, we conclude that the Westphalian settlement was flawed then and that it remains dangerous today. Simply put, in its effort to create a stable international order, Westphalia went too far in liberating states from moral restraints. Expediency overshadowed justice. By legitimating the drive for military power and the use of force, and by placing international stability on the precarious foundation of the successful operation of the balance of power, Westphalia enabled anarchy and amorality to take root in international affairs.[26]

The "reality" constructed on the destruction of Central Europe in the Thirty Years' War did not go unchallenged by those who would assert an international and domestic order based on morality and justice. Hugo Grotius (1583–1645), the so-called father of international law, was a contemporary of the men who constructed the Treaty of Westphalia. As explained by Karen Mingst, "Grotian thinking rejects the idea that states can do whatever they wish and that war is the supreme right of states and the hallmark of their sovereignty."[27] Yet advocates of a law-based international order would take a subordinate place over the centuries to those advocating a "state-first," national interest–first approach. The debate between those who advocated a broader ethic and those who advocated a narrow ethic remains to this day.

If we jump forward to the first half of the twentieth century and the interwar years when political idealism and advocates of international law and society were said to be in the ascendant as demonstrated by the newly created League of Nations, we still can hear the "reality" of the brutal mid-seventeenth century in the words of German historian Friedrich Meinecke. Explaining *raison d'état*, Meinecke intoned the following:

- *"Raison d'état* is the fundamental principle of national conduct, the State's first Law of Motion. It tells the statesman what he must do to preserve the health and strength of the State."[28]
- "Power belongs to the essence of the State."[29]
- "Power is not indeed 'evil in itself' . . . on the contrary it is naturally indifferent both towards good and evil."[30]
- "Within the State it is possible for *raison d'état* to remain in harmony with justice and morality, because no other power hinders that of the State."[31]
- But in regard to relations with other states, "Justice can only be upheld, if a power exists which is able and ready to uphold it. Otherwise the natural situation arises, where each tries to fight for the right he believes in, with whatever power-means he has at his disposal."[32]
- "That State . . . must create for itself its own imaginary right and necessity for existence, because no other authority can create this on its behalf."[33]
- States must "use and misuse a natural impulse [war] in one and the same breath."[34]

It is not too difficult to hear present-day national leaders using these same basic ideas when explaining, for instance, their fight against international terrorism or their fight against competing authorities (as in rebel groups) within their own borders. National leaders often evoke a realist world in which the state must fight to maintain its existence under conditions of anarchy. Having no higher authority to turn to should an injustice be done, each state must act in its own defense. One cannot undertake a defense without prior preparation; thus, the state must be constantly amassing military power in order to be ready for any challenges to its sovereignty. Indeed, there are times when the state must take action *before* a threat is realized in order to maintain its security and sovereignty.

Although the preceding discussion ultimately describes the realist worldview, both realism and liberalism assert that state sovereignty is fundamental to the international system. This is true despite the starkly different worlds envisioned by these paradigms. Liberalism (and its earlier variant, idealism, and later variant, pluralism) asserts that self-determining—sovereign—states can exist in harmony with other self-determining states in the international system. The key to this harmony is the mutual respect that should be given by all sovereign states to all other sovereign states, respect that is assured and reinforced through adherence to international laws and treaties and participation in international organizations. The UN system incorporates a broadly liberal view of international politics, yet membership is reserved exclusively for sovereign states.

States, Not Nations

If the national unit is the "standard unit of security"[35] in the contemporary international system, then we need to specify what the national unit is. "National" refers to things pertaining to countries or states. "National" in the sense of "national unit" or "national security" or "national interests" does not refer to things pertaining to "nations" in a strict sense.

"State" and "nation" are frequently used as interchangeable terms in the popular media and even by national governments and international organizations such as the United Nations. But scholars as well as activists seeking independent statehood for their nations note the important differences between these terms. Sheila Croucher, writing on identity and globalization, makes this useful shorthand distinction between state and nation: "the former refer[s] to a territorial-political unit and the latter to a human collectivity conscious of and in some way committed to its shared identity and mission."[36] We can add to Croucher's distinction.

A state is what we commonly refer to as a country. A state has an internationally recognized territory and population and an effective government. States and only states are sovereign; thus, states are the primary units of the contemporary international system and hold primary legal status. Recognition of statehood is conferred on a state by other legally recognized states. Since 1945, membership in the United Nations signifies recognition of statehood, although such membership is not strictly required; Switzerland has long been recognized internationally as a legal state, yet it joined the United Nations only at the start of the twenty-first century. Finally, states and only states can use violence to protect their interests.

A nation is a "human collectivity," but it is not necessarily a collectivity defined by territorial boundaries that are recognized internationally. A nation may claim a particular territory as its homeland and may even reside on that territory, but territory is recognized internationally as belonging to states. Nations are groups who have a sense of a common history and a sense of a common destiny. A nation may seek to become a state in order to better protect the nation against real and potential threats to the group's existence. With statehood comes the legal right to use violence to protect the nation and its interests. The desire to protect the nation is often manifested as nationalism, but states are also said to manifest nationalism, particularly states engaged in wars and foreign crusades. "Nationality," to throw another term into the mix, is not considered the same in international relations parlance as "ethnicity," as "nationality" connotes a relationship between the individual and the state. Ethnicity might be said to be the link between the individual and the nation.

Although "state" and "nation" are used interchangeably and often combined in the phrase "nation-state," the distinctions between the terms should not be easily dismissed. A "nation-state" denotes more or less perfect coincidence between the legal-political state and the sociocultural nation. Japan is a commonly used example of a nation-state. By contrast, the overwhelming majority of the world's states are multinational; that is, they contain within their borders more than one significant national grouping. Multinational states are not necessarily problematic: in many states, loyalty to the state coexists easily with loyalty to one's nation. For example, in the United States, positive feelings toward the United States as a whole generally do not interfere with or challenge positive feelings toward one's ethnic or group identity and vice versa. Thus, in a single summer, the city of Newport, Kentucky, can host a Fourth of July celebration in honor of the United States as well as host Celtic, French, Italian, and Latino heritage festivals (and, later in the fall, German Oktoberfest) without stirring up any rancor among its citizens.

But multinationalism can be the source of troubles within a state. Separatist nations may wish to break apart from a state and form their own state with their own government—that is, some nations may wish to be self-determining. The desire for self-determination, or statehood, is especially strong in cases where another group dominates the political, cultural, and economic life of the state and this other group uses its position of dominance to threaten the identity and existence of the minority nation.

The Components of a State

Earlier we defined a state as having a defined territory, population, and effective government. It is useful to deconstruct the state and its components in order to understand the difficulties posed by multinationalism and the nature of internal security problems faced today by many states.

Barry Buzan describes the state as having three components: a physical base, an "institutional expression," and an "idea" of the state.[37] The physical base of a state takes in the defined territory and population of our earlier definition. Since the beginning of the UN system in 1945, the territorial integrity of most sovereign states has not been threatened by other states. That is, with few exceptions, sovereign states have not attempted to remap other sovereign states by invading and annexing their territory. The Chinese takeover of Tibet in 1950 stands out as one of the few exceptions to this rule. In a few other cases—such as the Indonesian military takeover of East Timor in late 1975 and Morocco's efforts since 1976 to alter the demographic makeup of Western Sahara in order to annex it— states have attempted to assert control over territories as they were vacated by the colonial powers (the Netherlands in the case of East Timor and Spain in the case of Western Sahara).

The UN system is founded on the notion of respect for the territorial integrity of all states. States are thus proscribed from invading and conquering other states with the intent to annex the new territory and people. States that may wish to take over other states are deterred from doing so by the threat of a collective security response. (Collective security is discussed at length in chapter 8.) The 1990 invasion of Kuwait by Iraq was met with widespread international disapproval for this reason. Had Iraq attempted to take over Kuwait *prior* to 1945, it may have succeeded because no *global* organization existed dedicated to upholding the territorial integrity of its members.[38] Before 1945, Iraq's success in taking over Kuwait would have been contingent on its sheer military ability to do so (which it possessed in 1991) and its good relations with the relevant, interested "great powers." According to some accounts, the government of Saddam Hussein made strong hints that it intended to take over Kuwait in the summer of 1990. Having been told by the American ambassador that the U.S. government had no opinion on Iraq's differences with Kuwait but only wanted to see those differences settled quickly, the Iraqi government may have assumed that it was given a green light to proceed by the relevant, interested great power.[39] Unfortunately for Iraq, the U.S. government had not signaled a go-ahead. Facing international punishment as a result of the subsequent invasion of Kuwait, the Iraqi government claimed that it had no intention of annexing Kuwait and would leave once a friendly Kuwaiti government was established.

It is of course the case that the existence of the United Nations and its attendant membership obligations has not stopped all states from "disrespecting" the territorial integrity of other states. The same U.S. president—George H. W. Bush—who led the international community to war to punish Iraq for the invasion of Kuwait had ordered the invasion of Panama two years earlier in 1989. That invasion, launched for a variety of reasons, did not result in a UN-authorized war or military action against the United States. Indeed, no sanctions of any sort were levied on the United States for the invasion of Panama. Still, the United States did not annex Panama—a gesture of respect for the notion of territorial integrity—but instead replaced one government that had fallen out of favor with the United States with one more friendly to U.S. interests. That the United States could engage in such a violation of the sovereignty of Panama while Iraq could not in Kuwait is another indication that the notion of sovereign equality is more theory than reality.

As the examples of Panama in 1989 and Iraq in the wake of the 2003 U.S. invasion demonstrate, the territory of states may be more or less protected by notions embedded in international politics since the 1945 founding of the United Nations, but particular governments or officeholders may not. This brings us to the next component of a state.

In our definition of state, we included the component "effective government." Here, Buzan uses the term "institutional expression" to describe the second component of the state. The institutional expression of the state is the form and content of the government—the officeholders and the rules by which the officeholders come to power, the national laws, and the ways in which the laws are upheld and enforced. As a matter of principle, the shape and form of government within a particular country is not the legitimate business of any other state. But states are often quite involved in the domestic affairs of other states, attempting to shape and influence government type and policies, by overt or covert military action, the imposition of sanctions, the offering of rewards, and so forth.

The institutional expression of a state may be threatened internally as well. Governments that do not enjoy widespread internal legitimacy may come under political and even military attack from within their own borders. This leads us to Buzan's third component of the state—the "idea" of the state. He writes,

> The idea of the state is the most abstract component of the model, but also the most central. The notion of purpose is what distinguishes the idea of the state from its physical base and its institutions. The physical base simply exists. The institutions govern . . . but their functional logic falls a long way short of defining the totality of a state. . . . In a properly constituted state, one should expect to find a distinctive idea of some sort which lies at the heart of the state's political identity. What does the state exist to do? Why is it there? What is its relation to the society it contains?[40]

The idea of the state speaks to a positive linkage between society and state. Essentially, it indicates a measure of how legitimate the state is in the eyes of its population or how much and well the state is supported by the people. It is important to note that this may or may not relate to individual officeholders. In states with regular, routinized changes in officeholders (as in regular elections), popular support for the idea of the state may not be matched by popular support for a particular set of officeholders. The system may be viewed as legitimate even when the policies of officeholders are rejected. The "idea" of the state is not threatened by unpopular government officials who can be turned out of office in a no-confidence vote or new election.

Buzan proposes that the idea of the state can be understood in the nature of the relationship between the state and its society, and here we see the vexing differences between state and nation in more detail. Buzan suggests this relationship can take four forms: (1) the nation-state, (2) the state-nation, (3) the part nation-state, and (4) the multination state. In the nation-state, the idea of the state is the strongest because "here the nation precedes the state, and plays a major role in giving rise to it. The state's purpose is to protect and express the nation, and the bond between the two is deep and profound."[41] Examples Buzan gives of the nation-state are Hungary, Italy, and Japan.

In the second form, the state-nation, the state creates the nation in a "top-down" process. "This process is easiest to perform when populations have been largely transplanted from elsewhere to fill an empty, or weakly-held, territory."[42] In the state-nation, the state supports and promotes a national culture and national symbols through both rewards and coercion. This national culture generally is not directly at odds with citizens' original identities and cultures. The United States and Australia are the successful examples Buzan offers. He warns, though, that "newer entrants" into the process of state building, such as Nigeria (which is not a case of a transplanted or settler population), may have a harder time building a national superstructure over many and various primary identities.

The part nation-state is historically a rare occurrence in which a single nation is divided into two separate states. These states are comprised primarily of a single nation, making each a fairly "classic" nation-state. The part nation-state—here, think of North and South Korea—is the creation of external political actors and events. "The mystique of the unified nation-state frequently exercises a strong hold on part nation-states, and can easily become an obsessive and overriding security issue."[43]

Finally, the multination state contains "two or more substantially complete nations" within its borders.[44] Buzan proposes two subsets within this category: the federative state and the imperial state. In the federative state, the idea of nation-state is rejected. "Separate nations are allowed, even encouraged to pursue their own identities, and attempts are made to structure the state in such a way that no one nationality comes to dominate the whole state structure."[45] Buzan offers two examples: Canada, which still exists despite off-and-on-again efforts by the separatist Quebecois, and Yugoslavia, which no longer exists. The 2005 Iraqi government was conceived as a federation in order to accommodate and reassure different ethnic and religious groups about their place in post–Saddam Hussein Iraq.

The imperial multination state is more sinister. In the imperial state, one nation dominates the other(s) through a variety of means, such as the use of genocidal violence, massacre, forced relocations, imprisonment, and less obviously violent means, such as establishing a national education system dedicated to promoting a single language and culture and so on. The Soviet Union, despite claims to the contrary, favored ethnic Russians over all others. In a move taken from classic colonialism, Russians formed the primary administrative and privileged core within each of the Soviet republics, resulting in the presence of unwanted yet powerful Russian minorities in the newly independent post-Soviet states. In the case of Iraq, Kurds, Turkmen, and Arab Shi'ias were dominated by Arab Sunnis under British colonial rule and later under independent Iraqi governments up to and including that of Saddam Hussein. After 2003, the Kurds, Turkmen, and Arab Shi'ias feared a return to that status quo, while the Arab Sunnis feared that these other groups would seek revenge on them for the past.

The idea of the state is far less tangible than the territory and institutions of a state but the most critical in terms of national security. As Buzan explains,

> Some states will derive great strength from their link to the nation, whereas for others the tensions between state and nation will define their weakest and most vulnerable points. The importance of the nation as a vital component in the idea of the state has to be measured externally as well as internally. Unless the idea of the state is firmly planted in the minds of the population, the state as a whole has no secure foundation. Equally, unless the idea of the state is firmly planted in the "minds" of other states, the state has no secure environment.[46]

A "weak" state is one in which there is weak or missing loyalty to the idea of the state. In such a state, the national leaders will attempt to force compliance and loyalty through the use of government institutions. Political police, politically motivated violence by the government, and a high degree of control of the media are some hallmarks of a weak state. Clearly, coercive state- and loyalty-building practices "may have negative consequences for the security of many individuals and groups caught up in the process."[47] The more coercive and intrusive the state institutions become, the more reasons disaffected individuals and groups have to reject the state and the idea of the state being promoted by the national leaders.

The use of intrusive government institutions against people marked as threats to the state over time pushes more people into positions of hostility toward the state. In time, both the state and its disaffected population may take up arms in an effort to do away with each other. The difference between the two is that, generally speaking, states have a right to use violence against those who threaten their existence. When we move to international and human security, I will discuss norms and agreements that aim to recalibrate the international system away from an absolute right of states, but for now I stay in the state-first frame.

Building Internally Secure States

One of the legacies of Westphalia is that it is commonly accepted that states operate on a different "code" than do individuals or any other social group. This code distinguishes between appropriate and necessary state action and moral or ethical action, especially regarding the use of violence against threats. Thus, a state can order its own people to die for it in pursuit of national defense or in punishment for crimes "against the state" such as murder (although many states have abandoned the use of capital punishment for any crime). A state can determine that the people of other states must die so that it may better secure its interests. When soldiers die defending their country, the state—or the officials who represent the state—may mourn their loss while declaring their sacrifice to be noble and necessary. Some must make the ultimate sacrifice, it is said, in order to protect the greater good that is embodied in the state. When citizens of other countries die as a result of a state's actions to defend its interests, those lost lives are either "regrettable" when they are noncombatants or a sign of success when they are combatants. Lives lost in pursuit of national security are tallied on balance sheets as indications of the state's success or failure.

There is in this an absence of morality. The morality that we come to expect in our normal affairs with other human beings is suspended when considering how states make use of human beings for their own security needs. If a twenty-two-year-old American man were to come upon a twenty-two-year-old Japanese man in the Solomon Islands and kill him in hand-to-hand combat, this would offend our sense of what is good, moral, and legal. We would expect some sort of punishment for the killer. But transport these men back in time to World War II and make them soldiers: the American man would be expected to kill the Japanese man and vice versa. Both men would be excused from the normal bounds of what is moral behavior between human beings because they would no longer be individuals but agents of their states. Their cause would be the greater good, their conscience would be substituted for the national conscience.[48]

On matters of defending the state, political realists and liberals agree on some essential points: states have the right to self-defense, and sometimes war is necessary and appropriate. And, regretfully or not, war does not occur without the loss of human lives. As we try to understand basic national security as it derives from Westphalia, this fundamental point cannot be stressed enough: it is widely accepted that states operate by a different code than do human beings, and often that code is distinguished by its amorality.

Violence as Integral to the State-Building Process

Violence is one of the tools used by states to ensure security, whether the focus is internal or external security. Some scholars have asserted that violence is natural to the state-building process. State building here is taken to mean the development over time of effective institutional control of a defined territory. This process is not complete without the building of state legitimacy, as discussed previously.

Charles Tilly is widely quoted for his observation that states made war and war made states. Tilly's position, based on the study of the historical development of European states, is that state building is "organized violence."[49] In conflict-rife Europe, political units vied for survival against other political units. This struggle for survival required money and soldiers; no individuals or groups—internally or externally—gave up these resources willingly. Thus, to fight and survive external wars, nascent states used violence to force the people within their territories to supply the central authorities with much-needed money and soldiers. These treasures were necessary components of the external struggle to conquer the treasures of other would-be states while not being conquered. Internally, the successful state was one that expanded its reach into the whole of its territory, defeating peasant uprisings and aristocratic refusals to pay for "national" defense. The successful state was able to institute conscription and taxation systems in the face of considerable and often violent internal resistance. Defeating the internal resistance was essential to mobilizing the resources for defeating external challenges and further increasing state power and wealth through external conquest.

 In Tilly's analysis, the political units that survived over time succeeded in performing four essential tasks:

1. War making: Eliminating or neutralizing their own rivals outside the territories in which they have clear and continuous priority as wielders of force
2. State making: Eliminating or neutralizing their rivals inside those territories
3. Protection: Eliminating or neutralizing the enemies of their clients
4. Extraction: Acquiring the means of carrying out the first three activities—war making, state making and protection.[50]

Mohammed Ayoob argues that the violence that appears at times to be ubiquitous in former colonies should be understood in terms of this "natural" state-building process. Where European states had the luxury of time and freedom to "complete" this process, former colonies must navigate this process in a truncated time frame and under constraints imposed by globally accepted international principles. The European states that survived this process are today stable, modern states. Many political units did not survive to become stable, mature states. Thus, state building is conceived to be a violent political form of "natural selection."

The state-building process in former colonies was suspended during colonialism or was designed to facilitate the interests of the colonial power. On the conclusion of colonialism, former colonies found themselves thrust into a modern state system without the benefit of time and trial that produces stable, modern states (that is, without undergoing the same "natural selection" process as the European states). Additionally and critically, these new states achieved independence in an international system committed, by virtue of the United Nations, to the territorial integrity of states.[51] Nonviable political units that were largely colonial artifacts were recognized as juridically sovereign states even though they would not qualify empirically as sovereign states.[52] Taken together, the result is what Ayoob calls "disequilibrium":

> This disequilibrium lies at the root of the chronic political instability that we witness in most Third World states today. Instability, in turn, engenders violence and insecurity, as state-making strategies adopted by state elites to broaden and deepen the reach of the state clash with the interests of counterelites and segments of the population that perceive the extension of state authority as posing a direct danger to their social, economic, or political interests. Given adequate time, these conflicts of interest could be overcome peacefully through prolonged negotiations . . .
>
> However, given the short amount of time at the disposal of state makers in the Third World and the consequent acceleration in their state-making efforts, crises erupt simultaneously, become unmanageable as they overload the political and military capabilities of the state, and lead to a cumulation of crises that further erodes the legitimacy of the fragile post-colonial state.[53]

The violence in the state-building process in many countries has consequences for neighboring as well as distant countries. Conflict, weapons, and people (combatants as well as refugees) spill over borders, spreading instability and chaos. The ongoing conflict in the Democratic Republic of the Congo (DRC) illustrates this all too well. This conflict is explored in detail in extended discussion box 2.2.

Just as instability and chaos within a state may be contagious to neighboring states, an internally unstable state is ripe grounds for infection from international terrorism. International terrorist networks have made great use of the near anarchy found in some failed states and in states that have not fully extended effective institutional control over their entire territory. Before I address international terrorism as a threat to national security in more detail, though, it is important to note that terror was first used in the modern era as a *form of governance* designed to hasten this state-building process.

Among the many postinvasion apologies for the U.S. war against Iraq that began in March 2003, one claim was that the war was justified because of the human rights abuses committed by the regime of Saddam Hussein. That the deposed regime abused human rights is well known and not disputed. That this abuse created a moral imperative to invade Iraq was news. The violence used by the Hussein regime to maintain control of Iraq previously caused little or no concern for most other states. This lack of concern is the rule rather than the exception in an international system composed of sovereign states. Violent governance practices within states are the norm in the Westphalian system; many states at different times in their history have used violence to put down internal threats to the ruling regime. There are today international efforts under way to hold states accountable for good-governance practices that would include respect for human rights. These efforts include a responsibility of the community to intervene in states when the government cannot or will not protect its people from widespread violence. In this ethic, states have a responsibility to their people that is enforced by the international community. But this topic will be held for later in this book, as it is not the controlling norm.

Revolutionary France is credited as the birthplace of modern nationalism: France should and would be governed by the French people or nation rather than by a royal family. Revolutionary France caused dismay among the conservative governments of Europe that did not want the plague of government by the people to spread to their own subjects and lands. The French Revolution was a radical experiment that employed radical means to consolidate the new political system. Yet the means were radical only in degree, not in kind; the Revolution turned to state violence as a time-tested way to consolidate internal control.

Bruce Hoffman contends that the first modern use of terrorism was by the French revolutionary government. Terrorism was used "to consolidate the new government's power by intimidating counter-revolutionaries, subversives, and all other dissidents whom the new regime regarded as 'enemies of the people.'"[54] The use of state violence against internal threats was not new, but the claim that the violence was to defend against "enemies of the people" or to defend democracy was. Hoffman writes,

> Ironically, perhaps terrorism in its original context was also closely associated with the ideals of virtue and democracy. The revolutionary leader Maximilien Robespierre firmly believed that virtue was the mainspring of a popular government at peace, but that during the time of revolution must be

allied with terror in order for democracy to triumph. He appealed famously to "virtue, without which terror is evil; terror, without which virtue is helpless," and proclaimed: "Terror is nothing but justice, prompt, severe and inflexible; it is therefore an emanation of virtue."[55]

The *régime de la terreur* (Terror Regime) used terrorism—calculated, organized, deliberate violence designed to intimidate and cause fear in a target audience for political purposes—to create a "new and better society" to replace the old, corrupt political system. In this goal and in the use of violence, Hoffman suggests, the French revolutionaries were like their contemporary counterparts.

The use of terror or politically motivated violence intended to intimidate a population has a tipping point, whether practiced by states or terrorist or nationalist groups. Jessica Stern contends that most current-day terrorists probably will continue to avoid using weapons of mass destruction (WMD) in part because they wish to avoid alienating their target constituencies. The use of WMD by a terrorist group might be seen as going too far, causing repulsion for the terrorist group rather than increasing the legitimacy of its claims.[56] Thus, *up to a point*, the use of terrorism might gain terrorists sympathy and support, but past a certain point would-be constituents will reject the group because of its methods. This dynamic was seen in the fate of the French Terror Regime as well: the use of terror passed a critical threshold—the regime went too far in its use of violence and in very short time alienated its core constituents. Up to a point, the "cleansing" of French society of the remnants of the old regime was supported by the French people as necessary for instituting the new, better order. But in time, the acts taken in the name of the revolution and the people went too far, sowing the seeds for popular revolt against the revolutionary regime itself.

Hoffman writes that after the French people's rejection of the Terror Regime, "terrorism [by the state] became a term associated with the abuse of office and power—with overt 'criminal' implications."[57] Terrorism as an act of a state is associated with illegitimate totalitarian governments, such as that of Nazi Germany, Fascist Italy, and the Stalinist Soviet Union.[58] Such negative labeling comes from some of the same states who conveniently allied with totalitarian governments when it served their own interests. Here we can recall the long-term favorable U.S. relationship with Saddam Hussein's regime, a regime that openly used chemical weapons against its own people and Iranian troops without negative consequences for its relationship with the U.S. Reagan administration.

Further, such labeling comes from some states that themselves have used questionable means at home to defend "the people." The British Security Service MI5 was put to notorious use against political opponents

of the Margaret Thatcher government. As Peter Chalk and William Rosenau explain,

> For much of its existence, the Security Service received little outside scrutiny,
> and, during the 1980s, the agency mounted vigorous countersubversion
> operations against what Prime Minister Margaret Thatcher famously termed
> the "enemy within." Targets included Arthur Scargill, the left-wing leader of
> the national coal miners union who was alleged to have received financial
> assistance from Libya, and heavily politicized pressure groups, such as the
> Campaign for Nuclear Disarmament and the National Council for Civil Lib-
> erties. Such operations against legal and generally harmless left-wing activi-
> ties badly damaged the service's reputation.[59]

It must be said here that MI5 never engaged in the range and degree of
human rights abuses that were perpetrated by the Nazis on behalf of "the
people" or by other totalitarian states. And, once MI5's activities were
publicized, the British government instituted reforms to preclude the
political use of MI5 against legally constituted and acting groups, particularly those dissenting from the government's position. The point is not
to lump all states together but to be open about the fact that many, many
states have committed abuses of power in the name of protecting the state
or the people from a larger evil.

Between the French Revolution and the totalitarian regimes of the
twentieth century, Hoffman notes that terrorism was used by newfangled
nationalists in the nineteenth century in the cause of overthrowing
monarchies and instituting democracies. In the early twentieth century,
anarchists adopted terrorism as a means toward the goal of overthrowing
corrupt and oppressive states. And after World War II, terrorism was used
to achieve the self-determination of colonized peoples. In the present
time, terrorism has become the tool of those attempting to destabilize the
West and its agents, again in the name of oppressed people.[60] The theme
has been persistent: antigovernment groups attempting to overthrow the
yoke of illegitimate political authorities have recurred to the method
known as terrorism. Hoffman's analysis is that in the earlier periods, terrorism was targeted against "legitimate" targets, such as national governments, officeholders, or militaries, while in the most recent period, the net
is cast much wider, causing harm and death to innocents.

Setting aside the important topics of whether any group is ever justified
in its use of violence and whether innocent civilians should ever be targets of a terrorist attack, the common theme in the use of terrorism is a
claim that "the people" must be defended against an old, corrupt, and
illegitimate order. Whether used by revolutionaries, anarchists, or states
of different characters, the claim is that the use of violence to intimidate
and cause fear is necessary and even virtuous because the cause—the people—is virtuous. It is of course the fact that groups and regimes usurp the

cause of their people in order to forward their own more narrow interests and justify their actions.

Thus, violence is part of the process in which different groups contend for control of states and attempt to build and consolidate their power. Overthrowing the old order, starting a new order, defending the people— all are claims made to justify the use of violence for the pursuit of political objectives within countries. In the face of violent threats old and new, people will yield to their leaders in return for safety. This is part of the social contract: people give up some of their individual freedom in return for the protection provided by the group. Leaders of the group are entrusted with the protection of the people. State leaders know this and at times may manipulate this grant for their own purposes, sometimes to the point of the abuse of power. There is a tipping point, however, where the use of violence and coercion against old and new threats becomes counterproductive, generating the foundations of antigovernment sentiments and actions. I consider the implications of this and related topics in the next chapter on terrorism.

In early 1993, the U.S. Federal Bureau of Investigation and the Bureau of Alcohol, Tobacco and Firearms (ATF) launched a raid on a compound occupied by a millennialist cult, the Branch Davidians, in Waco, Texas. The goal was to seize what was suspected to be a large arsenal of weapons and explosives and to arrest the cult's leader, David Koresh. A millennialist cult is a religiously motivated group that believes that "the present age is corrupt and that a new age—the millennium—will dawn after a cleansing apocalypse."[1] Terrorism expert Jessica Stern explains that religiously motivated millennial terrorist groups believe "that humans can speed the process along" or assist God in bringing on the apocalypse or the end of human existence on earth.[2] Federal agents may not have been concerned that Koresh and his followers wanted to bring on the apocalypse, but they did suspect that Koresh was arming and training his followers to kill federal and state agents.[3]

Koresh's followers in the Waco compound numbered only between 100 and 125, so there was no issue of any meaningful threat to the entire U.S. government or to the existence of the United States. But threatening to kill government agents and taking steps to carry through on these threats are illegal, criminal actions. Additionally, as Stern points out, terrorist groups learn from and take cues from other terrorist groups—once one group crosses some threshold of violence, others will follow suit.[4] Federal authorities wanted to quash Koresh's ability to launch a "war" on federal agents in part to discourage and deter any would-be copycat activities by other radical, antigovernment groups.[5]

On February 28, 1993, around 200 law enforcement personnel (primarily ATF agents) launched a raid on the compound. The agents walked into an ambush and sustained four deaths and numerous other casualties during a "withering" gunfight.[6] After a truce was called and casualties attended to, a fifty-one-day standoff ensued. On April 19, federal authorities attempted to end the siege by using tanks to punch holes through the walls of the main building in order to inject tear gas as a prelude to storming the compound. Within minutes, the Davidians had set the compound on fire, killing some eighty adult sect members and possibly twenty children.

The entire episode from start to finish was a Justice Department operation, so Attorney General Janet Reno took full responsibility for deciding to launch the final raid on April 19. There was considerable praise as well as criticism for the manner in which the siege was ended. Critics claimed that heavy-handed tactics—especially the use of tanks—were unproductive when dealing with antigovernment cults. But this was before the terrorist attacks of 9/11. In the aftermath of 9/11 and since the creation of the Department of Homeland Security, it is likely that federal authorities would not be criticized much for using force against millennialist groups who show signs of planning mass violence.

Notes

1. Jessica Stern, *The Ultimate Terrorists* (Cambridge, Mass.: Harvard University Press, 1999), 71.

2. Stern, *The Ultimate Terrorists*, 71.

3. Daniel Browning, "ATF Reveals Basis for First Raid on Branch Davidians," *St. Louis Post-Dispatch*, April 22, 1993, A1.

4. Stern, *The Ultimate Terrorists*, 75.

5. Decisive action against one antigovernment group sends a signal to other groups about the consequences of certain activities. Unfortunately, groups might be inspired to take revenge on behalf of the targeted group. The Branch Davidian episode partly inspired the bombing of the federal building in Oklahoma City, Oklahoma, on the second anniversary of the final assault on the Davidians' compound.

6. Pierre Thomas, "Raid on Cult Exploded in First Minute," *Washington Post*, March 27, 1993, A1.

This discussion is not just a study of the instability in the Democratic Republic of the Congo (DRC) but also a brief look into civil wars in several African countries. All of these civil wars have been marked by strong international involvement, the lack of clear and effective institutional control by the relevant governments, and bloody disagreements over the "idea of the state" in every country. This discussion focuses primarily on two countries, although many more countries are caught in and implicated in this example of the contagion of instability and chaos.

The DRC is the large country located in the center of the African continent. Its territory is about a fourth of the size of the United States, or about the size of western Europe. The DRC borders Congo, Central African Republic, Sudan, Uganda, Rwanda, Burundi, Tanzania, Zambia, and Angola. In its independence era, it has been known as Congo, Zaire, and now the Democratic Republic of the Congo. For simplicity's sake, I'll use the name DRC in this discussion, acknowledging that the name has changed over time, depending on the ruling regime/government.

The DRC was a Belgian colony from 1884 to 1960. In 1960, the United Nations deployed a peacekeeping operation (the UN Operation in Congo, or ONUC by its French name) to assist the withdrawal of Belgian troops and to help the new government establish law and order. The country soon dissolved into civil war as Katanga province attempted to secede. ONUC was then charged with helping the DRC maintain its territorial integrity and political independence, and then in subsequent UN Security Council resolutions the peacekeeping force was charged with preventing civil war (where it already was occurring) and securing the removal of all foreign troops and mercenaries.[1] At its height, ONUC numbered over 19,000 troops; it also sustained 250 fatalities. ONUC withdrew from the Congo in 1964. In 1965, Mobutu Sese Seko seized power and ruled the renamed Zaire until he fled from a rebellion thirty-two years later.

The chaos, conflict, foreign involvement, and UN peacekeepers present at the DRC's beginning were there as of 2006. The most recent interstate war there can be traced most directly to the Rwandan genocide in 1994.[2] Rwanda's own independence from Belgium was precipitated by an ethnic war between the colonial-favored Tutsi minority and the Hutu majority. On its independence in 1962, Rwanda became a Hutu-dominated state. "During the succeeding decades, Hutu leaders conducted numerous pogroms against the Tutsis, creating a major refugee problem for neighboring Tanzania, Uganda, Burundi, and Zaire."[3] In time, the Rwandan Tutsi refugees in Uganda formed a rebel army.

The Rwandan Tutsi exiles honed their military skills when they joined with Ugandan rebels in 1981 to topple the Ugandan government. In 1988, these exiles formed the Rwandan Patriotic Front (RPF), and in 1990 they launched a war on the Hutu Rwandan government. Among the Tutsi exile fighters was Major Paul Kagame. Kagame, who received military training from the U.S. Army, became the leader of the RPF after its commanding officer died in initial military forays against the Hutu Rwandan government in 1990.[5]

In 1993 the United Nations brokered a cease-fire between the RPF and the Rwandan government forces. The cease-fire allowed for the deployment of a UN peacekeeping operation whose primary mission was to keep arms from flowing into Rwanda from neighboring countries. In April 1994, the Rwandan Hutu president's plane was shot down under mysterious circumstances. All persons on the plane were killed, including the Tutsi president of Burundi. Hutu extremists took over the Rwandan government on the pretense of the downing of the plane and initiated a genocide campaign that resulted in the deaths of 800,000 people (Tutsis and moderate Hutus) over several weeks. The UN peacekeeping force was ordered to stand down as the genocide took full force. The RPF renewed its fight against the government army and ultimately ended the genocide by overthrowing the Hutu government. See chapter 9 for more discussion of this case.

When it was clear that the RPF would defeat the Hutu forces, France led Operation Turquoise, a UN-approved peace enforcement mission, into Rwanda. (Chapter 9 discusses the differences between peacekeeping and peace enforcement.) Operation Turquoise effectively operated to protect the *génocidaires* from retribution by the RPF. Over a million Hutus, including the *génocidaires*, fled into French-protected camps and then across the border into UN refugee camps in the DRC. This is where the story of the DRC picks up again.

The Rwandan Hutu refugees in the DRC camps proved to be serious trouble for the United Nations, for the nongovernmental humanitarian assistance organizations that ran the camps, and for the host country. A few passages from the secretary-general's report of November 18, 1994, establish the chaos:

An estimated 1.2 million people fled Rwanda over a four-day period in mid-July to the Kivu region of Zaire, in one of the largest and most sudden movements of refugees in modern history. . . . The camps, which sprawl over miles, are overcrowded, chaotic and increasingly insecure. The refugees live in makeshift huts and are completely dependent on United Nations and relief agencies for basic needs assistance. . . .

The former Rwandese political leaders, Rwandese government forces soldiers and militias control the camps, though the degree of control varies from area to area. They are determined to ensure by force, if necessary, that the refugees do not repatriate to Rwanda. They also make it difficult for relief agencies' activities in the camps and prevent relief supplies from reaching those in need. It is believed that these elements may be preparing for an armed invasion of Rwanda and that they may be stockpiling and selling food distributed by relief agencies in preparation for such an invasion. There have already been some cross border excursions. Security is further undermined by general lawlessness, extortion, banditry and gang warfare between groups fighting for control of the camps. As a result of these threats to security, non-governmental organizations responsible for the distribution of relief supplies in the camps have begun to withdraw.[5]

The displaced Rwandans in the DRC included approximately 50,000 former Rwandan regular forces, 10,000 militia, 800 members of the former Presidential Guard, and 230 Hutu Rwandan political leaders from the toppled government. Because of the sudden flood of people over the border, Zairian troops and police were unable to control who and what came in; thus, these combined Rwandan Hutu forces came into the DRC fairly well equipped with weapons, vehicles, and communications devices.

Some of the camps in the DRC were designated by humanitarian groups as "military" right away, leaving aid workers reluctant to render any assistance to these camps.[6] In the camps designated "refugee," relief workers were threatened, coerced into providing assistance to armed factions, kidnapped, and murdered. In short order, violent clashes occurred between Zairian troops and Rwandan militia running the camps. Zairian officials wanted to stop the Rwandans from looting local natural resources and had decided to force the Rwandans to return to their country if they would not repatriate voluntarily.[7]

A year and a half after the Rwandan Hutus fled into the DRC, the refugee camps were still nearly full. In December 1995, in a report related to a postgenocide UN peacekeeping operation in Rwanda, the secretary-general reported that the UN High Commissioner for Refugees (UNHCR) and the Zairian government had restored and maintained security in the refugee camps, although the camps clearly were being used to launch organized attacks across the border into

Rwanda. These attacks led to Rwandan government accusations of Zairian complicity with the Hutu rebels/refugees. The secretary-general concluded,

> The core issue for Rwanda remains national reconciliation. This requires the rapid creation of conditions that would facilitate the safe return of 1.6 million refugees to their homes in dignity and the bringing to justice the perpetrators of the genocide. After nearly a year and a half in camps in Zaire and the United Republic of Tanzania, the refugees have placed formidable socio-economic and environmental burdens on the host countries, and this has sometimes severely strained the latter's goodwill. In addition, increasing infiltration and sabotage activities by the former Rwandese Government Forces and militia have heightened tension both within Rwanda and between Rwanda and its neighbors.[8]

By early 1996, warnings appeared in the secretary-general's report about an imminent international war between the DRC, Rwanda, and Uganda. In the final report regarding the UN peacekeeping operation in Rwanda, the secretary-general noted,

> Since my last report, relative calm and stability have continued to prevail throughout Rwanda, with the exception of areas bordering Zaire. In those areas the situation is tense as a result of an increase in the level of insurgent activities by elements of the former Rwandese Government Forces (RGF).[9]

The "marked increase" in insurgent activity coming from the DRC caused the Rwandan government to increase its troop strength and patrols along the border. The government of Zaire, the secretary-general reported, had attempted to improve relations with Rwanda by turning over some Rwandan government military equipment confiscated from the Rwandan Hutu forces. Yet some 1.1 million refugees remained in Zaire,[10] presumably under the control and direction of the Hutu leaders, and the number of returnees was very low.[11]

The UN presence in Rwanda ended in March 1996 at the request of the Rwandan government. According to a nongovernmental organization, the International Crisis Group (ICG), the end was also coming for the Mobutu government in Zaire, in part because Rwanda and Uganda had had enough insurgent activity from Hutu groups across their border. Rwanda and Uganda launched a military operation—a war, an intervention, an invasion—into Zaire. Jeffrey Herbst concludes that

> the effectiveness of this operation (the refugee camps were emptied, millions of Hutu were returned to Rwanda, and the armed

Hutu groups lost some of their best sanctuaries and their lifeline to international assistance) stands in stark contrast to the endless dithering by non-Western powers over intervention first in Rwanda in 1994 and then in Zaire in 1996 as the refugee crisis became dramatic.[12]

The ICG reports on the cascading events coming from this war:

Claiming that Hutu *génocidaires* had taken refuge within eastern [DR] Congo, Rwanda and Uganda backed a May 1997 rebellion in Congo, removing Mobutu Sese Seko, the Congo's leader since 1965, and replacing him with Laurent Kabila. However, when Kabila moved to purge Tutsis from his government, Rwanda intervened in the Congo for a second time, this time with the intention of removing Kabila. Rwandan troops backing Congolese Tutsi rebels invaded in August 1998, leading Kabila to seek assistance from Zimbabwe, Angola and Namibia. Kabila managed to avoid the fate of his predecessor, Mobutu, but the Congo was launched into a conflict in which an estimated 3 million died [as of mid-2004], most of them from war-related diseases and starvation. The countries involved, and later the non-governmental actors, signed up to a ceasefire at Lusaka, Zambia, in July 1999 and the UN Security Council sent a peacekeeping mission (MONUC) to the Congo in 2000.[13]

The UN peacekeeping force was dispersed throughout the DRC, but the eastern provinces bordering Uganda, Rwanda, and Burundi remained relatively unstable and outside the parameters of the 1999 Lusaka accords. MONUC lacked the capacity and mandate to control these areas. To cap the lawlessness and bring the east back under control, the United Nations authorized the deployment of a French-led European Union peace enforcement operation, Operation Artemis, in May 2003.[14] Artemis was deployed to Bunia, an anarchic city on the DRC-Ugandan border. For the space of a few months, Artemis used overwhelming force to compel weapons off the street and bring Bunia under control. Artemis was successful in the short term and then turned Bunia back over to MONUC and government control.[15]

But the UN peacekeeping operation still lacked the necessary capabilities to keep the eastern provinces pacified and compel the actors there to stay within the Lusaka Accords process. In the spring of 2004, interethnic violence escalated, forcing a restructuring and shifting of MONUC's resources, but to no avail. Further, the peacekeepers themselves were increasingly targeted for violence and killed.

The violence in the DRC once again spilled over into other countries in the summer of 2004. In June, rebel Congolese commanders who had been participating in the creation of a new unified Congolese national army seized Bukavu, a city on the DRC-Rwandan border. These rebels claimed to be acting to protect Congolese Tutsis from ethnic cleansing. The Congolese national army retook the city, but the government claimed that Rwanda had instigated the rebellion.[16] The DRC government ordered 10,000 troops to the Rwanda border to forestall further provocations. The UN peacekeepers in the area were unable to stop the rebellion but did return fire with the rebels after the Bukavu uprising was ended. Rwanda and the DRC traded accusations and threatened to widen the war once more, with other countries in the region taking sides.

The Bukavu uprising spilled over into Burundi with disastrous results. Congolese Tutsis had fled the fighting—not into Rwanda, which was more proximate, but into Burundi. These Congolese Tutsi refugees gathered in a UN-run camp in Gatumba, Burundi, about five kilometers from the Congolese border.[17] The camp was intended for Burundi returnees—that is, for Burundians who had fled *their* country's civil war and had returned after a peace agreement had been signed. The UN deployed a peacekeeping force in Burundi in May 2004 to facilitate the peace process and to protect civilians.[18] When Bukavu erupted in violence in June 2004, the newly established UN peacekeeping force and humanitarian personnel in Burundi were confronted with frightened Congolese refugees who fled across the border.

Two months later, 160 of these Congolese Tutsi refugees were massacred in one night in the UN Gatumba camp. The victims included children and babies. None of the Burundian returnees were harmed in the attack.[19] None of the authorities responsible for protecting the people in the camp—not the UNHCR, the UN peacekeepers, or the transitional Burundian government and army—did anything to stop the massacre.[20] A preliminary UN report suggested that the perpetrators were members of a rebel Burundian army working with Mai-Mai fighters (that's another story) and Rwandan Hutu rebels, both acting out of the eastern DRC.[21]

The government of Rwanda and some members of the transitional Burundian government began to threaten to launch forces into the eastern DRC to chase down the killers of the refugees. I will leave the case study at this point in time. This case shows how chaos and instability in one country can have disastrous consequences for neighboring countries. This case also demonstrates how difficult it is to generate an effective international response, a topic discussed in later chapters on international and human security.

Notes

1. United Nations Department of Peacekeeping Operations, "United Nations Operation in the Congo," http://www.un.org/Depts/DPKO/Missions/onuc.htm (accessed December 1, 2005).

2. International Crisis Group, "Conflict in Eastern Congo," http://www .icg.org (accessed September 8, 2004).

3. Donald C. F. Daniel and Bradd C. Hayes with Chantal de Jonge Oudraat, *Coercive Inducement and the Containment of International Crises* (Washington, D.C.: United States Institute of Peace Press, 1999), 114.

4. Daniel and Hayes, *Coercive Inducement and the Containment of International Crises*, 115.

5. Report of the Secretary-General on Security in the Rwandese Refugee Camps, S/1994/1308, November 18, 1994, 2–3.

6. Keith B. Richburg, "No Relief for Wounded Hutus," *Washington Post*, August 23, 1994, A13.

7. "Zaire Troops Clash with Rwandans in Camps," *New York Times*, November 27, 1994, 26; Chris Megreal, "Soldiers Turn on Refugees in Zaire," *Guardian* (London), November 30, 1994, 20.

8. Report of the Secretary-General on the United Nations Assistance Mission for Rwanda, S/1995/1002, December 1, 1995, 10.

9. Report of the Secretary-General on the United Nations Assistance Mission for Rwanda, S/1996/149, February 29, 1996, 1.

10. Report of the Secretary-General on the United Nations Assistance Mission for Rwanda, S/1996/149, February 29, 1996, 7.

11. Report of the Secretary-General on the United Nations Assistance Mission for Rwanda, S/1996/149, February 29, 1996, 6.

12. Jeffrey Herbst, "African Peacekeepers and State Failure," in *Peacekeeping and Peace Enforcement in Africa*, ed. Robert I. Rotberg et al. (Washington, D.C.: Brookings Institution Press, 2000), 28–29.

13. International Crisis Group, "Conflict in Eastern Congo."

14. United Nations Security Council, S/RES/1484, May 30, 2003.

15. Laura Neack, "Peacekeeping, Bloody Peacekeeping," *Bulletin of the Atomic Scientists*, July/August 2004, 46.

16. Rory Carroll, "War Fears as Congo Rushes in Troops," *Guardian* (London), June 22, 2004, 13.

17. Kate Holt and Sarah Hughes, "Slaughter of the Innocents," *Independent* (London), August 25, 2004, 2, 3.

18. United Nations Security Council, S/RES/1545 (2004), May 21, 2004.

19. United Nations Department of Peacekeeping Operations, "ONUB Condemns Gatumba Massacre," press release, ONUB/PIO/PR/28/2004, August 14, 2004.

20. Holt and Hughes, "Slaughter of the Innocents."

21. Anne Penketh, "Annan Pushes UN for $1 BN Expansion of Congo Force," *Independent* (London), September 8, 2004, 32.

3

Terrorism

When we think of state building as a process, we imply that there is some starting point, then some intermediate steps or stages of various sorts, and then some ending. There is also the implication that state building is developmental—that states move from less institutionalized, less effective, and less legitimate to more institutionalized, more effective, and more legitimate. As I have discussed, this process involves violence; states—national leaders or ruling regimes—have used and probably will continue to use claims about internal existential threats to justify the use of violence against internal enemies. But the intended end point is a stable state in which the population accepts the legitimacy of the political system and the roles played by government in their lives. In a stable state, the institutions of governance permeate the country and render effective law and order within the state's borders.

In such a stable "mature state," there will be no significant internal threats to the survival of the state. As noted earlier, in countries not beset by civil war or insurgency, where national power has been firmly consolidated in the hands of a central government, national militaries are generally not used to provide for and maintain internal security. Such use of the military is not required in stable states. Militant antigovernment groups may be present in stable states, but they are generally handled as law enforcement problems rather than existential threats.

The "global war on terror" blurs this internal-external distinction even in stable states with effective and minimal law and order institutions. For example, in the 2004 U.S. presidential campaign, the sitting vice president warned repeatedly that if the challenger should win the election, the new administration would make the mistake of viewing terrorism as a criminal and law enforcement problem rather than a military one. At the same time, a senior counterterrorism official within the Central Intelligence Agency (CIA) criticized the Bush administration for failing to understand that al-Qaeda had changed from a terrorist organization to a "global Islamic insurgency." Terrorist organizations are countered with law enforcement activities aimed at eliminating known leadership, whereas insurgencies are adept at developing new leadership and thus should be countered with military measures aimed at the entire insurgency.[1] Meanwhile, terrorism experts, such as Bruce Hoffman, insist that fighting terrorism is *both* a law enforcement and a military problem and that the former approach may be more important than the latter. Fighting terrorism, Hoffman writes, requires good and actionable information, and good and actionable information

> is discerned not from orders of battle, visual satellite transmissions of opposing force positions, or intercepted signals but from human intelligence gathered mostly from the indigenous population. The police, specifically trained to interact with the public, typically have better access than the military to what are called human intelligence sources. Indeed, good police work depends on informers, undercover agents, and the apprehension and interrogation of terrorists and suspected terrorists, who provide the additional informational critical to destroying terrorist organizations.[2]

As with any national security issue, discussions of terrorism are embedded in political debates. Who is a terrorist? What is terrorism? What should governments do to counter terrorism, whether international or homegrown? These are questions that are not answered easily.

Defining Terrorism

Defining a thing that is political is never simple. Indeed, the politics in the act of defining can never be left behind. As Hoffman notes, "Different departments or agencies of even the same government will themselves often have very different definitions for terrorism." "Not surprisingly, each of the . . . definitions reflects the priorities and particular interests of the specific agency involved."[3] Political interests and agendas influence how state agencies define terrorism.

National leaders, too, use the term "terrorism" for political purposes. For example, governments frequently claim that homegrown antigovernment groups are linked to international groups. Such claims are designed to delegitimize the groups and to elicit support from interested third parties. During the Cold War, authoritarian states (in Latin America particularly but not exclusively) would label antigovernment groups "communist" in order to justify extreme and repressive measures against their own citizens and gain assistance from the United States. In a replay of history, in the U.S.-declared global war on terror, national leaders may claim al-Qaeda problems where none may exist for the same reasons. When the Bush administration publicly linked financial and military assistance to being "with us" in the war on terror and called for punishing states that were not "with us" in the war on Iraq, incentive was provided for sometimes disingenuous, politicized claims about local grievances being generated by international terrorism.

It is the case that antigovernment groups have had and will have external ties to sympathetic outside groups. Antigovernment groups act like states in this regard; as the often-quoted expression goes, the enemy of my enemy is my friend. To counter the wealth and power of the government it opposes, an antigovernment group looks to whatever resources it can muster, and sometimes these come from foreign groups and states.

Hoffman tells us that terrorism is driven by that fundamental Westphalian goal—power. Terrorism is "ineluctably about power: the pursuit of power, the acquisition of power, and the use of power to achieve political change. Terrorism is thus violence—or, equally important, the threat of violence—used and directed in pursuit of, or in service of, a political aim."[4] Hoffman also says that terrorism is "designed to have far-reaching psychological repercussions beyond the immediate victim or target," "conducted by an organization with an identifiable chain of command or conspiratorial cell structure," and "perpetrated by a subnational group or non-state entity."[5]

Although this definition does not cast judgment on whether the use of terrorism is justifiable, Hoffman makes it clear that "terrorism [and terrorist] is a pejorative term. It is a word with intrinsically negative connotations that is generally applied to one's enemies and opponents, or to those with [whom] one disagrees and would otherwise prefer to ignore."[6] Here, another often-quoted expression comes to mind: one person's terrorist is another person's freedom fighter. This expression is attributed both to U.S. President Ronald Reagan and to Palestinian Authority leader Yassir Arafat—no political soul mates by any definition.

"Freedom fighter" is a term that conveys legitimacy. If a group is fighting for freedom, then the cause is good—and perhaps the methods are justifiable, if not "good." One may reject in principle the method of violence but be sympathetic to the reasons behind the use of violence. During the struggle against apartheid in South Africa, the African National Congress (ANC) first attempted to fight for democracy and justice through legal and social action, but when this failed, the ANC committed itself to the armed overthrow of the apartheid government. Toward this goal, the ANC sought and accepted military and financial assistance from the Soviet Union, among other sympathetic sources. Thus, although the ANC was engaged in what the South African government called acts of "terrorism" with the aid of America's prime enemy, the Soviet Union, Americans were increasingly sympathetic to the ANC because the antiapartheid cause was seen as good and moral.

During the 2005 World Summit at the United Nations, states attempted to reach an agreement on a definition of terrorism, among other agenda items. Some states wanted a definition that condemned any attacks on civilians as terrorism; others objected to this because such a definition would lump together terrorism and legitimate struggles for national liberation. The founders of some modern states, after all, used terrorism in their independence struggles against colonial and occupying powers. Political circumstances change, and in the words of Eqbal Ahmad, "The terrorist of yesterday is the hero of today, and the hero of yesterday becomes the terrorist of today."[7] A rigid definition of terrorism might not give states the flexibility needed to promote and support regime change in other countries or otherwise adjust to changing circumstances.

For example, the United States financially and militarily supported the mujahideen in Afghanistan who were fighting against the Soviet Union and its client government during the 1980s. The U.S. government declared the mujahideen "freedom fighters," fully aware and supportive of the international composition of the group. Some of these freedom fighters were Afghani; some, like Osama bin Laden and his recruits, were Arab and hailed from Middle Eastern countries. Once the Soviets were defeated and withdrew from Afghanistan, these same international fighters dispersed to other countries armed with the heady accomplishment of having beaten a superpower. They also were armed figuratively with a violent ideology and literally with weapons and expertise. When some of these "Arab Afghans" started appearing in the Bosnian War on the side of the Bosnian Muslims, a sense of unease and alarm began to grow in the West. The U.S. government, in time, insisted that the Bosnian government expel the Arab fighters. This unease was replaced with outright condemnation after the 1998 al-Qaeda attacks on the U.S. embassies in Tanzania and Kenya and the 2000 al-Qaeda attack on the USS *Cole*. Later, Russian officials started claiming that these same Arab "terrorists" were assisting and then fomenting the war in Chechnya. American political authorities, too, would credit "foreign terrorists" and "foreign fighters" with the violence and insurgency in Iraq after the U.S. invasion. "Foreign terrorists" and "foreign fighters" are code words for international terrorists belonging to or associated with those same mujahideen who once served the same cause of and drew financial and military support from the United States. (See extended discussion box 3.1 for more on Chechen-Russian relations and international terrorism.)

In the 1980s, the targets of the mujahideen were the occupying army of the Soviet Union and an "illegitimate" Afghan government. Both were seen as justifiable targets—in the view of the mujahideen and the United States. Today these fighters often target people who do not fit easily into a category that is considered legitimate in armed struggle. As Jessica Stern explains, "Terrorism is aimed at *noncombatants*. This is what makes it different from fighting in a war."[8]

But who is a noncombatant and who a combatant? These are more confounding concepts, as Stern tells us:

> A soldier on a battlefield is unquestionably a combatant, but what if the soldier's country is not at war, and he is sleeping in a military housing complex, as nineteen US soldiers were when they were killed by a bomb in Dhahran, Saudi Arabia, in June 1996? What if he is riding a bus that also carries civilians, as an Israeli soldier was when a suicide bomber attacked in Gaza in April 1995?[9]

The recent American trend of using military subcontractors in multiple supportive roles in military operations only makes this issue more difficult. Are the subcontractors combatants if the only reason they are present in an area is to facilitate U.S. military operations, or do they retain noncombatant status? The answer to this question is complicated by the particular mission the military is on. If subcontractors are attached to U.S. peacekeeping troops deployed in a UN mission, politically motivated violence against the subcontractors might be called terrorism. But if those subcontractors are the targets of politically motivated violence while assisting U.S. troops battling insurgents in Iraq, they might not be called the victims of terrorism.

The invasion of Iraq also brings up the disquieting problem of warfare as terrorism. Stern's definition of terrorism as "an act or threat of violence against noncombatants with the objective of exacting revenge, intimidating, or otherwise influencing an audience"[10] can lead to the conclusion that certain acts of state warfare are also properly labeled terrorism. In Stern's words,

> States have also used terrorism as an instrument of war, by deliberately attacking civilians in the hope of crushing enemy morale. In late 1940 the British Chiefs of Staff determined that Germany's morale was more vulnerable than its industry, and decided to bomb the centers of key German cities. Historians estimate that these attacks killed some 300,000 Germans, most of them civilians, and seriously injured 780,000 more. In Dresden alone, in the spring of 1945, when the war was virtually won, the bombing killed nearly 100,000 people.[11]

In war, terrorizing the enemy's population may be the explicit political goal of military action. Stern recounts the view of a U.S. military commander regarding the use of atomic weapons by the United States against Japan in August 1945: "There were only two ways to win the war—either by going in after them or by shock. The atomic bomb was the shock action."[12] The intended audience of this shock was not just the Japanese government and people; the United States wanted to put the world on notice that it possessed the ultimate weapon.

Shocking the government and population of Iraq was also integral to the U.S. invasion in 2003—as in the famous "shock and awe" bombing campaign that was designed not to kill thousands upon thousands of civilians and noncivilians but, instead, to *threaten* the deaths of thousands upon thousands. This threat was levied in order to cause the government to collapse and/or surrender. The extended audience, according to the Bush administration, consisted of international terrorists and the governments that harbored them. Do states engage in acts or threatened acts of violence "against noncombatants with the objective of exacting revenge, intimidating, or otherwise influencing an audience"? Undeniably—but we must recall the operating principle that states claim a right to do what they need to do to defend their interests.

The Internationalization of Terrorism

Terrorists can be "homegrown" and with strictly local motivations and goals (such as the overthrow of illegitimate central authorities or the pursuit of national self-determination), but homegrown terrorists increasingly have connections to international actors. Experts seem to agree that global and local terrorist groups have formed a loosely knit and shifting network. This amorphous nature of terrorism makes government response difficult. Intragovernment efforts to stop terrorism must be more coordinated—blurring the standard domestic-international or internal-external divide—and intergovernment efforts also require greater coordination.

To say that terrorism has internationalized is not to suggest that there is a single monolithic terrorist group—say, al-Qaeda—that poses the primary challenge today. The threat al-Qaeda itself posed by 2006 had become less and less tangible.[13] Instead, al-Qaeda was a threat because of its capacity for inspiration—in terms of both message and operational methods—and because al-Qaeda had facilitated networking between global jihadists and local antigovernment groups.

In December 2004, a CIA advisory group warned that the focus of counterterrorism efforts should not be on al-Qaeda and affiliated groups but on the factors that spawn such terrorism, such as perceived Western domination of Islamic countries.[14] The group concluded that "experts assess that the majority of international terrorist groups will continue to identify with radical Islam."[15] Further, global communications as well as "informal networks of charitable foundations, *madrassas, hawalas,* and other mechanisms will continue to proliferate and be exploited by radical elements; alienation among unemployed youths will swell the ranks of those vulnerable to terrorist recruitment."[16]

The CIA advisory group predicted that terrorist recruitment would not be limited to predominantly Muslim areas but would spread to places like western Europe, where "religious identity has traditionally not been as strong" among immigrant groups.[17] The American invasion of Iraq set this into full swing:

> Intelligence officials fear that for a new generation of disaffected European Muslims, Iraq could become what Afghanistan, Bosnia and Chechnya were for European Islamic militants in past decades: a galvanizing cause that sends idealistic young men abroad, trains them and puts them in touch with a more radical global network of terrorists. In the past, many young Europeans who fought in those wars came back to Europe to plot terrorist attacks at home.[18]

European officials estimated that by 2004, "hundreds" of young militant Muslim European men had joined the war in Iraq, assisted by recruiters who appeared within months of the American invasion.

The British International Institute for Strategic Studies (IISS) agreed with this ominous assessment of the wider impact of the war in Iraq. In December 2004, IISS concluded that "Iraq may be serving as a valuable proving-ground for 'blooding' foreign jihadists, and could conceivably form the basis of a second generation of capable leaders (for instance, Zarqawi) and middle-management players."[19] The CIA group assessed the situation similarly: "The [al-Qaeda] membership that was distinguished by having trained in Afghanistan will gradually dissipate, to be replaced in part by the dispersion of the experienced survivors of the conflict in Iraq." Further, "Iraq and other possible conflicts in the future could provide recruitment, training grounds, technical skills and language proficiency for a new class of terrorists who are 'professionalized' and for whom political violence becomes an end in itself."[20]

As local grievances merge with internationally experienced operatives, the targets of terrorism may become less precise as Western states and hated local regimes get lumped together. For example, the internationalization of terrorism resulted in the targeting of Australia and Australians because of the John Howard government's extraordinarily close association with U.S. foreign policy.[21] Howard's conservative government took office in 1996 and quickly dropped its liberal predecessor's Asian-directed foreign policy orientation. The Howard government instead cast Australia as the "deputy" to the United States and insinuated that its job would be to keep Asians in line.[22] This self-deputizing was not fully embraced by the Clinton administration but was celebrated in the prelude to the Iraq war by the Bush administration. Toward the goal of distinguishing Australia from Asia, Australia led a multinational peace enforcement operation in 1999 into Indonesia's East Timor (now the country of Timor-Leste). Australia's troop presence in East Timor was a primary motive behind the bombings of two Bali nightclubs in October 2002, bombings that killed 202 people, including eighty-eight Australians.[23] Australia's hawkish stance on the global war on terror, Howard's proclamation of the right to launch preemptive attacks on neighbors who harbored threats, and Howard's strong support for the Iraq war probably contributed as well to the bombing of the Australian embassy in Jakarta, Indonesia, in September 2004.

These attacks on Australian citizens and interests suggest that in the twenty-first century, international terrorism will be aimed at both primary targets and their affiliates and allies. This may have been demonstrated in the Madrid commuter train bombings in March 2004. These bombings, which claimed 200 lives and wounded another 1,500, were said to be in retaliation for Spain's participation in the American-led coalition that invaded Iraq. The center-right government of Jose María Aznar had defied strong Spanish public opinion against the war to participate in the U.S.-led coalition. The bombings might have been the last straw for the Spanish people, who voted the conservative Spanish government out of office within days of the bombings in favor of the Socialist Party led by José Luis Rodriguez Zapatero. Zapatero had made a campaign pledge to withdraw Spanish troops from Iraq, and on taking office he promptly ordered the withdrawal to be complete by May 2004, just two months after the Madrid bombings.

The internationalization of terrorism also creates the situation in which countries that have no real homegrown terrorism may become the haven for terrorists planning acts against other countries. Rand analysts Peter Chalk and William Rosenau discuss this phenomenon as it applies to Canada:

> Over the past decade, terrorists linked to Hamas, Hizbollah, Egyptian Islamic Jihad, the GIA, al Qaeda, PIRA, the Kurdish Worker's Party (PKK), the Liberation Tigers of Tamil Eelam (LTTE), Babbar Khalsa, and the Dashmesh Regiment are known to have entered Canada—generally posing as refugees—to engage in various front and organizational support activities. Principal pursuits have included fund-raising, lobbying, weapon procurement, diaspora mobilization, money laundering, and people or commodity transit.[24]

Chalk and Rosenau conclude that "with the possible exception of the United States and the United Kingdom, there are more international terrorist organizations currently active in Canada than anywhere else in the world."[25] As if to confirm this finding, Canada's 2004 national security document stated that one of Canada's core national security interests was "ensuring Canada is not a base for threats to our allies."[26]

It is an odd twist of circumstances that makes Canada a "nest" for terrorism, just as a failed or failing state may serve as a terrorist haven. The situations are different, of course. A failed or failing state—such as Afghanistan under the Taliban and perhaps even through 2006—is one that does not exert full institutional control over its entire territory. The lack of effective authority creates conditions in which terrorists can come and go and do as they wish with impunity. Advanced, highly developed countries such as Canada offer advantages to terrorists on a different order than do failed states. Important resources such as modern communications, transportation, financial institutions, technologies, and some types of weapons are procured easily in modern, open societies. At the same time, however, the openness of a Canada is similar to the openness of a failed or failing state. Where a failed or failing state is open and porous because the central authority is unable to exert full control over its territory, advanced liberal democracies are open and porous by design.

The social contract between the government and society in a liberal democracy intentionally limits the reach of government. Freedom of speech, movement, association, and other civil liberties are cherished and protected—and these liberties are indivisible. All persons residing within a liberal democracy enjoy the same civil liberties (although civil rights such as voting are extended only to citizens)—that is, all persons enjoy more or less the same freedoms whether the persons have good or malign purposes. In totalitarian or police states, governments keep suspected individuals and groups under surveillance and/or locked down (imprisoned), making terrorism harder to organize, prepare, and execute. Thus, despite Bush administration claims to the contrary, Saddam Hussein's Iraq was a particularly inhospitable place for terrorists. Only in Kurdish-controlled areas in the 1990s could one find active terrorist groups. International terrorists have few incentives to locate their operations in totalitarian states, while liberal democracies offer great advantages and protections against government intrusions.[27]

Canada's social contract also includes a strong sense of Canada as a good international citizen, willing to do its part to make the world more humane and secure for human beings. This results in an external security policy aimed at promoting international and human security and an internal security policy aimed at maintaining Canada as a welcome, open refuge for immigrants. Yet this refuge "has been effectively used by both peace-abiding and extremist elements from around the globe."[28]

As we will see shortly in our discussion of counterterrorism efforts, the social contract struck between the Canadian government and society greatly limits what Canadian authorities can do in the name of counterterrorism. This is true for and appropriate in all liberal democracies. It may be doubly difficult, however, for Canadian authorities to conduct certain types of counterterrorism operations within Canada given the circumstance that terrorist activities within Canada are not aimed at Canada. Canadians have demonstrated a high ability to empathize with citizens of other places, but the lack of terrorist attacks against Canada or Canadians may slow the hand of those who would increase counterterrorism operations at home. Further, economic openness, like political openness, creates opportunities for terrorists. Canada, the United States, and all other highly developed countries are porous by virtue of the magnitude of things and people crossing over and to some extent erasing national borders. Consider this description of the United States:

> If America is riddled with holes and targets, it's because a big society designed to be open is hard to change—impossible, probably. In 2000 more than 350 million non-US citizens entered the country. In 1999 Americans made 5.2 billion phone calls to locations outside the United States. Federal Express handles nearly five million packages every business day, UPS accounts for 13.6 million, and until it became a portal for terror, the Postal Service processed 680 million pieces of mail a day. More than two billion tons of cargo ran in and out of US ports in 1999, and about 7.5 million North Americans got on and off cruise ships last year [2001].[29]

Very few societies today remain closed; most are intentionally open in order to facilitate economic transactions that are critical to national economic well-being. Thus, economic openness enhances economic well-being—a core interest of any state—but the trade-off is a loss of a certain degree of government control of national borders.

The Increasing Lethality of Terrorism

The 9/11 terrorist attacks on the United States killed more people in a single episode than any before or since anywhere. In this regard, this episode stands alone among terrorist incidents. These attacks began the Bush administration's global war on terror and caused many to declare that we had entered a new and more dangerous era.[30] The high-casualty follow-on Bali and Madrid bombings—as well as other less lethal but still deadly bombings in other parts of Indonesia, Turkey, Saudi Arabia, and Morocco, and the London bombings of 2005—seemed proof of this new age of global terror.

The growing number of terrorist attacks and the growing number of people killed and injured in the twenty-first century is evidence to some analysts that terrorism has taken on a different cast. The Organization for Economic Cooperation and Development (OECD) warned about the possibility of unrecoverable economic losses from "megaterrorism" just two days before the terrorist attacks on the London transit system on July 7, 2005.[31] Robert Art calls this new kind of terrorism "grand terror." Until the early 1990s, Art writes, "the goals of traditional terrorists were strictly political, precisely defined, and directed toward specific goals such as ending political repression and economic injustice for a group, or attaining statehood for an ethnic minority." The number of deaths caused by such traditional terrorists was limited: "The aim of traditional terrorists was to cause enough death to rivet attention to their political cause, but not so much death as to cause a political backlash that would hurt that cause."[32]

Stern noted two years before the 9/11 attacks that a "new breed" of terrorism had appeared. This terrorism by "ad hoc groups motivated by religious conviction or revenge, violent right-wing extremists, and apocalyptic and millenarian cults" was inclined to acts of extreme violence. "Religious [terrorist] groups," Stern noted, "are becoming more common, and they are more violent than secular groups."[33]

Beyond the frightening doomsday scenarios of religious groups attempting to emulate divine retribution or spark a final war to end all wars, the lethality of terrorist attacks might be increasing for more "practical," rational reasons. Art proposes that terrorists "believe that governments and their citizens have become inured to killing and that therefore stepping up the killing is necessary to regain political attention."[34] This fits with Martha Crenshaw's assessment that the choice to use terrorism is fundamentally rational and strategic and results from political learning. "The practitioners of terrorism often claim that they had no choice but terrorism, and it is indeed true that terrorism often follows the failure of other methods."[35] Terrorists learn what authorities will do when confronted with opposition, particularly violent opposition. "Terrorists also learn from the experiences of others, usually communicated to them via the news media. Hence the existence of patterns of contagion in terrorist incidents."[36] Stern also notes this last point: "When it comes to methods, terrorists tend to *copy others*, so the use of WMD [weapons of mass destruction] by one terrorist group or by a nation may spark similar incidents" by others.[37]

In all the discussions of the increasing lethality of terrorism, this last point seems the most disturbing. From the late 1960s through the mid-1980s, terrorist groups crossed a line that previously prohibited the killing of women and children. After several groups crossed this line, other groups quickly followed.[38] Crossing the line gets the attention of authorities and societies. The taking of Middle School No. 1 in Beslan, Russia, should alarm authorities outside Russia less because of the Russian claims of international terrorism than because of the threshold crossed. Few things could terrorize and disrupt a society more than killing a school full of children.

What might hold terrorists back from crossing another line and using WMD? Stern asserts that steep technical obstacles make WMD use by terrorists improbable.[39] If technical obstacles could be overcome, little might hold some groups back. Stern worries that groups that claim to be following a higher (divine) authority may become "morally disengaged from the consequences of their actions" and even more willing to push the envelope in terms of terror tactics.[40] Moral disengagement is easier for "groups with amorphous constituencies," such as those affiliated with Osama bin Laden.[41]

Religion scholar Karen Armstrong issues a similar warning about the dangers of antinomian religious fundamentalist groups. Antinomianism is a doctrine typically associated with Christian groups that purports that the New Testament frees Christians from obedience to any laws of any origin. Armstrong identifies strong antinomian beliefs in fundamentalist Christian, Jewish, and Muslim groups. She argues that antinomian groups have risen historically in "times that were so desperate that something entirely new was required. Old values no longer applied; there had to be a new law, and a new freedom that could only be achieved by a flagrant disavowal of the old norms."[42] The twentieth century showed a marked increase in such groups and their nihilism, with 9/11 "simply the latest and most ferocious offensive conducted by fundamentalists in their ongoing battle for God."[43] This point was driven home for Armstrong by the fact that the terrorist who piloted the first plane into the World Trade Center had been drinking vodka that morning:

> Muslims are forbidden by their religion to drink alcohol. The idea that a Muslim martyr could go to meet God with vodka on his breath is as bizarre a thought as that of Baruch Goldstein, the Jewish fundamentalist who gunned down twenty-nine Muslims in the Great Mosque of Hebron in 1994 and was himself killed during the attack, enjoying a breakfast of bacon and eggs before carrying out the action. Most fundamentalists live strictly orthodox lives, and alcohol, nightclubs, and loose women are aspects of the *jahiliyyah*, the ignorant, godless barbarism that Muslim fundamentalists . . . have vowed not only to abjure but also to eliminate. The hijackers seem to have gone out of their way not only to disobey the basic laws of the religion they have vowed to defend but to also trample on the principles that motivate the traditional fundamentalist.[44]

Armstrong attributes a twentieth-century increase in antinomianism to the rise of modernity—the very kind of threat that requires abandoning the old moral code in order to defend it. Unlike others, however, Armstrong warns that the antinomian threat in the twenty-first century is not a clash of civilizations between modern and backward societies but rather an internal, intrasocietal dispute between modernists and fundamentalists. Armstrong writes, "As if to underline this fact, the American Christian fundamentalists Jerry Falwell and Pat Robertson almost immediately proclaimed that the [9/11] tragedy had been a judgment of God for the sins of the secular humanists in the United States—a viewpoint that was not far removed from that of the Muslim hijackers."[45] Indeed, Islamist terrorists associated with al-Qaeda have shown no reluctance to kill other Muslims not just around the world but even in their holy lands in their war against modernity.

Defending the Homeland against Terrorism

Despite the old saying that an ounce of prevention is worth a pound of cure, governments tend not to do much about the threat of terrorism until something tangible occurs, such as an attack or the uncovering of a plan for an attack. Here, I should qualify this discussion to indicate that my focus is on more or less open societies in which the national officeholders are accountable in some way to the broader public. Totalitarian governments of various sorts are already organized to meet real and imagined threats to their existence, whether posed by terrorists or by antigovernment groups. These governments are constantly on watch for potential sources of internal threats to their rule. Democratic states with open societies, conversely, tend to be more reactive than proactive to potential internal threats.

In one sense, the reactionary nature of a democracy's response to terrorism is related to the fundamental social contract struck between the people and the government. Democracies are intentionally open societies, and the role of government in open societies, in many respects, is to promote and maintain the openness. Not only does this openness create conditions that are hospitable to terrorist activities, as discussed earlier, but the openness means that governments typically do not engage in acts of prevention, waiting instead until an attack provokes the need for a "cure." Unfortunately, the cure that is chosen may be as momentous as the terrorist attack. As Laura Donohue warns, "When an open society has been taken advantage of [by terrorism] the immediate response is to close it."[46]

Democratic governments are responsive governments by design, and a terrorist attack prompts a government not just to respond

> but it must be *seen* to respond. And not just to terrorism in general, but to each significant attack. Following the 1974 Birmingham bombings [in the United Kingdom], for example, Westminster introduced the Prevention of Terrorism (Temporary Provisions) Act. After the August 15, 1998 Real IRA bombing in Omagh, Northern Ireland, the United Kingdom adopted the Criminal Justice (Terrorism and Conspiracy) Act and the Republic of Ireland introduced the 1999 Criminal Justice Act. . . . Following the 1995 attack by

Timothy McVeigh on the Murrah Federal Building in Oklahoma City, the United States' Congress adopted the 1996 Antiterrorism and Effective Death Penalty Act. And within weeks of September 11th, America witnessed, amongst other provisions, the adoption of PL 107-56, the "United [sic] and Strengthening America by Providing Appropriate Tools Required to Intercept and Obstruct Terrorism (USA PATRIOT) Act of 2001."[47]

As is true for any security issue, government responses to terrorism tend to take two forms: those dealing with internal vulnerabilities and those dealing with external vulnerabilities. Because of the difficulties involved in trying to close down all the possible external sources of terrorism, governments may conclude that they can be more effective turning inward. Donohue details the extent of such activity in the United States in the wake of the 9/11 attacks:

> Between September 11, 2001, and January 11, 2002, . . . Congress proposed more than 450 counterterrorist resolutions, bill, and amendments. (This compared with approximately 1,300 total in the course of US history.) Within four months of the attacks, more than two dozen new measures became law. President Bush issued 12 Executive Orders and 10 Presidential Proclamations related to the attacks. Only a handful addressed the war in Afghanistan. Most dealt with the domestic realm, the consequences of September 11, and the United States' preparedness for future terrorist attack.[48]

Donohue warns that these emergency laws, which have the impact of abridging civil liberties, become regularized over time as temporary emergency measures become permanent.[49] Since terrorism remains a distinct possibility and since governments are supposed to protect their citizens from terrorism, "security forces become reluctant to relinquish" powers. Meanwhile, calls to restore a preattack political order (that is, restore curtailed civil liberties and limit government intrusiveness) are met with derision and questions about whether the source of the calls is appropriately patriotic.[50] Civil liberties get curtailed, noncitizens get legally scapegoated, presumptions about innocence and free speech rights get eroded, and power becomes concentrated in the hands of the executive in order to more effectively deal with terrorists. Counterterrorist measures in liberal states move these states away from the liberal ideal of minimalist government—that essentially is no more than a sum of its parts—toward the antiliberal ideal of a maximalist government—which takes on more importance than its parts—all in the name of preserving and protecting "the people."

There is a built-in dynamic that encourages this movement away from minimalism and toward the maximalist state. Measures aimed at improving the government's internal investigatory and arrest powers tend to be more intrusive on civil liberties than those designed to improve how a government is organized to conduct counterterrorism. Yet attempts to reorganize government bureaucracies get frustrated by entrenched interests who do not want power and money shifted away from their agencies. Individual rights, conversely, are more easily curtailed because individuals (citizens but especially noncitizens) have less immediate political clout than do government agencies. Thus, for political reasons, we might expect a government to approve the curtailing of individual liberties via an increase in police investigatory and detainment powers rather than reorganize itself to make counterterrorism efforts more efficient and effective.

This dynamic and some potentially sinister results have been apparent in the United States in the post-9/11 era. The USA PATRIOT Act was rushed through Congress less than two months after the 9/11 attacks. It passed the Senate by a vote of 98 to 1 and the House by a vote of 357 to 66, with no discussion, debate, or hearings. In one of the most dramatic actions taken in the immediate aftermath of 9/11, Congress moved to curtail some civil liberties rather than reorganize intelligence agencies that had failed to detect the 9/11 plan prior to the attacks. Some of the USA PATRIOT Act's provisions "effectively [tore] down legal fire walls erected . . . during the Watergate era, when the nation was stunned by disclosures about presidential abuses of domestic intelligence gathering against political activists."[51]

Subsequent to increasing the surveillance powers of government, Congress acted to establish the Department of Homeland Security to better secure the territorial United States. This reorganization, however, took considerably longer than the USA PATRIOT Act, with the department coming into official existence in late January 2003. This department's mission is to "prevent terrorist attacks within the United States, reduce America's vulnerability to terrorism, and minimize the damage from potential attacks and natural disasters."[52] It includes operations as different as the Customs Service, parts of the Immigration and Naturalization Service, the Federal Emergency Management Agency, the Plum Island Animal Disease Center, and the Federal Computer Incident Response Center, among the twenty-two different operations organized into four directorates. Homeland Security does not include the agencies that gather and analyze intelligence or those that would act on certain types of intelligence.

In its short existence, Homeland Security has come under criticism for its public service announcements (some featuring duct tape and plastic sheeting to protect the air in private homes in the case of a chemical or biological attack), color-coded risk alerts, and seemingly politicized announcements about nonspecific threats.[53] More tellingly in the struggle to reorganize and better centralize disparate agencies was the finding issued in a fall 2004 report by the department's own inspector general. It noted that three years after the 9/11 attacks, the government had yet to bring together the more than a dozen different terrorist watch lists used by various government agencies into a single, comprehensive list available to all.[54] The lack of such a comprehensive list was a critical failure that prevented the thwarting of the 9/11 attacks.

Are there examples of how governments organize themselves to conduct counterterrorism and defend the homeland that might serve as templates for the U.S. government? This was a central question asked in a Rand study published in 2004. Authors Peter Chalk and William Rosenau analyzed the domestic intelligence operations of four democracies—the United Kingdom, France, Canada, and Australia—to identify strengths and weaknesses in each and to draw comparisons to the United States. In each of the four cases, the domestic intelligence agencies had no power of arrest and were separated from (but worked closely with) law enforcement agencies. The primary missions of these agencies involved the gathering of information for regular threat assessments aimed at threat mitigation.[55] The comparable U.S. agency, the Federal Bureau of Investigation (FBI), "while superbly qualified to investigate terrorist incidents *after* the fact, was grossly ill equipped to *prevent* attacks, given its strong law enforcement and prosecutorial culture."[56]

Because their primary missions are tied to internal threat mitigation, the domestic intelligence agencies in the United Kingdom, France, Canada, and Australia all put emphasis on the generation and use of human-based information gathered through local communities via local informants. For example, France's primary internal intelligence agency is the Direction de la Surveillance du Territoire (Directorate of Territorial Security [DST]). Its mission includes protecting economic and scientific infrastructure as well as broad counterterrorism.[57] Toward this goal, the DST develops locally generated human intelligence through the use of informers and the active monitoring of all immigrants, "especially those with an Islamic or North African background. All noncitizens are required to carry an identity card, and French nationals running hotels and guesthouses must inform authorities of the arrival and departure of any immigrants to whom they provide lodging."[58] This information is fed into a centralized database developed in part through DST's extensive working ties with the National Police (in urban areas, acting under the Ministry of the Interior) and the National Gendarmerie (in rural areas, acting under the Ministry of Defense). The DST also assists investigating magistrates as they conduct pretrial investigations into whether terrorist crimes have been committed.[59]

A less intrusive example is that of the Canadian domestic counterterrorism agency, the Canadian Security Intelligence Services (CSIS). Prior to the establishment of the CSIS in 1984, counterterrorism was conducted by the Royal Canadian Mounted Police (RCMP). That the RCMP was in charge of domestic intelligence was the motivation for creating CSIS: "There were mounting concerns that vesting a nonaccountable intelligence function within a domestic police agency that retained full powers of arrest threatened the democratic ethos of the Canadian way of life— particularly the right of all citizens to exercise legitimate political dissent."[60] The CSIS produces time-sensitive threat assessments aimed at forewarning and advising federal, provincial, and municipal government agencies. It takes care to advertise its mission and goals at the national and local levels in order to reassure citizens and to encourage and develop local-level intelligence.[61] Such efforts to reassure the public are seen as critical to establishing the trust necessary for negotiating with and within migrant communities. As discussed earlier, this is important in Canada, where some refugee and migrant communities increasingly are suspected of participating in recruitment and fund-raising activities for a variety of terrorist organizations.

Democratic governments must strike a sometimes precarious balance between the demands for greater internal security and the demand for government that upholds the values of liberalism. Some governments find the balance easier to strike, and some do not. Sometimes governments underestimate the dangers of terrorism, and sometimes they overestimate the dangers at the expense of individual liberties. Ultimately, the sovereign state claims an absolute right to tip the balance in favor of protecting the country over the cost to individuals. It is the case that many states have traveled far, so to speak, from Westphalia, and their citizens will not accept extreme trade-offs for security, as the Canadian case suggests. In the next chapter, I continue the discussion of national security by considering how states identify external security threats—another balancing act requiring more trade-offs.

The months of August and September 2004 were especially bloody in Russia because of four spectacular terrorist attacks. On August 24, two passenger airplanes were downed almost simultaneously by suicide bombers, killing ninety. On August 31, a suicide bomber took ten lives at a subway stop in Moscow. Then, on September 3, a three-day hostage taking at Middle School No. 1 in Beslan ended in explosions and free fire that killed at least 330 people, including many children. Ultimately, all these attacks were attributed by the Russian government to an alliance of "international" and Chechen "terrorists." Indeed, the government of Vladimir Putin initially claimed that some "Arabs" were among the terrorists who took Middle School No. 1 hostage.

Were the Chechens who opposed Russian rule in Chechnya inspired, trained, and/or funded by international terrorism, especially that associated with al-Qaeda? This was one of the many urgent questions needing answers after these bloody two months in Russian. Whether one considered the Chechen problem to be "homegrown" or foreign inspired might determine to some degree one's prescriptions for solving the Russian-Chechen conflict. At times, the Putin government claimed that the Chechen problem was domestic and thus none of the outside world's business; at other times, the government linked the Chechen problem to international terrorism and thus expected the outside world to be sympathetic to whatever Russia did in self-defense.

Russian-Chechen relations have been marked by great animosity since Russia's takeover of the Caucasus in the mid-nineteenth century. The Chechens have resisted Russian domination ever since. During the Russian Revolution, the Chechen and Ingush people declared themselves to be the independent state of Dagestan (a state that would be populated primarily by Sunni Muslim people), an effort that did not stand. Dagestan was divided by Soviet authorities to dilute the resistance, creating in part the Chechen-Ingush Autonomous Soviet Socialist Republic. The Chechen and Ingush peoples were troublesome for the Soviet Union and were accused of collaborating with the Nazis during World War II. For this they were deported nearly en masse to Siberia and central Asia in 1944. The Chechen-Ingush Autonomous Soviet Socialist Republic was not restored until 1957 by then Soviet leader Nikita Khrushchev, at which time the Chechens and Ingush were allowed to return. The experience of mass deportation was added to the long list of grievances held by the Chechens and Ingush peoples against the Russians.

As the Soviet Union was imploding in late 1991, a vote held in the Chechen-Ingush Autonomous Soviet Socialist Republic brought to the presidency a nationalist Chechen who promptly declared Chechnya to be independent of the Soviet Union. When the Soviet Union collapsed, Chechnya was considered by Russian authorities (and the other states in the international system) to be one of the twenty-one autonomous republics *within* Russia. Yet Russian authorities did virtually nothing to demonstrate Russian legal authority over Chechnya. It operated as a more or less independent country until late 1994.

In December 1994, President Boris Yeltsin ended Russia's careless policy toward the independence-minded Chechnya by launching a massive military invasion. Russian firepower was concentrated on the capital, Grozny, which was also the site of an important oil field and pipeline and the home to approximately half the Chechen population. It took the Russian military two months to regain control of Grozny after leveling and depopulating it. In the fighting that raged on throughout Chechnya for two more years, perhaps 100,000 Chechens were killed in a population that numbered only about 1 million.

Despite the fact that Chechens were Sunni Muslim, the self-declared independent state of Chechnya, by the constitution adopted in 1992, was to be a secular, parliamentary state. Further, despite rumors to the contrary, during the first Chechen war (1994–1996), the secular nationalist struggle remained central to the rebel cause, and "essentially no fighters had a strong sense of the larger international Islamic movement."[1] Although there was a minority of Chechens who were interested in radical Islamism,[2] foreign fighters and foreign assistance were not features of the Chechen struggle until after the first war concluded. The first war ended after some 5,000 Chechen rebels recaptured Grozny in 1996, just as the Russian public and media turned decisively against the war. The Russians and Chechens signed a cease-fire that allowed Chechnya to continue to act autonomously but without resolving the longer-term status of the republic.

In the interwar period, Chechnya was marked by lawlessness and banditry. As might be expected, into this confusion came foreign influence, especially in the form of financial support from Islamic charities in Arab states, Europe, and North America.[3] Osama bin Laden took notice of Chechnya at this time, suggesting that it was an incubator of religious war, as were Bosnia and Tajikistan.[4] Some al-Qaeda fighters came to Chechnya during this time. Perhaps in response to the influx of foreign jihadists and money, Chechen President Aslan Maskhadov declared in early 1999 that Islamic sharia law would be imposed over a three-year period. "Chechnya's period of independence, when the republic was lawless, appears to have been the peak of the transit of fighters, cash and ideology from abroad."[5] Also at this time, Islamic radicals dominated the Chechen rebels. These radicals staged an armed incursion into the neighboring Russian republic Dagestan in the summer of 1999 designed to consolidate a larger Islamic separatist state.[6]

The second Chechen war began in the fall of 1999 after apartment block bombings in Russia were blamed on Chechen terrorists. Some media sources later suggested that Russian authorities may have had a hand in these bombings to justify renewed military operations in Chechnya.[7] Regardless, the second war no doubt was prompted by the threats posed by continued Chechen lawlessness to Russia's access to natural gas and oil as well as the need to shore up popular support for Vladimir Putin's transition from acting to elected Russian president.

The second war in Chechnya—in all its enormous slaughter and stalemate—was still active when the terrorist attacks on the United States occurred on September 11, 2001. Prior to 9/11, the United States and the European Union regularly called on Russia to modify its actions in Chechnya and seek a political rather than military solution. Putin took the 9/11 attacks as an opportunity to admonish the Americans and Europeans regarding Chechnya, reminding them that Russians were under attack by international terrorists as well. In a quid pro quo, the American administration began to moderate its tone on Chechnya, echoing Russian claims that the problems there were attributable to terrorism, while Putin announced his support for the Bush administration's newly declared global war on terrorism. Russian officials even modified for a short time their opposition to U.S. military presence in the former Soviet republics in central Asia in order to give the Americans forward basing for operations in Afghanistan.

During the second Chechen war, Russian officials repeatedly complained that Chechen fighters were regrouping in the Pankisi Gorge area of neighboring Georgia. "Russia [had] alternately threatened Georgian officials and negotiated with them to solve the rebel occupation of the gorge, which also [was] home to an estimated 5,000 to 7,000 Chechen refugees."[8] In early 2002, the U.S. government announced that it would be supporting the Georgian government with military training and equipment to use against the fighters, who American officials said included Arabs who had trained in al-Qaeda camps in Afghanistan. Publicly dismissing some Russian fears about American troops so close to Russia, Putin declared that the American efforts in Pankisi were part of the war on terrorism and helpful.[9]

That Chechen rebels were taking haven in the Pankisi Gorge seems indisputable, but the presence of Arabs or al-Qaeda fighters was less so. Georgia posed a different political problem to the Russians, one that the Putin government seemed happy to link to terrorism, Chechnya, and the post-9/11 world. Since the breakup of the Soviet Union, Georgia had been disinclined to acknowledge Russia's dominance. In response, Russia gave support to Abkhazian separatists in their fight against Georgian authorities, and then Russia forced Georgia to allow 7,000 Russian "peacekeepers" to assist in maintaining a cease-fire that was struck between the government and the separatists.[10] At the same time, Georgia reluctantly joined the Russian-led Commonwealth of Independent States.

In the meantime, Georgian officials had struck a decidedly pro-American foreign policy stance. Key to the Georgian-American relationship was oil. "Georgia [was] also ground zero in a significant post-Cold War struggle between Russia and the United States, over the direction oil from the Caspian Sea region will take as it makes its way to Europe. The United States [had] backed Georgia's efforts to host pipelines that would keep the oil from going through Iran and Russia."[11] Establishing a U.S. military presence in Georgia prior to 9/11 was unthinkable, but after 9/11, Russian claims about foreign terrorists in Pankisi gave the Americans and the Georgians the opening they had wanted.

Although Putin publicly stated that the U.S. military presence in Georgia served everyone's interests and threatened none, he continued to threaten Georgia over the Chechen fighters in the Pankisi Gorge. On the anniversary of 9/11, Putin used Bush's language of the previous year to inform the UN Security Council that he reserved the right to launch preemptive strikes against Georgia if it did not do more to clean out Pankisi. Putin claimed "that Georgia's harboring of Chechen fighters gave Russia the right to act in self-defense under Article 51 of the United Nations Charter and the antiterrorism resolution passed" by the Security Council after the 9/11 terrorist attacks.[12] Georgia's parliament, in response, condemned Putin's comments as well as Russian military aircraft incursions into Georgian airspace as threats of aggression. The Bush administration indicated that it would not support any unilateral military action by Russia against Georgia,[13] but the threats continued to be issued.

Indeed, the threats levied against Georgia seemed to be a diversion from the homegrown problems associated with Chechnya, as demonstrated the following month. In October 2002, Chechen rebels took 763 people hostage in a Moscow theater. Russian authorities ended the hostage taking by pumping an unnamed gas into the theater, resulting in the deaths of over one hundred hostages and the rebels.

Some of the hostage takers in this episode were identified as "black widows," or Chechen women whose relatives were killed by Russian forces in the Chechen wars. None were foreign jihadists. Similarly, the suicide bombers who brought down two passenger airliners in August 2004 were Chechen women. The hostage takers in the siege in Middle School No. 1 in Beslan in September 2004 were both men and women, and all were apparently Chechen or Ingush despite official claims about "Arabs" being present.

After the disaster at Beslan, Putin met with foreign journalists to discuss the events in Russia. As reported in the London newspaper *Guardian*, Putin did not tolerate questions that linked Russia's policies in Chechnya to the terrorist attacks.[14] "The president made it clear that he [saw] the drive for Chechen independence as the spearhead of a strategy by Chechen Islamists, helped by foreign fundamentalists, to undermine the whole of southern Russia and even stir up trouble among Muslim communities in other parts of the country." Russian officials also renewed their threats against Georgia in light of the Beslan terrorist attack, ruling out nothing except the use of nuclear weapons.[15]

This discussion began by asking whether the Chechens who carried out the terrorist attacks in Russia in August and September 2004 were foreign inspired, trained, or affiliated.[16] Chechen animosity toward Russians goes back more than a century, and Chechen efforts to throw off Russian domination go back just as far. Any links that existed between Chechen rebels and international terrorist groups appeared to be in the service of long-standing Chechen nationalist goals. Any claims by the Russians about international terrorists in Chechnya similarly appeared to serve Russian political interests.

Notes

1. C. J. Chivers and Steven Lee Myers, "Chechen Rebels Mainly Driven by Nationalism," *New York Times*, September 12, 2004, 1.

2. Scott Peterson, "Al Qaeda among the Chechens," *Christian Science Monitor*, September 7, 2004, 1.

3. Chivers and Myers, "Chechen Rebels Mainly Driven by Nationalism."

4. Chivers and Myers, "Chechen Rebels Mainly Driven by Nationalism."

5. Chivers and Myers, "Chechen Rebels Mainly Driven by Nationalism."

6. Peterson, "Al Qaeda among the Chechens."

7. Patrick Cockburn, "Russian Intelligence Produces Apartment Bombing Evidence," *Independent* (London), March 17, 2000, 19; Johann Hari, "Beheaded Hostages, Slaughtered Children, and the Misguided War on Global Terror," *Independent* (London), September 22, 2004, 31.

8. Sharon LaFraniere, "US Military in Georgia Rankles Russia," *Washington Post*, February 28, 2002, A16.

9. Patrick E. Tyler, "Russia's Leader Says He Supports American Military Aid for Georgia," *New York Times*, March 2, 2002, 9.

10. LaFraniere, "US Military in Georgia Rankles Russia."

11. David Filipov, "US Troops Help Ex-Soviet State Fight Militants," *Boston Globe*, March 19, 2002, A1.

12. Steven Lee Myers, "Echoing Bush, Putin Asks UN to Back Georgia Attack," *New York Times*, September 13, 2002, 9.

13. Ian Traynor, "Putin Threatens to Invade Georgia," September 13, 2002, *Guardian* (London), 14.

14. Jonathan Steele, "Angry Putin Rejects Public Beslan Inquiry," *Guardian* (London), September 7, 2004.

15. "Russia to Hit Foreign Lairs?" *Reuters/Toronto Sun*, September 13, 2004, 42.

16. "Victims of a Conflict without End," *Economist*, Economist.com, September 7, 2004.

4

Identifying External
Security Threats

C onsider these proclamations from different national leaders on the
national security issues confronting their states:

- "The enemy is not a single political regime or person or religion or
  ideology. The enemy is terrorism . . .
    "We will disrupt and destroy terrorist organizations by . . . defend-
  ing the United States, the American people, and our interests at home
  and abroad by identifying and destroying the threat before it reaches
  our borders. While the United States will constantly strive to enlist
  the support of the international community, we will not hesitate to
  act alone, if necessary, to exercise our right of self-defense by acting
  preemptively against such terrorists, to prevent them from doing
  harm against our people and our country." (U.S. President George W.
  Bush, September 2002)[1]
- "In the defence area the Juche Idea means Self-Defence, it's a basic
  point to warrant the protection of the country using an invincible
  military power that will protect the motherland and revolutionary
  achievements from the aggressive Yankee imperialism and its ser-
  vants." (Government of North Korea website, 2004)[2]
- "We have shown weakness in the face of danger. And the weak get
  beaten up." (Russian President Vladimir Putin, Address to the
  Nation, September 2004)[3]

- "Any time the United Nations and the international community fail to disarm [our enemies] . . . and to contain them, we shall do it ourselves, and this will not take long, or it is even happening now." (Rwandan President Paul Kagame, November 2004)[4]

The pursuit of external security, like the pursuit of internal security, is an absolute right of the state. Article 51 (Chapter VII) of the UN Charter upholds this right even as it seeks to establish the means by which external security can be guaranteed collectively:

Nothing in the present Charter shall impair the inherent right of individual or collective self-defence if an armed attack occurs against a Member of the United Nations, until the Security Council has taken measures necessary to maintain international peace and security.[5]

The UN Charter envisions a world in which external security is guaranteed by mutual respect for the territorial integrity of all states as well as by the threat of collective security or the collective punishment of aggressors. I examine international security later in this book, but no discussion of national security post-1945 is complete without acknowledging the important context of the UN system.

The United Nations is a system based on reciprocal exchanges. In exchange for the promise of protection through collective security, states agree "that armed force shall not be used, save in the common interest."[6] This relinquishing of the use of armed force in the pursuit of a state's foreign policy goals does not, as noted previously, impair the state's "inherent right" of self-defense. Furthermore, as I discuss in later chapters, the UN system is a *voluntary* system of reciprocal exchanges, and states are more or less bound by membership obligations (some states seem more bound than others, some less bound). Thus, the use of armed force in statecraft remains a present reality in international politics, as much as the use of state violence remains present in state-building and state-maintenance activities within states. States threaten and use armed force—and they erect stockpiles of armaments for these purposes.

Collective security itself could not be maintained credibly without the threat of some military punishment; thus, even the UN international security system is dependent on the presence of military power and capabilities. Beyond self-defense and regional defense, the need to contribute to international security explains in part why two prominent states currently prohibited by their own laws from acquiring offensive military capabilities—Japan (by virtue of its Peace Constitution) and Germany (by virtue of its Basic Law)—still maintain formidable military capabilities.

International Anarchy and the Security Dilemma

As discussed in chapter 2, what we have come to accept as the reality of international politics was born on the bloodied fields of Central Europe during the Thirty Years' War. "The war bred a pessimistic mood: evil was seen as ubiquitous and *realpolitik* seemed to offer the only viable tactics for advancing one's interests in a callous world."[7] The long legacy of Westphalian principles demonstrates "that when a practice (such as war making) becomes widespread, these customs tend to become obligatory."[8]

What we call the Westphalian peace treaty initiated a system between states that did not attempt to guarantee international peace but instead "created a war called 'peace.'"[9] The first element of this system that came to be taken as a given was that the international system was characterized by anarchy, which is to say that "there is no international political authority invested with a legitimate monopoly of force capable of enforcing peace, protecting states against aggression, and guaranteeing that their rights will not be violated."[10] Given the predominant value placed on state sovereignty in international politics, no overarching international political authority *could* be created. International treaties could be struck and accords arranged, but these would be premised on the understanding that national security interests might at any time require a state's departure from such treaties and accords.

Anarchy does not imply chaos, nor does it imply a lack of rules and order. Instead, the order that was struck after Westphalia was founded on the realist notion of the balance of power. The *Penguin Dictionary of International Relations* tells us that "balance of power," like "power" itself, is both "pervasive and indispensable" in characterizations of international politics as well as "by no means clear" and "open to a number of different interpretations."[11] Balance of power refers to the distribution of power across the international system, especially or particularly among the greater or major powers (although this could apply equally to regional systems and regional powers). This balance is more than a distribution of power because it is also a system by which great powers attempt to prevent any one of their ranks from becoming hegemonic. War is not necessarily the first resort in such a system, as war is not always the most efficient way to maintain the balance. Thus, great powers calibrate and recalibrate the balance through arms acquisitions, negotiations, short-term alliance formation, and then, if necessary, war. After great power war, the order must be restruck, but the "new" order is decidedly old in terms of its membership, as the balance-of-power system pays an odd respect to the notion that defeated and chastened great powers must be allowed to reenter the arrangement.

The balance-of-power system did not ensure peace but regularized war as a means by which some European states consolidated their power over other Europeans and ultimately over the world. The world wars of the first half of the twentieth century can be understood in some sense as balance-of-power wars, although by this time the European great powers had been joined by the United States, China, and Japan.

The balance-of-power system also did not preserve a stable status quo or equilibrium. John Mearsheimer maintains this is "because the international system creates powerful incentives for states to look for opportunities to gain power at the expense of rivals, and to take advantage of those situations when the benefits outweigh the costs. A [major] state's ultimate goal is to be the hegemon in the system."[12] Writing in the midst of a great power war—World War II—Nicholas J. Spykman made this same observation:

> The truth of the matter is that states are interested only in a balance (imbalance) which is in their favor. Not an equilibrium, but a generous margin is their objective. There is no real security in being just as strong as a potential enemy; there is security only in being a little stronger. There is no possibility of action if one's strength is fully checked; there is a chance for a positive foreign policy only if there is a margin of force which can be freely used.[13]

These same sentiments were present in U.S. domestic politics in the aftermath of the 1972 signing of the nuclear arms control agreement, the Strategic Arms Limitations Treaty (SALT) I, between the United States and the Soviet Union. For the Soviet Union, SALT I signaled that the superpowers were essentially equal, that their power was essentially balanced. This was seen as a Soviet achievement after decades of playing catch-up with the Americans. To American conservatives within the Republican party especially, SALT I was an ominous sign. Essential equivalence was something to be feared; peace with the Soviets could be achieved only through strength over them. Ronald Reagan would ride to the U.S. presidency on a "peace through strength" bandwagon.

As I will discuss later in this book, elements of the balance-of-power system get incorporated into the UN collective security framework, although the free use of war to regulate the distribution of power across the great powers is prohibited.

An additional concept needs to be added here before we go on to examine states' responses to threats, and that is the realist concept of the security dilemma. As explained by Glenn Snyder,

> The term is generally used to denote the self-defeating aspect of the quest for security in an anarchic system. The theory says that even when no state has any desire to attack others, none can be sure that others' intentions are peaceful, or will remain so; hence each must accumulate power for defense. Since no state can know that the power accumulation of others is defensively motivated only, each must assume that it might be intended for attack. Conse-

quently, each party's power increments are matched by the others, and all wind up with no more security than when the vicious cycle began, along with the costs incurred in having acquired and having to maintain their power.[14]

Consider this quote from a 1907 British security document concerning German-British relations and how it captures the essence of the security dilemma:

> So long, then, as Germany competes for an intellectual and moral leadership of the world in reliance on [its] own national advantages and energies England can but admire, applaud, and join in the race. If, on the other hand, Germany believes that greater relative preponderance of material power, wider extent of territory, inviolable frontiers, and supremacy at sea are the necessary and preliminary possessions without which any aspirations to such leadership must end in failure, then England must expect that Germany will surely seek to diminish the power of any rivals, to enhance [its] own by extending [its] dominion, to hinder the co-operation of other States, and ultimately to break up and supplant the British Empire.
>
> Now it is quite possible that Germany does not, nor ever will, consciously cherish any schemes of so subversive a nature. [Its] statesmen have openly repudiated them with indignation. Their denial may be perfectly honest, and their indignation justified . . .
>
> But this is not a matter in which England can safely run any risks . . .
>
> Meanwhile it is important to make it quite clear that a recognition of the dangers of the situation need not and does not imply any hostility to Germany.[15]

By this same logic, should Germany perceive hostility and threat from Britain's actions (and, by this logic, why should it not?), Germany would be justified in acting on such threat, although this response would naturally lead England to perceive greater threat and step up its own actions in response.

In chapter 1, we examined the case of Australia's refusal to allow the landing of some Afghan boat people in August 2001. Australia's ongoing efforts to manage the security threat posed by boat people (as potential terrorists) resulted in a December 2004 policy announcement that threatened its neighbors. The Australian prime minister declared that Australia would begin to enforce a 1,000-nautical-mile maritime security zone to protect against shipborne terrorists who would threaten Australian territory and offshore oil interests in the Timor Sea. Any ship entering the zone would be required to produce detailed information on its cargo, crew, and destination(s) when challenged by the Australian navy.[16] By the declared size of the zone, the territorial waters and even the sovereign territory of Indonesia, Timor-Leste, Papua New Guinea, and New Zealand would be violated by Australia.

Officials in Indonesia and New Zealand, as well as those in Malaysia whose waters and territory would not be directly affected, quickly warned Australia not to violate other states' sovereignty or international maritime law.[17] Although Australian officials tried to reassure the neighbors, some were not so easily placated. Indonesia had had prickly relations with Australia since the 1970s and Indonesia's annexing of East Timor. When ethnic conflict erupted around East Timor's independence referendum in September 1999, Australian Prime Minister John Howard declared Australia to be the "deputy" of the United States in Asia as Australia led a multinational military intervention force into East Timor.[18] These bad relations were intensified over the August 2001 Afghan boat people episode when Australian officials implied that Indonesia had encouraged the people smuggling that sent illegal migrants toward Australia. Adding more fuel to the fire since 2002 were repeated pronouncements by the Australian prime minister that Australia reserved the right to launch preemptive strikes in neighboring countries to prevent terrorist attacks.[19] If any specific country were to feel threatened by the new Australian maritime security zone, it would be Indonesia. By realist logic, Indonesia would be foolhardy *not* to respond with some heightened military posture to Australia's newest affront.

The tsunami disaster that struck on December 26, 2004, put the tense security dynamics between Australia and Indonesia into a different but not necessarily more cooperative light. The earthquake and tsunami took their hardest toll on the Indonesian province of Aceh. Aceh was the scene of a thirty-year-old separatist rebellion. Indonesian military officials had banned foreign presence in Aceh—specifically aid groups and media—prior to the disaster. After the tsunami struck, foreign humanitarian groups and militaries were permitted in Indonesia but within certain well-defined limits. American and Australian military forces were permitted to render disaster relief, but these foreign military personnel operated without traditional sidearms or self-defense weaponry in order to assuage Indonesian sensitivities. Further, Indonesian authorities ordered the foreign troops to leave Indonesian territory by March 26, and until then all foreign military assistance would be under the operational control of the Indonesian military.[20] Despite the country's loss of over 100,000 people in the tsunami calamity, the compelling human needs could not override government concerns over potential threats to Indonesian sovereignty.

Just as the ongoing security dilemma and bad relations between Indonesia and Australia would not be abated by the humanitarian disaster that struck in late December 2004, Indonesian government forces would not hesitate to use the disaster to continue to wage the fight against the Aceh separatists. Humanitarian aid groups were allowed into Aceh to provide disaster relief, but officials declared that these efforts were restricted to two main cities and had to be conducted under military oversight:

As well as announcing the restrictions on movements outside the two main cities, the military said . . . that it was requiring aid agencies to tell the military where they are planning to deliver assistance. During the civil conflict, food has been a target of both the military and the rebels, and precise information about where food is being delivered for civilians could be of help to the military in its battle against the separatist insurgents.[21]

Not all states appear to be seized by the dynamics of the security dilemma to be sure. But whenever central authorities are faced with what they perceive to be serious threats to their existence, sovereignty, status, or prestige, we are sure to see elements of this self-defeating cycle as well as trade-offs with other national values.

A critical problem for national leaders is how to gauge threats in a system that is by definition abundant with threats. Further, national leaders must somehow convince other states that their actions are simply defensive and not intended to be threatening (unless the game of threats is on, and in a realist world this is the operative assumption). In sorting out threats, Klaus Knorr makes the distinction between *actual* threats (which he says can be precise as well as vague), *potential* threats, and *systemic* threats. The determination of whether a threat is actual or potential is always made more dangerous by systemic threats:

> Today's friendly neighbor may become dangerous tomorrow, because, for example, he has acquired additional territory or superior technology or a strong ally or a different government. The observation that interstate changes in intentions and capabilities can unpredictably lead to dangerous threats follows from the very structure of the international system in which each unit is militarily sovereign. We call this, therefore, the *systemic* threat. It means that, over the longer run, no state-actor can ever be certain of its security.[22]

What do states *do* when perceiving actual or potential threats in the face of the "reality" of the security dilemma and the ongoing systemic threat? There are a variety of stances a state may take, as I examine next.

Balancing Power, Balancing Threats

As discussed earlier in this chapter, the balance of power refers both to the distribution of capabilities across the actors in the system and to how great powers regulate their own relations in order to prevent one of their own from becoming hegemonic. In a situation such as the current international system where one state holds predominant power, the expectation derived from balance-of-power theory is that other major states will amass more power and ally against the predominant power to restore a multipolar equilibrium to the system.[23] The balance-of-power system works on the basis of short-term alliances between like-minded states or, to use a phrase popular in some circles, short-term coalitions of the willing.

Despite the persistence of balance-of-power ideas, power itself is not always immediately threatening. The power held by any given state may *not* be perceived as threatening, even in a world in which one assumes that the broader systemic threat is a "reality" to which one must respond. Even preponderant power need not result in the perception of threat. In the 1990s, Josef Joffe suggested that American preponderance might not prompt balancing behavior by other major powers (China, Russia, and the European Union) because the nature of American preponderance was nonthreatening. "America is different," Joffe wrote,

> it irks and domineers, but it does not conquer. It tries to call the shots and bend the rules, but it does not go to war for land and glory. . . . Those who coerce or subjugate others are far more likely to inspire hostile alliances than nations that contain themselves, as it were.[24]

Joffe borrowed Joseph Nye's notion of "soft power"[25] to explain that "this type of power—a culture that radiates outward and a market that draws inward—rests on pull, not on push; on acceptance, not on conquest. Worse, this kind of power cannot be aggregated, nor can it be balanced."[26] Because of the nature of American power and the benefits of cooperating with the United States, other major powers did not need to balance against it because of the absence of any perceived threat.

However, policies change, as do expected responses to policies. The declared Bush policy of preventive/preemptive war (discussed in chapter 6) enunciated in the September 2002 National Security Strategy of the United States of America and reinforced in the March 2006 strategy paper signaled that the United States would no longer "contain" itself. The U.S. invasion of Iraq in March 2003 demonstrated that the United States would not only "irk and domineer" but would also "conquer." Indeed, in late 2004 the outgoing U.S. secretary of state declared that the Bush administration would continue to wage an "aggressive" foreign policy into its next term in office.[27] This was reinforced by Bush's second inaugural speech, when he declared that U.S. national security depended on ending tyranny around the world, a call that could be interpreted as a threat of more military action.

Russia had been a strong opponent of the U.S. war in Iraq, as had China to a lesser degree. At the end of 2004, as a second Bush administration was assured and after a very damaging diplomatic scuffle over Ukrainian elections, Russia announced that it would hold the first-ever large-scale joint military exercises with China in late 2005.[28] This announcement was met with concerns over whether the two would sign a formal military alliance. Meanwhile, advisers to the U.S. president were urging a policy stance in

which China was viewed more as a growing rival than a strategic partner.[29] Then, in the summer 2005, the Shanghai Cooperation Organization—a regional alliance composed of Russia, China, Kazakhstan, Kyrgyzstan, Uzbekistan, and Tajikistan—demanded that the United States
indicate a deadline for ending its use of bases in Kyrgyzstan and Uzbekistan.[30] These bases were considered essential to the U.S. war in
Afghanistan and were part of a longer-term U.S. strategy of securing
access to central Asian oil and natural gas.[31] The demand—dismissed by
the United States—signaled the choosing of sides in a developing great
power game. The United States was not able to persuade Uzbekistan to
change its mind. The beginnings of a shifting power balance were evident
in 2005, prompted by changing perceptions of U.S. power in light of
changing U.S. policy and practice.

A related issue is that *some* power capabilities held by *some* countries are
not perceived to be threatening in the same way as those same capabilities would be perceived if held by other countries. If one's allies or
friendly trading partners hold a certain type of weapon system, the threat
posed (if one is perceived at all) is far less than that posed when that
weapon is held by a state (or group of states) with which one shares a history of enmity. Even regarding "rogue" states, it is possible to judge that
one rogue is better or worse than another; thus, certain power capabilities
may be more tolerable when held by the lesser rogue than if held by the
greater rogue. Other dynamics may come into play, of course; as I'll discuss shortly, the response given to a lesser rogue's unwanted behaviors
may be more reactionary than that given to the greater rogue's unwanted
behaviors.

Even among one's friends, there may be a hierarchy of interests that
allows for some friends to possess greater power capabilities than other
friends. According to Jungmin Kang and others, this differential treatment
of friends is partly to blame for South Korea's secret nuclear weapons
activities:

> South Korea's hidden actions exemplify the impulse toward proliferation
> that arises in response to the discriminatory treatment the United States
> shows to different states, permitting, for example, Japan to have tons of plu-
> tonium while South Korea may have none, and Japan to explore mixed oxide
> fuels for reactors while South Korea may not. The disparity in the application
> of ostensibly universal nonproliferation norms is keenly felt by Koreans who
> remain resentful of Japan's big power status and its colonial aggression in
> Korea.[32]

What secret nuclear weapons activities had been prompted, in part, by
this discrimination, which allowed some American friends to be more
powerful than others?

[In the fall of 2001] under pressure from the International Atomic Energy Agency (IAEA), South Korea publicly disclosed its past secret nuclear research activities, revealing that it had conducted chemical uranium enrichment from 1979 to 1981, separated small quantities of plutonium in 1982, experimented with uranium enrichment in 2000, and manufactured depleted uranium munitions from 1983 to 1987. The South Korean government had violated its international agreements by not declaring any of these activities to the IAEA in Vienna.[33]

South Korea's activities, it must be remembered, occurred in the context of at least two different security dilemmas: a more historical one with Japan and an ongoing one with North Korea.

That some countries—whether friend or foe—are perceived to present more or less of a threat than others when in possession of certain types of capabilities raises two related analytical topics: balance-of-threat theory and threat perception. Stephen Walt has contended that states balance not against power itself but rather against certain types of power and certain types of intentions. Offensive capabilities amassed by a state or a group of states with perceived aggressive intentions prompt balancing behavior, not the mere possession of certain types of power.[34] How one defines offensive capabilities and aggressive intentions depends on one's interpretation of facts. This then raises the more difficult issue of threat perception.

As Knorr explains, a threat is an ambiguous thing; thus, accurate threat perception is a vital yet formidable task:

> Even an ultimatum may be a bluff, and marching troops can be ordered to stop. The crucial point is that a threat is usually not observable. It is a cognitive construct. But unless it is a product of psychopathology, this construct is derived from things which, in principle, can be observed—that is, the behavior of governments and the capabilities of states. Unfortunately, these observable realities rarely have unmistakable meaning. They are ambiguous, and also they change over time.[35]

How do we judge whether an act means what we think it means, and at what cost do we hesitate until more unambiguous information is available? These questions underscored comments made by the U.S. national security adviser in 2002 during the Bush administration's public construction of its case to go to war with Iraq: "The problem here is that there will always be some uncertainty about how quickly [Saddam Hussein] can acquire nuclear weapons. But we don't want the smoking gun to be a mushroom cloud."[36] To wait for better information on which to act may be wise, but to wait too long in some "games" is to never have a second chance. Yet the American failure to find any weapons of mass destruction (WMD) in Iraq suggests that the decision to act "before it was too late" was a judgment call based on an inaccurate reading of the intelligence at the very least.

Knorr contends that threat perception is beset by two general difficulties: First, there is the intrinsic or intellectual problem of developing good and reliable information from the past or present and projecting this onto the future.[37] As the terrorist attacks of 9/11 would indicate, gathering, analyzing, and "connecting the dots" between reliable bits of intelligence sometimes seems beyond the capabilities of the most powerful states.

Intelligence also must be weighed against what is known, and this may lead to other problems. It is of course understandable that decision makers attempt to understand the past as a key to understanding the future, but overreliance on history can cause one to fail to see changes in capabilities that would prompt new types of reasonably expected behaviors. Knorr explains that in October 1973, Israel was surprised by an Egyptian and Syrian military attack (the opening of the 1973 Arab-Israeli war). The surprise resulted, in part, from Israel's assumption that these Arab states would not launch and in fact were not capable of launching a surprise attack. "This assumption was based in part on the belief, derived from plenty of previous experience, that the Arab countries were incapable of maintaining political and military secrecy, which is a prerequisite for achieving surprise. This time, however, the Arab governments had the capability."[38]

Bush administration allegations about the threat posed by Iraq's stockpiling of WMD before the March 2003 invasion were in part based on relatively recent historical revelations. After the first Gulf War of 1991, international weapons inspectors were surprised to learn how far along Iraq's nuclear weapons program had been. Citing this surprise, Bush administration officials claimed that the international community should assume that Iraqi WMD research and production were still under way more than ten years later and despite an international inspections regime and that the Iraqi regime's claims to the contrary were merely attempts to deceive the international community. But, Knorr cautions decision makers, "the past does not repeat itself automatically."[39] Opponents may increase their capabilities in ways not envisioned as the 1973 Arab attack on Israel demonstrated. Or the opponent's abilities may become degraded substantially, or it may have abandoned the pursuit of certain offensive capabilities, as the Iraqi regime apparently did prior to the 2003 invasion.[40]

The Bush administration appeared incapable of imagining a different interpretation of facts—thus, the Bush administration did not or would not accept that the Iraqi regime may have abandoned its WMD ambitions while still attempting to enjoy the threatening perception that it was close to WMD possession. This leads to Knorr's second observation about the difficulties of threat perception: threat perception is compounded by the intervention of individuals' and groups' emotions, predispositions, and attitudes, all of which serve to distort the interpretation of what information is known.[41] Rigid preconceptions, wishful thinking, selective retrieval, and use of information in ways consistent with "an actor's treasured self-image,"[42] as well as groupthink and bureaucratic rewards structures that suppress or distort information, all are impediments to accurate threat perception.

Accurate threat perception is not just impeded by intrinsic/intellectual and predispositional difficulties. Knorr proposes that we also take into account "situational strangeness" or "cultural strangeness," which causes decision makers to be unable to accurately understand what they are observing about the opponent.[43] The distortions get magnified when an opponent is attempting to deceive its own public for its own domestic political purposes. Further, when the opponent's government sends mixed or conflicting signals, the threatened state may impose its own understanding on the signals: "If one finds the usual untidiness of government intolerable, one may try hard to superimpose careful design on ambiguous behavior."[44] Thus, the Bush administration claimed it saw intentional deceit and concealment when the Iraqi government claimed to have no WMD programs or stockpiles, while the Iraqi government also engaged in elaborate efforts to mislead international inspectors. These same misleading activities could have just as easily been efforts to retain the mystique of regime power over the Iraqi people as well as over its foreign opponents in order to hide the hollowness of the regime's real power or even the unraveling of the regime's hold on power. Rather than perceiving efforts to cover the hollowness of Saddam Hussein's power, the Bush administration perceived (or claimed to perceive) efforts to hide actual WMD.

The dispute among the major powers over whether the Iraqi regime posed a threat sufficient to warrant invasion and regime change revealed a great power split—based in part on the perception of a more aggressive, unilateralist United States—that could result in the emergence of a multipolar balance-of-power system over time. One fundamental calculation in deciding whether to balance against American power—or any country's power—is whether that power is perceived to be aggressive and threatening. But the use or threatened use of power does not always lead other countries to perceive their *own* values to be threatened. States may conclude that a perceived threat can be managed in ways short of amassing power for balancing purposes. In addition, balancing is not an option available to all states. Thus, I next consider responses other than balancing.

Accommodation

State responses to perceived threats involve calculations of interests and costs—what and how much of one's values are perceived threatened is weighed against how much cost one is willing to incur to defend the threatened values. Sometimes the costs of defending one's interests are calculated to be greater than the costs of accommodating the demands of the state that issues the threat. Sometimes there is not much of a threat to one's values, but the threatening state's demands might be accommodated for other purposes. Accommodation is defined in the *Penguin Dictionary of International Relations* as "the process whereby actors in conflict agree to recognize some of the others' claims while not sacrificing their basic interests. The source of conflict is not removed but the aggression it often generates is presumed to be."[45] Accommodation is considered similar to appeasement but without the negative connotations associated with the latter term.

Peter Karsten describes accommodation as a logical response involving one-sided, unidirectional "concessions that are taken in order to preserve a part of what is threatened, to avoid war, to avoid making increased provisions for deterrence-defense, or to win 'clients.'"[46] In responding to perceived threats, the state, "whether systematically or not, ordinarily engages in some assessment of the nature of the threat, then estimates the prestige, treasure, manpower, and other resources that it will need to spend in order to counter or eliminate that perceived threat."[47] Stronger powers have a greater range of possible responses to threats than do weaker powers, but even stronger powers may elect to accommodate rather than confront the sources of threats, especially if the costs of and/or risks involved in confrontation or deterrence are considered greater than the risk itself.[48]

The possession of nuclear weapons by the secretive North Korean regime seemingly would constitute an important threat to any number of countries. Starting in the 1990s and continuing into the new century, stronger powers such as the United States and China, as well as medium power Japan and less powerful South Korea, have all advocated some accommodation in response to the threat that North Korea would develop nuclear weapons. In 1994, the United States signed a bilateral agreement with North Korea called the Agreed Framework. In the first phase of the agreement, North Korea would freeze all nuclear weapons–related activity. In the second phase, the United States and its allies would construct two light-water nuclear energy reactors and supply heavy fuel oil. By the third phase, North Korea would dismantle all weapons-related activities.[49] The IAEA would be allowed to conduct inspections and construct permanent surveillance cameras at sensitive sites in North Korea. The construction of the nuclear reactors never occurred, nor did a pledge to begin talks aimed at normalizing diplomatic and economic relations. Yet the Agreed Framework was more or less intact, with North Korea's nuclear weapons program remaining in deep freeze until the more aggressive Bush administration replaced the more accommodating Clinton administration in 2001.

The George W. Bush administration's antipathy to the North Korean regime was displayed with flair in the famous "axis of evil" proclamation in Bush's State of the Union Address in January 2002. This speech also unsheathed the Bush doctrine of preemptive strikes against rogue states before they could fully acquire nuclear weapons capabilities (this doctrine and preemptive and preventive war will be discussed in chapter 6). During the course of 2002, as the Bush administration highlighted the imminent threat from Iraq, it also refused to engage in discussions with North Korea. In early December 2002, North Korea responded to the Bush administration by kicking out the IAEA inspectors and dismantling the inspection cameras. North Korea indicated that it would move ahead with its nuclear weapons program unless the Bush administration would sign a nonaggression pact with it. Declaring that the North Korean threat lacked credibility, the Bush administration downplayed any worries that North Korea would restart its weapons program. By January 2003, North Korea announced that it was withdrawing from the Nuclear Nonproliferation Treaty and had reopened the long-shuttered nuclear facility at Yongbyon. Caught by some surprise, the Bush administration declared that the situation warranted multilateral diplomatic efforts since military options were untenable.[50] The administration declared that the Bush doctrine against proliferation by rogues was intact but that each case was different and that some cases could not be managed successfully using military power.

The Bush administration had blamed the Clinton administration for being too accommodating with North Korea and thus that Clinton, not Bush, was responsible for the 2003 "noncrisis." Yet the Clinton administration had had plans on the table for a military strike against North Korea should it fail to live up to the Agreed Framework.[51] Instead, the Bush administration insisted that the only viable option for resolving the "noncrisis" was through six-party talks with six-party accommodations (and it would not discuss a nonaggression pact as North Korea demanded). Moreover, the administration insisted that the North dismantle its weapons program before talks could begin on economic and energy issues.

This hard line toward North Korea could be seen as more style than substance. As the Bush administration remained adamant on its terms and stalled on talks—despite pleas from South Korea, China, Japan, and Russia for the Americans to be more accommodating and flexible—the North Korean government apparently moved forward in converting a formerly sealed stockpile of 8,000 spent nuclear fuel rods into weapons-grade plutonium. The Bush administration could not but have known that delay would give North Korea time to build nuclear weapons. By the reckoning of the head of the IAEA, North Korea had produced five or six nuclear weapons by the end of 2004.[52] It seems logical to conclude that the administration was prepared to accept—that is, accommodate—a nuclear-armed North Korea despite the Bush doctrine.

The fact that accommodation has occurred in one international event, according to Karsten, does not automatically or inevitably lead to new threatening acts—that is, the state that is accommodated is not necessarily emboldened to push for more. The Bush administration had argued that accommodating North Korea on any issue would lead to even more North Korean demands. Karsten's research suggests that in some cases accommodation can reverse threatening behavior and put into play a different relational dynamics. Similarly, the state that makes the concessions cannot be expected to make further accommodations or concessions in the future.[53] Thus, North Korean leaders would be misunderstanding accommodation were they to expect that American leaders could be pressed for continual concessions. Accommodation, like all political acts, is "a product of circumstance and setting."[54] Changes in perceptions about the nature of the threat, defensive and offensive capabilities, as well as domestic and international politics, create situations in which new calculations about interests and costs are made with the possibility of different responses.

Bandwagoning

Sometimes when states attempt to threaten the values of another, the motivations behind the threats may be mixed. Threatening states may be attempting to wrestle concessions from another state with no real intention to make good on the threat. Stronger states may acknowledge this when making concessions to smaller powers; the concessions made in this instance become the price not of securing the values against the threat but the price of securing the cliency or passivity of the smaller power. The stronger power may find making concessions useful not for security purposes but for other foreign policy goals. The smaller power may prove a useful client in a grander scheme, or the smaller power may need to be neutralized and encouraged to sit out when the grander scheme is set into play. Thus, threats may be made not to actually threaten but to achieve some other goal.

Theories about balance of power and balance of threat assume that states must respond to efforts by a state or group of states to increase power. Efforts to increase power are assumed to be threatening, and threats require responses. There is in this an assumption that most states are status quo states content with the international system and their place in it. But the previous paragraph indicates that states are not always threatened by other states' efforts to increase their power. And we cannot assume that all states *are* content with the status quo and will feel prompted to defend it. Along a different line already discussed in this chapter, we also cannot assume that all states will feel threatened even by explicit threats cast their way. How one interprets a threat and how one interprets opportunities in the environment are important factors to keep in mind. Not all responses involve acting out of self-preservation to secure one's interests. Sometimes states join threatening states—or bandwagon with them—in order to maximize their own power rather than enhance their own security.[55]

Randall Schweller characterizes bandwagoning as being based on very different motivations from balancing. Balancing, he suggests, is behavior aimed at "self-preservation and the protection of values already possessed." The primary goal is to avoid losses in the face of a significant external threat. Bandwagoning, conversely, is behavior aimed at "self-extension: to obtain values coveted." Bandwagoning, then, is for profit and requires no significant external threat as prompt.[56] Indeed, there *is* a threat, but the threat is not to the bandwagoning state; the threat emanates from another, revisionist state and is perceived as being aimed at yet another state or states. The state that chooses to jump on the bandwagon is choosing to assist in some way in *making* the threat in order to profit from the potential system-level changes that may result.

The state that chooses to bandwagon should not be assumed to be actively engaged in the fight to alter the status quo. The bandwagoning state may be allowed to "free ride" on the actions of the revisionist state; here Schweller suggests that the revisionist state accepts free riding as the price of blocking the free rider from joining the side defending the status quo.[57] Implicit in this is the idea that the bandwagoning state is not altogether unhappy with the status quo (it could have chosen to join those who defend it) but is enticed more by the opportunity to profit from revision. Bandwagoning can also take another free-rider form in "piling-on" behavior that comes near the conclusion of a conflict when it is clear that the revisionist state will win.[58] End-of-game piling on can be understood as a response to future punishment or a future threat; Schweller explains that it may be motivated by the desire to avoid punishment for not actively participating on the winning side of the fight. By way of example, as World War II drew to a close, many states signed on to a U.S.-British document that declared war on Germany and Japan. Only states that declared war on Germany and Japan would be allowed to join the soon-to-be-created United Nations (as discussed in chapter 8). The punishment for not declaring war was the threat of being left out as the new international order was constructed.

Alliances and Coalitions

Schweller's discussion of bandwagoning turns on the idea that "alliance choices . . . are often motivated by opportunities for gain as well as danger, by appetite as well as fear."[59] This sense of alliance formation differs from the more conventional understanding that alliances are formalized mutual defense pacts among friends (or countries with strong common ties) and against adversaries conceived primarily as states. The topic of allying as a possible response to threat has appeared throughout this discussion thus far, but now we will look explicitly at alliance behavior and the choice to act multilaterally or unilaterally against perceived threats.

In the most fundamental sense, the decision to act multilaterally or unilaterally to achieve security is linked to the worldview held by national leadership. When national leaders see the world in liberal terms, multilateralism is the preferred and best method for action against commonly shared security problems. When national leaders see the world in realist terms, unilateral action is deemed the last, best defense. Yet even realists will act multilaterally through military alliances and coalitions when it advances their interests, and liberals will act unilaterally when immediate security threats are perceived.

Alliances "are formal associations of states for the use (or non-use) of military force, intended for either the security or the aggrandizement of their members, against specific other states, whether or not these others are explicitly recognized."[60] Glenn Snyder explains that alliances are a "formal subset" of alignment. "Alignment amounts to a set of mutual *expectations* between two or more states that they will have each other's support in disputes or wars with particular other states."[61] The post–World War II era was unusual in the history of the modern state system in that states made use of peacetime military alliances. Previous balance-of-power systems generally depended on coalitions or groups of states formed in wartime in response to revisionist threats. Formalized alliances—particularly those concluded in peacetime—were eschewed because of their obvious limitations and restrictions; states had to have the flexibility to realign as needed in order to regulate and maintain the system.

A few quick examples illustrate the differences in these concepts. The World War II grouping of the United States, Great Britain, France (in the form of the French resistance), and the Soviet Union was an ad hoc coalition of states formed in wartime to maintain the system against the revisionist ad hoc coalition of Germany, Italy, and Japan. The North Atlantic Treaty Organization (NATO), formed in 1949, was a peacetime military alliance formed against the threat posed by the Soviet Union and its allies (which formed their own formalized alliance in 1955, known as the Warsaw Pact). The group of states that united in 1991 to compel Iraq to end its illegal occupation of Kuwait was an ad hoc coalition, but because it was formed on the basis of UN Security Council resolutions and enjoyed widespread multilateral support it is typically termed a modified collective security response to a threat to the international system (collective security and the 1991 Gulf War will be examined in chapter 8).

What was the nature of the group involved in the invasion of Iraq in March 2003? By the Bush administration's terminology, it was a "coalition of the willing." This coalition was formed for the purposes of the invasion when a collective response was not forthcoming from the UN Security Council because of great power disagreement over the necessity of the war. These "multinational forces" involved in the invasion consisted primarily of U.S. military forces and a much smaller contingent of British forces with even smaller numbers of troops from other countries, such as Poland and Ukraine. The exact membership of these "multinational forces" in the "coalition of the willing" remained ambiguous and the contributions of each members to the cause unclear since, in the Bush administration's words, some members did not want to go public about their participation.[62]

As already noted, old-style realists embedded in the balance-of-power system preferred informal coalitions because of the flexibility these allowed. At any given point in time, revisionist activities by a state or group of states might require a new counteraligning coalition to protect and preserve the status quo. The knowledge that one had no and should have no permanent friends and that one's previous coalition partners may join a future adversarial coalition kept international relations embedded in suspicion.

Despite the preference for informal coalitions, Snyder maintains that there were still incentives in the multipolar balance-of-power system for states to seek allies. Alliances (and here, importantly, he refers to informal alliances or coalitions rather than formal alliances), armaments, and territorial aggrandizement, Snyder asserts, are the most prominent methods used by states to accumulate power when stuck in the grasp of the security dilemma.[63] But alliances themselves present variations on the security dilemma. Specifically, state A runs the risk that its ally, state B, will abandon it in the face of a significant threat to A. There is the additional risk that A will become entrapped in its alliance commitments to B, perhaps even to the point of fighting a war on behalf of B that does not directly involve A's interests. Snyder explains that these risks vary inversely, and

> reducing one tends to increase the other. Thus a . . . strategy of strong commitment to an ally reduces the risk of abandonment by reducing *his* fear of abandonment; he is discouraged from defecting by his confidence in one's support. But this very support may encourage him to excessive boldness in disputes or crises with the adversary, thus exposing one to the risk of a war that one would not wish to fight. Conversely . . . [a] strategy of weak or vague commitment, or a record of failing to support the ally in specific conflicts, tends to restrain the ally and to reduce the risk of entrapment; but it also increases the risk of abandonment by casting doubt on one's loyalty, hence devaluing the alliance for the ally. Thus, the resolution of the alliance security dilemma—the choice of strategy—requires chiefly a comparison and trade-off between the costs and risks of abandonment and entrapment.[64]

There are related problems as well. If one chooses a strategy of weak commitment in order to minimize the risk of entrapment, one increases one's bargaining ability over an ally. State A can squeeze greater concessions or payments out of B if B doubts the strength of A's commitment.[65] On the other hand, "a strong commitment to the ally tends to solidify the adversary alliance by increasing the degree of threat to it."[66] This, in turn, increases the costs of abandonment and thereby increases one's dependency on an ally.

Snyder contends that in the formal military alliances of the Cold War—specifically in NATO—the risk of abandonment by one's allies was very low if not altogether unlikely because of the shared understanding of the strength of the adversarial alliance.[67] Entrapment was still possible especially for smaller allies locked into the global politics of the superpowers, but without the countervailing risk of abandonment, the Cold War period was not marked by what Snyder calls the "alliance dilemma." Instead, the threat posed by the adversary alliance (which is another way of suggesting the classic security dilemma) ensured alliance stability and members' commitment *and* even permitted allies to engage in strong policy disagreements without consequence for the alliance.[68]

In the absence of the strong adversary alliance, the cement of the alliance dissolves, and strong policy differences work to erode faith in the commitment of allies all over again. Thus, after the end of the Cold War, the disintegration of the Soviet Union, the end of the Warsaw Pact, and the admittance of many former Warsaw Pact members to NATO, real and persistent questions were raised about the durability of NATO. The organization had begun to reinvent itself as a peacekeeping and/or peace enforcement arrangement in the mid- to late 1990s specifically in regard to the conflicts in the Balkans, but NATO appeared to have found a renewed mutual defense purpose with the 9/11 attacks on the United States. On September 12, 2001, the NATO governing council invoked the Article 5 mutual defense clause for the first time in NATO's history. But very quickly, new doubts about the future of the alliance were raised by the Bush administration's unilateralist preference to limit the involvement of NATO in Afghanistan in order to limit attendant obligations to shared decision making in the war[69] and then by serious disagreements among the NATO allies about whether the next "front line" in the war on terror went through Iraq.

To use Snyder's terminology, we might say that the Bush administration's approach to NATO demonstrated strong realist fears of entrapment or being tied down by allies in the prosecution of the war on terror and in pursuit of its longer-term foreign policy goals. This fear of entrapment was not balanced against the risks of abandonment in the face of a considerable adversary. Instead, the Bush administration signaled that it found little comfort in or need for formal alliances given its own sense of power and purpose in the world. Within weeks of the terrorist attacks on the United States, the secretary of defense offered the Bush administration's new view on alliances and coalitions in the war on terrorism:

> This war will not be waged by a grand alliance united for a single purpose of defeating an axis of hostile powers. Instead, it will involve floating coalitions of countries, which may change and evolve. Countries will have different roles and contribute in different ways. Some will help us publicly, while others, because of their circumstances, may help us privately and secretly. In this war, the mission will define the coalition—not the other way around.[70]

The meaning of this announcement was reinforced by the 2002 National Security Strategy of the United States of America, in which it was declared that the United States would not "hesitate to act alone, if necessary, to exercise our right of self-defense by acting preemptively" in the war on terror.[71] The 2006 strategy paper maintained the right to act alone while striking a humbler tone about the value of working with allies and partners.[72]

We might also interpret the French and German opposition to war in Iraq in terms of their worries over entrapment by their aggressive ally the United States. If the French and Germans were to follow the United States into war in Iraq, where would the trail lead next—to Iran? Syria? Since the adversary threat was not fully understood and the enemy not fully or easily identified, the costs to France and Germany of American abandonment were similarly vague and imprecise.

Without an adequately understood and commonly perceived threat, continuation of the NATO alliance would seem to hold few positive incentives to any of its major partners. In this regard, NATO's persistence might be attributed in part to fossilization, rendering it permanent long after its purpose had vanished. Yet NATO also may persist by virtue of the enthusiasm of its new members, who may use it as a formal vehicle for piling-on behavior. When some of the newest NATO members contributed small numbers of troops to the "multinational forces" in the "coalition of the willing" in Iraq, they may have been bandwagoning with the sole remaining and primarily unilateralist, aggressive, and slow-to-forget superpower in the hope of reaping future rewards and avoiding future punishment.

I continue the discussion of external security threats in the next chapter by considering defense and war.

5

Defending against
External Security Threats

All states' national security policies are aimed at protecting their territory and population, political independence and autonomy, and economic well-being. Countries define each of these—and the perceived threats to each of these—in different ways, sometimes directing their efforts inward and sometimes outward. Even within particular countries, different regimes (that is, the highest national decision makers) define these values and threats differently. Another important idea to keep in mind is that the protection of any one value or set of values often comes at the expense of one or more others. This last idea is basic to my discussion here. Defending national values involves manipulating a variety of the tools of statecraft, but my discussion will be primarily about using military force to defend a country's core values.

Defense in its most essential form involves the ability to withstand a physical attack on one's territory. This understanding "rests on an essentially autarkic notion of the state as a unit self-contained and self-reliant in all the major political, economic and cultural elements of life. Its principal military need is to defend its domestic universe from disruption by external military attack or internal disorder."[1] One obvious shortcoming of this notion of national defense is that it is a remnant of "the largely bygone days when most important state interests could be protected by military force."[2] In a broader sense—for some but not all countries—national defense has come to involve the use of military force to protect core values or interests, whether those values are located within the state's borders or not. But for now, we will stay with the idea of defending one's own territory from attack in order to expand on the concept of defense and the related term "deterrence."

Another obvious shortcoming of the term "defense" conceived as the ability to withstand an invasion attempt is that such an attempt is more and more unlikely given the sheer magnitude of the military power necessary to invade and conquer another country successfully. Historical examples of more powerful states invading and attempting to occupy less powerful states such as the Soviets in Afghanistan in the 1980s and the Americans in Iraq after March 2003 demonstrate how much overwhelming force and power are required to carry this out. Most countries do not face potential enemies who possess this kind of military power.

Instead of the threat of an invasion attempt, most states must protect against the possibility of an enemy using force or violence to cause unacceptable *damage* to territory, population, or critical infrastructure. Such an attack might be carried out through the use of aircraft, ballistic or short-range missiles, covert special operations, suicide attacks, and so on. The attacker could be a state as easily as a nonstate actor (and here the identity of the attacker would in part determine the form and method of the attack), and the attacker need not possess power capabilities on par with the target's. This last statement is especially true in an age of defending against transnational terrorism committed by nonstate actors.

Defending against such an attack—an attack not intended to invade and conquer but simply to cause harm—requires the use of more than military force. On the military side, one may defend by hardening national infrastructure against such threats, but this may be a task of nearly imponderable complexity in this era of vast interdependencies. One may also attempt to eliminate all the possible sources of such attacks or at a minimum the immediate potential sources through the use of preemptive or preventive military force against targets in other countries. This policy, too, poses its own complications, as I will take up in chapter 6.

Another possible response is to *deter* such an attack by levying a counterthreat against the would-be attacker. A deterrence strategy involves dissuading an attack by threatening would-be attackers with dire retaliatory consequences. Just as an attacker may not possess the military power to attempt to invade and conquer a country and thus resorts to the use of force to hurt the opponent in order to exact a political price, the targeted country may not possess the military power to be able to thwart an invasion attempt but may well have the military power to hurt a would-be attacker. That is, the ability to credibly threaten damage to one's opponent is more attainable than the ability to defend against or threaten invasion. With this in mind, our discussion of military defense will involve more than the traditional and perhaps outdated notion of national territorial defense against invasion, focusing more on deterring and preventing attacks that fall short of full-scale invasion.

The Defense Dilemma: Trading Off National Values

Military power is central to the defense of the state and its values. Yet "military power holds the ambiguous role in world politics of being simultaneously the decisive threat to life and order and the instrument of protecting both."[3] Barry Buzan explains that this power

> lies at the heart of the national security problem. States in an anarchy require military power both for their own defence and for the broader security purposes of system management. But once acquired, such power generates a counter-security dynamic of its own which threatens both individual states and the order of the system as a whole.[4]

Military force threatens the international system through the proliferation of weapons (generated by the security dilemma) and through the destructive potential of those weapons (particularly weapons of mass destruction).[5] Military force threatens individual states through the same security dilemma and destructive potential of weapons as well as through what Buzan calls the "defense dilemma."

In December 2004, the highest court in Great Britain, the Law Lords, overturned parts of the Anti-Terrorism, Crime and Security Act of 2001, which had been enacted after the 9/11 terrorist attacks on the United States. The law had permitted the British Home Office to detain indefinitely and without charge foreigners suspected of terrorist activities. The Law Lords found the law to be a violation of European human rights laws, but the ruling went even further. One of the judges wrote, "The real threat to the life of the nation, in the sense of a people living in accordance with its traditional laws and political values, comes not from terrorism but from laws such as these."[6] To put it another way, the law, designed to defend Britain, posed more of a threat to the British nation and its core values than that which it was designed to counter. The particular response to the terrorist threat embodied in the legislation ran counter to the critical values of the nation.

This, in a nutshell, is an illustration of the defense dilemma. Buzan describes the defense dilemma as "contradictions between the pursuit of military defense and national security" when the "cost of [defense] compromises other security objectives."[7] For instance, as the Soviet Union attempted to counter the security threat posed by nuclear arms development and stockpiling by the United States, its economy was undermined and overstretched, contributing in part to the internal collapse of the country. The pursuit of defense against an enemy's weapons arsenal may come at the cost of the loss of the state. The trade-off in such a case is extreme, but even the most well-intentioned policymakers may put into play the ultimate defense dilemma with disastrous consequences.

The example of the British Law Lords striking down the antiterrorism law in the name of the British nation suggests a necessary widening of the concept of the defense dilemma. I will use "defense dilemma" as a term that characterizes the contradictions that arise between the pursuit of national security through military defense and the protection of other fundamental national values. The wording of the Law Lords' ruling is worth repeating: "The real threat to the life of the nation . . . comes not from terrorism but from laws such as these."[8] Trade-offs are unavoidable in any political enterprise, but some trade-offs go more to the heart of a country's continued existence as an entity dedicated to upholding certain fundamental values. Striking the right balance is in many respects an art form the results of which may be admired by few. In March 2005, the British Parliament struck a difficult compromise on a new antiterrorism law to replace that which the Law Lords struck down. The compromise bill came after a historic thirty-one-hour debate in the upper chamber of Parliament, and as compromises go, few seemed happy with or even certain about its provisions.[9]

Some of this trade-off has been explored in chapter 3, but it merits revisiting here. As Benjamin Franklin put it, "They that can give up essential liberty to obtain a little temporary safety deserve neither liberty nor safety." The burdens of defending one's interests in any kind of war—hot or cold, internal or external—always come at some cost and often at the cost of core national values and interests—thus the inescapable situation of the defense dilemma.

Deterrence and Nuclear Weapons

Nuclear weapons put the security dilemma and the ambiguous role of military weapons as both protectors and destroyers of life into the starkest relief. That nuclear weapons exist leads some states to conclude that they have no choice but to obtain them, even while recognizing that their longer-term interests might be better secured in a nuclear weapons–free world. We hear this unfortunate conclusion in Jaswant Singh's explanation of India's 1998 nuclear weapons tests and its continued development of a nuclear arsenal and ballistic missiles. Singh writes, "India's nuclear policy remains firmly committed to a basic tenet: that the country's national security in a world of nuclear proliferation lies either in global disarmament or in exercise of the principle of equal and legitimate security for all."[10] Unless and until the nuclear "haves" renounce nuclear weapons and all the world's states join together to eliminate nuclear weapons, India maintains that all states have the legitimate right to obtain whatever is necessary to provide for their own security. After all, "India still lives in a rough neighborhood"[11] in which some of the neighbors show no inclination to dismantle their own nuclear weapons.

Most of our understandings and expectations about the behavior of states possessing nuclear weapons arise out of the development of the American-Soviet nuclear relationship. The American-Soviet nuclear relationship in its first years was asymmetrical, with the United States in possession first of a monopoly on and then a predominance of nuclear destructive capability. In the time that the Soviets lacked sufficient weapons and delivery systems to threaten substantial damage to U.S. territory, the United States possessed what is called first-strike capability. This is the capability to substantially eliminate the enemy's ability to retaliate to any degree. One result of this first-strike capability was the U.S. threat of massive retaliation in response to any Soviet efforts to increase Soviet territory or influence. This asymmetry characterized the relationship until around the start of the 1970s.

By 1972 and the signing of the Strategic Arms Limitation Treaty (SALT I), the Soviet nuclear weapons program and arsenal had developed to the point of essential equivalence to that of the United States in terms of nuclear destructive capacity (which includes both warhead stocks and reliable delivery vehicles). The Soviet Union had achieved second-strike capability, or the ability to absorb a nuclear attack by the United States and still have sufficient nuclear weapons remaining to retaliate and inflict comparable and unacceptable damage. The United States, too, possessed second-strike capability; thus, a superpower war theoretically would ensure a situation of mutual assured destruction (MAD). The *mutual* recognition of MAD meant that the idea of direct war of any sort between the superpowers was "unthinkable." By virtue of both sides acquiring second-strike capability, the superpower relationship reached the "maturity" of stable nuclear deterrence.

Understood this way, MAD freed the superpowers from the inevitable self-defeating drive of the security dilemma. Both sides in such a relationship should and would understand the consequences of their mutual actions and thus would be mutually deterred, restrained, and *reassured*. Further, neither side would be provoked by uncertainty and the lack of trust to continue arming and taking other more provocative moves.

Of course, despite the "achievement" of MAD and many arms control and disarmament treaties signed between the two superpowers, neither seemed so reassured by their "mature" relationship that they stopped arming. Even after the Cold War ended and the Soviet Union collapsed, Russia and the United States continued to develop or planned to develop new nuclear weapons systems.

More important, to borrow an idea from Nobel laureate Thomas Schelling, there is perversity in the admission that each country's people and territory are hostage to the other side—that one ultimately *cannot* defend one's core values—and perversity in the idea that each side in the Cold War *intentionally* moved to achieve such a situation. Labeling this situation "mature" denotes a judgment that this is a good situation, that it is a good thing that one's enemy has the capability to destroy one's people and territory. Expanding on this logic, one might imagine that the world would be better off if more countries—particularly those engaged in long-standing rivalries—possessed sufficient nuclear weapons to achieve stable deterrence.[12] That is, it would be a really good thing if lots or most countries could utterly destroy their enemies and vice versa. Nuclear proliferation, using this logic, should be a foreign policy goal of all states rather than a phenomenon that states attempt to curtail.

Schelling notes another perversity in this:

> Major war [between the nuclear superpowers] is often discussed as though it would be only a contest in national destruction. If this is indeed the case— if the destruction of cities and their populations has become, with nuclear weapons, the primary object in an all-out war—the sequence of war has been reversed. Instead of destroying enemy forces as a prelude to imposing one's will on the enemy nation, one would have to destroy the nation as a means or a prelude to destroying the enemy forces. If one cannot disable enemy forces without virtually destroying the country, the victor does not even have the option of sparing the conquered nation. He has already destroyed it.[13]

And, because one's opponent has second-strike capability, the victor has also ensured the destruction of its own country.

Is there a problem with any of this? Yes, to be sure! One obvious problem lies in the nature of deterrence. Deterrence turns on perception. To be deterred, state A must perceive that state B in fact *will* exact massive punishment on A should A attempt some aggression against B. State A will not be deterred if it does not believe or no longer believes that B would carry out its threat. Deterrence will not work without credibility. To maintain credibility, B must remain belligerent in its tone toward A to communicate that the threat is credible *and* durable.

But the threat must be more than rhetoric and perception. State B's threat must be demonstrated to have a foundation in capability—B must actually possess the weapons it threatens to use. This can be accomplished through old-fashioned military parades, military exercises, weapons shows, and so forth. Or, if a state wishes to create uncertainty about whether it possesses such weapons, it may leak ambiguous information to encourage speculation. But possession or suspected possession may not be enough to build credibility. State A may perceive B to be reluctant to use what it possesses. To make its threat most effective, B must demonstrate its willingness to use the weapon in question. In Schelling's words,

> Unhappily, the power to hurt is often communicated by some performance of it. Whether it is sheer terroristic violence to induce an irrational response, or cool premeditated violence to persuade somebody that that you mean it and may do it again, it is not the pain and damage itself but its influence on somebody's behavior that matters. It is the expectation of *more* violence that gets the wanted behavior, if the power to hurt can get it at all.[14]

Even with some demonstrated capacity and willingness to use it, state A should not expect that B's preferences remain static. States are led by humans, and humans change their minds or lose their taste for certain "games." Thus, A may determine that B has lost its resolve to carry through on its threat, and thus A perceives a green light where there was once red or perhaps the uncertainty of yellow. Country A's perception of B's intention to carry through can change, making A more rather than less likely to initiate war because A has been presented with a ripe opportunity.

We can also imagine a scenario in which state A believes B's threat to be intact, credible, and persistent yet A's situation may have changed, making A willing to take the risk and initiate conflict. Perhaps A's leadership has suffered internal or external political setbacks that make it feel as if it has nothing left to lose. Nothing about stable deterrence requires either side to stop pursuing technological advancements, and so perhaps B is on the verge of acquiring a weapon system that would give it first-strike capability. For example, a missile defense system that shields B from A's second-strike retaliation would give B the opportunity to initiate and win nuclear war. Sensing that B may be on the verge of such a technological advance, A may determine that it should strike and ensure the destruction of both sides rather than concede victory to B. Beyond these recalculations, computer errors, false warnings, unauthorized use of nuclear weapons, accidental firings, and third-party firings of nuclear weapons can quickly alter the environment, giving one side or the other reason to reassess the costs of nuclear war and MAD. For states seeking to defend their interests through nuclear deterrence, these are cautionary words.

Further, each party in a relationship characterized by stable deterrence is assumed to be an economic actor (as suggested by state A's recalculations of B's intentions mentioned previously), and it is assumed that each party "understands" the other side's motivations and behaviors. Richard Betts explains the errors in these assumptions:

> Theorists who have elaborated the concept of deterrence have usually done so in detached terms of adversaries who understand each other and, while opposing each other's interests, at least share the sense of the purpose of each

other's deterrent threats. In practice significant confusion . . . existed [in the Cold War] not only between Washington and Moscow, but within the United States, between the United States and its allies, among theorists, and among services and bureaucracies about the purposes and logic of deterrent threats.[15]

Given that policymakers understand that their own decisions are derived in a manner that does not approximate a more or less straightforward, input-output, cost-benefit calculation, why would they assume anything about the rationality of their opponent's decision-making process? Yet assuming rationality is the easiest way to "understand" the opponent, and so this "logic" guides nuclear deterrence.

Let's consider another problem with deterrence. During the Cold War, there was an unwritten "rule" that nuclear-armed countries would not use nuclear weapons against countries lacking these weapons. This rule was publicly exposed in the 1964 U.S. presidential election campaign when the sitting Democratic president used a television commercial— once—to suggest that his "radical" Republican opponent would use nuclear weapons against North Vietnam to end the conflict there but start a larger nuclear war. During the Cold War, linkages between states made it likely that the use of nuclear weapons by one of the superpowers against a nonnuclear opponent would necessitate the entry into the conflict of the other superpower—and therefore nuclear war. Not wanting to provoke nuclear war, the superpowers were deterred from using nuclear weapons even against nonnuclear foes. This was not just an accidental result of linkages in the world; the U.S. policy of extended deterrence intentionally threatened nuclear retaliation for any attacks on its allies.

After the Cold War and especially after the start of the U.S. "global war on terror," it has become less clear how a nuclear state would be restrained from using nuclear weapons against a nonnuclear opponent. In July 2001, the U.S. Department of Defense and Department of Energy completed a study on the modification of nuclear weapons for the purposes of attacking hardened bunker complexes and buried tunnels.[16] The study concerned potential enemies North Korea, Iraq, and China but got considerable media coverage in late 2001 as the military found it difficult to find al-Qaeda leaders in the caves of Afghanistan. The new nuclear weapon—called the Robust Nuclear Earth Penetrator—would "pack a relatively small punch, just enough to destroy reinforced steel-and-concrete command centers and vaporize stocks of biological and chemical weapons deep beneath the earth's surface."[17] These new nuclear weapons would be developed not to reinforce deterrence but rather for use in war. These weapons were not just an idea on a Pentagon wish list—the Bush administration requested funding in 2004 to develop these weapons to use in its preemptive/preventive war policy. Holding the line for the moment was a Republican member of Congress from Ohio who refused to put the administration's request into the budget passed out of his energy subcommittee. He gave two reasons for refusing the administration's request. First, he said, "We cannot advocate for nuclear nonproliferation around the globe and pursue more useable nuclear weapons options at home."[18] Second, developing such weapons would almost guarantee their use by someone.[19]

An additional question is, How many nuclear weapons are necessary to establish a situation of stable deterrence? When a country wishes to threaten "unacceptable damage," is such damage measured in terms of total destruction of the target (for which a major nuclear arsenal would be required), or would the destruction of a major city (which would require only a few warheads) be "unacceptable" to the target? To minimize the possibility of either kind of attack, should countries target the opponent's nuclear weapons facilities—a counterforce strategy—or target the opponent's cities—a countervalue strategy? Since nuclear facilities are likely to be hidden and dispersed throughout a country while cities may be dispersed but certainly are not hidden, a countervalue strategy would seem to be the easiest strategy. But how many of the opponent's cities would one need to target to establish an effective threat? How much of this needs to be communicated so that the opponent understands the nature of the threat being levied against it? Does the *opponent* measure "unacceptable damage" in terms of total destruction, or would the destruction of a major city be unacceptable? The uncertainty in all this is likely to cause each side to target as many cities as possible. But will this forestall a nuclear war or just ensure that, should it come, the war would be total?

Yet another issue is whether the possession of nuclear weapons by both sides of an international rivalry deters conventional war between the two. Historian John Lewis Gaddis famously declared the Cold War to be the "long peace" because both the bipolar structure of the international system and the stable, mature nuclear relationship between the superpowers guaranteed that there would be no major power wars.[20] Another unwritten but well-understood "rule" of the Cold War system was that the Americans and Soviets would take care never to confront each other in direct and sustained military hostilities. But there were wars during the "long peace," and the superpowers contributed their share and beyond to those. Nuclear deterrence did not deter the superpowers from contributing to local conflicts or even supplanting local grievances with their own grievances whenever it suited their interests.

The post–Cold War period offers an episode that suggests that nuclear weapons do not deter direct conventional war between nuclear foes. In 1998, India and Pakistan engaged in "tit-for-tat" nuclear explosions to test and demonstrate their operational nuclear weapons capabilities. Singh explains the testing this way: "India had to ensure that its nuclear option, developed and safeguarded over decades, was not eroded by self-imposed restraint."[21] Nuclear test ban treaties leave countries uncertain about their nuclear arsenals, an uncertainty that might restrain them from considering the use of nuclear weapons (will they work? should we risk it?) or might create concerns that one's nuclear threat may lack sufficient punch (will my opponent think my nukes won't work? can we risk that?). Whatever the reasons for the 1998 detonations, these tit-for-tat nuclear tests were followed by increased ballistic missile production and testing by both countries.

Contrary to Cold War–based expectations, the nuclear weapons tests of 1998 seemed to signal the *opening* of the door to more direct conventional confrontations between old foes India and Pakistan. An ongoing issue between these opponents was the political status of Jammu and Kashmir province of India. Upendra Choudhury contends that Pakistan became increasingly bold in its overtures against India via disputed Kashmir *concurrent with the development of its nuclear weapons capability*:

> Over the years, militant opposition to Indian rule of Kashmir has undergone a transformation. Conflict was initiated, and at first waged, by local Kashmiri militants, although Pakistan had always considered Kashmir an "unfinished agenda of partition" as well.
>
> Since the late 1980s, when Pakistan acquired a nuclear capability . . . it has pursued a proxy war in Kashmir without fear of Indian retaliation. In the mid-1990s, the struggle was taken over by foreign mercenaries recruited from as many as 14 Islamic nations, believed to be under the guidance of Pakistan. Throughout this period, the Pakistani army was not directly involved in operations against India.
>
> But the Kargil war in 1999 demonstrated that Pakistan was not averse to raising the stakes through direct intervention. Similarly, Pakistan once supported terrorism and arson only in Jammu and Kashmir, but more recently it has supported terror activities in other parts of India, including New Delhi. India's tolerance was breached when allegedly Pakistan-based terrorist outfits attacked the Indian parliament on December 13, 2001. Deciding it could no longer live with the proxy war, India massed troops on the Indo-Pakistani border.[22]

There is some dispute among Pakistanis about who in Pakistan planned the incursion that became the Kargil war in the spring of 1999. Kargil is a town just inside the Indian side of the Line of Control separating Indian and Pakistani forces in Kashmir. The Line of Control was established in July 1972 as part of the cease-fire agreement ending hostilities in the 1971 Indian-Pakistani war. The Line essentially follows an earlier cease-fire line established in 1949 at the conclusion of the first Indian-Pakistani war. Kargil also sits on the major road running through the Indian Himalayas.

In the winter of 1999, Pakistani regular troops and Islamic militants crossed over the Line of Control and established themselves in Indian bunkers abandoned during the harsh mountain winter. When Indian troops returned in the spring, Pakistani forces pinned them down in the environs of Kargil with artillery and rockets.[23] "Pakistan took India by surprise and for two months a few hundred Pakistanis kept 60,000 Indian troops, backed by bombers, at bay."[24] The U.S. Clinton administration intervened, causing Pakistani Prime Minister Nawaz Sharif to announce in mid-July that Pakistan would withdraw its troops across the Line of Control. Whether the incursion was planned by the Pakistani military—as Sharif suggested—or not, it derailed a peace initiative between Pakistan and India begun that February, and the Pakistani withdrawal under American pressure gave cause to the military to depose Sharif in mid-October. Pakistan's chief of the army, General Pervez Musharraf, led the coup against Sharif. The war served no apparent purpose for Pakistan, but it did belie the idea that nuclear-armed enemies will be deterred from engaging in direct military conflict for fear of nuclear war.

Complicating any discussion of Kashmir and the nuclear relationship between Pakistan and India is China. Adding China into this discussion also suggests that deterrence as a policy is flawed because nuclear-armed enemies may not be engaged in just a two-opponent "game." This is a final, critical problem with deterrence that is often overlooked. What tends to get forgotten in discussions of Kashmir is the Chinese presence. China militarily occupies 38,000 square kilometers of Kashmir as well as 90,000 square kilometers in another Indian state as a result of a border war in 1962.[25] India suffered a major military defeat in that war and since then has perceived China to be a primary security threat. India's nuclear arsenal thus is partly directed against the Pakistani threat and partly directed against the Chinese. Moreover, China "has been the principal provider of nuclear and missile technologies to Pakistan" as a counterweight to India.[26] China's own nuclear security interests take into account India, Russia, and the United States.

The United States has contributed to the insecurity of the subcontinent, further demonstrating the dangerous shortcomings of nuclear deterrence strategies that do not take into account multiple parties and interests. According to the "Nuclear Notebook" published by the *Bulletin of the Atomic Scientists*, Pakistan was estimated to have between twenty-four and forty-eight nuclear weapons at the start of 2002,[27] while India held fewer, approximately thirty to thirty-five.[28] Both sides could deliver nuclear weapons using aircraft and ballistic missiles, but the balance was in India's favor because it also had in development or possibly even had deployed naval nuclear weapons by 2001–2002.[29] In 1990, the United States had stopped sales of F-16s to Pakistan over concerns that Pakistan was pursuing the development of nuclear weapons. In response to the 1998 nuclear tests, the United States imposed military sanctions on both Pakistan and India, but these were lifted after the "global war on terror" was begun in late 2001. Pakistan began lobbying, at that point, for the United States to sell it more F-16 aircraft, the vehicles "most likely to be used by the Pakistani Air Force to deliver nuclear weapons."[30] In late March 2005, the U.S. government announced that it would resume sales of F-16s to Pakistan—sales without limits—and offered to make high-tech combat aircraft available to India as well.[31] A devastating earthquake in October 2005 caused Pakistan to alter its plans to buy seventy-seven F-16 aircraft from the United States, but the point is made.[32]

As an aside, the U.S. decision to recalibrate this nuclear enmity with the delivery vehicle of choice for Pakistan apparently was not informed by two reports issued by the National Intelligence Council of the Central Intelligence Agency that suggested that Pakistan was on the path to becoming a "failed state." Key excerpts from these reports on the future of India and Pakistan and their relationship appear in extended discussion box 5.1.

Containment

Deterrence is not just a strategy aimed at stopping an attack; it is also a strategy used to stop an opponent from doing other undesirable activities, such as expand its sphere of influence and power. That is, deterrence can be the method by which an opponent is contained. Containment of the Soviet Union and its allies was the primary post–World War II objective of U.S. foreign policy. Whether Iraq's ambitions were sufficiently contained was a primary point of contention prior to the U.S. invasion of Iraq in 2003. In neither of these cases was the containment of the opponent accomplished strictly through military deterrence, but military deterrence was the primary means.

The U.S. containment policy aimed at the Soviet threat was first articulated in a 1947 article in *Foreign Affairs* by "Mr. X," or George Kennan. Kennan was an American diplomat posted to Moscow when he wrote that the Soviets/Russians were bent on expansionism at the expense of the Western world. The Soviet style of expansionism, unlike the expansionism of "individual aggressive leaders like Napoleon and Hitler," was "more sensitive to contrary force, more ready to yield on individual sectors of the diplomatic front when that force is felt to be too strong, and thus more rational in the logic and rhetoric of power. On the other hand it cannot be easily defeated or discouraged by a single victory on the part of its opponent."[33]

Because of the nature of the Soviet threat and mind-set, Kennan advised, "it is clear that the main element of any United States policy toward the Soviet Union must be that of a long-term, patient but firm and vigilant containment of Russian expansive tendencies." Any government dealing with Russia "should remain at all times cool and collected and . . . its demands on Russian policy should be put forward in such a manner as to leave the way open for a compliance not too detrimental to Russian prestige." With this in mind, Kennan believed that "the Soviet pressure against the free institutions of the Western world is something that can be contained by the adroit and vigilant application of counter-force at a series of constantly shifting geographical and political points."

Kennan called for a multifaceted approach to containing the Soviets involving sensitivity and flexibility in the short term and a "firm and vigilant" long-term perspective. But the application of U.S. containment policy became heavily militaristic, with key emphasis placed on the formation of interlocking military alliances encircling the communist countries and the construction of hundreds of military bases with the forward deployment of U.S. troops. As Samuel Huntington described it, "Containment and deterrence reflected a territorial concept of security, in which a line was drawn about territories of the 'free world' whose collective security against communist aggression was considered essential to the security of the United States."[34] This line was defended through a policy of extended deterrence. "If the United States was to deter the expansion of communist states, it would have to make clear and firm its commitments to come to the defense of other countries if they were attacked, and it would have to have the military capabilities to respond to aggression by imposing unacceptable costs upon the aggressor."[35] The unacceptable costs, of course, would be borne in a nuclear attack.

Containment was not aimed exclusively at the Soviet Union and its allies. The United States engaged in a dual containment policy in the post–World War II world that not only locked its enemies in place but locked its allies in as well. Benjamin Schwarz writes that the American grand strategy was to "relieve" would-be great power challengers of high defense costs in order to "relieve" them of—deny them—the military capacity to challenge U.S. predominance.[36] This idea carried over to the post–Cold War period after the containment of the Soviet threat was historical. Schwartz notes that a 1992 Pentagon Defense Planning Guidance paper, written by Paul Wolfowitz (one of the primary architects of the U.S. invasion of Iraq), suggested that U.S. allies, particularly the major powers, should be contained in their ambitions from "ever aspiring to a larger regional or global role" while the United States provided "adult supervision." The first President Bush rejected this guidance, and the second President Bush incorporated it into his national security strategy.

Just as U.S. containment policy was implemented primarily in military terms against Kennan's prescriptions, it also was not exercised with the kind of finesse and nuance that Kennan suggested. Specifically, there was an all-or-nothing attitude among the American foreign policy elite that disallowed nuance, especially when states attempted to stay nonaligned during the Cold War. In 1955, influential political commentator Walter Lippman wrote that "all nations must join our alliances or be considered as fellow-travelers on their way to becoming Communist satellites."[37] In 1956, U.S. Secretary of State John Foster Dulles intoned in a speech that the containment-based mutual defense treaties, "with forty-two countries of America, Europe and Asia . . . abolish as between the parties, the principle of neutrality, which pretends that a nation can best gain safety for itself by being indifferent to the fate of others. This has increasingly become an obsolete conception and, except under exceptional circumstances, it is an immoral and shortsighted conception."[38] This absolutism, like the containment of major power contenders, did not go the way of the Cold War. In his speech to a joint session of the U.S. Congress within weeks of the 9/11 terrorist attacks, President George W. Bush said these (in)famous words: "Every nation, in every region, now has a decision to make. Either you are with us, or you are with the terrorists."[39]

Going well past the counsel of George Kennan, the policy of containment became the vehicle by which American global military predominance was established and then consolidated. In September 2001—a decade after the collapse of the Soviet Union and the Soviet threat—there were some 725 American military bases outside the United States. This number, writes Chalmers Johnson, underreported the extent of U.S. military presence in the world "since some bases exist[ed] under leaseholds, informal agreements, or disguises of various kinds."[40] Since the terrorist attacks of 9/11, even more American military bases have been created. To Johnson, containment was less about a Soviet threat (or a terrorist threat post-9/11) than about establishing an American empire:

> Whether or not most of these bases would have proved of real importance in a Soviet-American war, their possession was justified as a crucial part of a policy of "containing" Communism. It was sometimes argued as well that the bases needed to be retained just to keep them out of Soviet hands. Containment and strategic denial became the rationales for a new version of imperialism that replaced the old and discredited practice of colonialism. Military bases, vaguely legitimized through alliances and mutual security pacts, became the institutional form this new imperialism took.[41]

Toward the goal of maintaining American predominance, containment of any potential challengers can be expected to remain a primary foreign policy strategy employed by the United States.

A containment strategy is primarily about the exercise of force and power intended to limit the ability of some other actor to freely choose its own behaviors. Generally, containment is aimed at limiting unwanted foreign policy behaviors, but sometimes containment is designed to curtail the activity of a government within its own territory.

The UN prohibitions against Iraq after the 1991 Gulf War were designed in the first instance to limit threatening international behavior by Iraq and to compensate Kuwaiti victims for Iraq's invasion of their country, and only then were prohibitions imposed to limit the territorially bound activity of the Iraqi government. These prohibitions amounted to the containment of Iraqi ambitions and behaviors; thus, they are worth a brief look. These were, however, multilateral and thus somewhat different from unilateral containment policies. On the other hand, the United States and the United Kingdom used the post–Gulf War resolutions on Iraq as the legal basis for the 2003 invasion.

At the conclusion of the 1991 Gulf War, UN Security Council Resolution 687 (April 3, 1991) welcomed "the restoration to Kuwait of its sovereignty, independence and territorial integrity and the return of its legitimate Government." Resolution 687 also noted that during the crisis and war over Kuwait, Iraq had threatened to use weapons of mass destruction, conducted unprovoked attacks against other countries, and threatened to use terrorism and take hostages outside of Iraq. All these activities were noted as being against various international conventions signed by Iraq and threats to international peace and security. In light of all this, the Security Council imposed certain conditions on Iraq in order to limit its ability to threaten its neighbors and the international peace. Specifically, Iraq was required to "unconditionally accept the destruction, removal, or rendering harmless, under international supervision" of chemical and biological weapons and stocks of related agents and all ballistic missiles with a range over 150 kilometers. Further, Iraq was to "unconditionally agree not to acquire or develop nuclear weapons or nuclear-weapon-usable material or any subsystems or components" or to develop and maintain any facilities designed for nuclear weapons–related purposes. These restrictions effectively formed the bulk of what was known as the "sanctions regime" designed to contain the threat Iraq posed to other states.

In order to ensure Iraq's compliance with the prohibitions, Iraq was required to provide full reports on the whereabouts of restricted materials and facilitate on-site international inspections, destruction, removal, or rendering harmless of all such materials. (The costs of inspections and related activities would be paid by the Iraqi government according to UN Security Council Resolution 706, August 15, 1991.) The reports of these international inspections commissions would form the basis for periodic Security Council review of the prohibitions. Every sixty days, according to Resolution 687, the Council would review "the policies and practices of the Government of Iraq, including the implementation of all relevant resolutions of the Council, for the purpose of determining whether to reduce or lift the prohibitions." The noted prohibitions, including those restricting "the import of commodities and products originating in Iraq and the prohibitions against financial transactions related thereto," would be ended as soon as the Council found Iraq to be in full compliance.

Later Security Council resolutions established how Iraq would pay compensation to Kuwait and others for all damages incurred in Iraq's occupation of Kuwait and established the "oil for food" fund that would allow the sale of petroleum products for the importation of food and other essential civilian needs, such as medicines. Thus, the Security Council sought to limit Iraq's threatening behaviors to neighbors and make it pay compensation for previous actions against neighbors without incurring great Iraqi civilian suffering in the process (which, it turns out, occurred nonetheless).

Within days of Resolution 687, the Security Council also passed a resolution that was aimed at the domestic behavior of the Iraqi government. The prompt was a humanitarian crisis involving Iraqi Kurds. As Thomas Weiss explains,

> After the Allied victory on February 27 [1991], a power vacuum facilitated uprisings by former soldiers—the Shiites in the south and the Kurds in the north. Southern Iraq was the first insurrection, where the Shiites took the lead and captured the port of Basra and subsequently the major cities in southern Iraq. On March 4, the Kurdish uprising began in Rania and later spread to virtually all major cities in the region. Among the factors leading to the Kurdish uprising was the call by US president George H. W. Bush for all minority groups and citizens to revolt and depose the authoritarian regime of Saddam Hussein . . .
>   Evidence shows that Hussein had anticipated the revolts and placed various forces on reserve, rather than dedicate them to the Kuwaiti front . . .
>   The result was disastrous and predictable: vicious repression.[42]

Weiss estimates that the number of deaths resulting from the uprisings and subsequent repression by Iraqi government forces was between 20,000 and 100,000.

In the wake of the uprisings and government response, some 2 million Kurds fled their homes, moving toward Iran and Turkey. Kurds who fled to Iran were given safe refuge, although Iran was strapped for resources and in short order denied adequate international aid for the refugees because of its bad relations with the United States.[43] Meanwhile, NATO ally Turkey physically restricted the Kurds from seeking haven in Turkey. "Human rights abuses by Turkish border guards and the life-threatening winter conditions of the border-mountain region led to an increasing death rate—between 400 and 1,000 per day."[44] The impending disaster for the Kurds in the north was brought to the attention of the world by the media that had amassed in the region for the Gulf War.

On April 5, 1991, the Security Council passed Resolution 688, noting its grave concern over "the repression of the Iraqi civilian population in many parts of Iraq, including most recently in Kurdish-populated areas, which led to a massive flow of refugees towards and across international frontiers and to cross-border incursions which threaten international peace and security in the region." In this resolution, the Council warned that it "*insists* that Iraq allow immediate access by international humanitarian organizations to all those in need of assistance in all parts of Iraq" and appealed "to all Member States and to all humanitarian organizations to contribute to these humanitarian relief efforts."

The United States took Resolution 688 as authorization for a military intervention to assist the Kurds in northern Iraq. Acting with the support of key allies, the United States launched Operation Express Care to offer immediate humanitarian relief and longer-term security to the Kurds. Weiss asserts that "the Security Council's language did not explicitly sanction the intervention, but the intent was clear."[45] The U.S. plan was to get the Kurds back to their home villages as quickly as possible (especially before the start of the spring planting season) and to force the permanent military withdrawal of the Iraqi military. "The solution was the creation of a security zone in northern Iraq to be patrolled by Allied aircraft, which in turn would form the basis to enforce the no-fly zone in June, which interdicted Iraqi flights above the thirty-sixth parallel. In August 1992, another no-fly zone was created in southern Iraq, below the thirty-second parallel, to protect the Shiites."[46]

This liberal reading of Resolution 688 was not contested by any significant international actors in 1992. The use of military force to impose restrictions on the internal behavior and movement of Iraqi government forces was accepted as part of the fuller package of containing the Hussein regime. What started as prohibitions to contain Iraq in its foreign affairs thus moved seamlessly into prohibitions to contain Iraq in its domestic affairs. This move limiting the domestic sovereignty of the Iraqi government was initiated by the United States and resisted by no other members of the United Nations. After this, the sanctions regime against the Iraqi government proceeded apace, and the periodic use of military force by the United States and sometimes Great Britain became a regular feature of this regime. Over time, other actors did begin to question the effectiveness and sometimes the humaneness of the containment policy and its military enforcement.[47]

Containment—and here we would adopt from the Iraqi example the expanded notion of containment aimed at both external *and* internal behavior—via sanctions is highly contentious. Does containment actually work in terms of limiting the foreign and domestic behavior of the targeted regime? Before she was national security adviser and then secretary of state in the George W. Bush administration, then candidate Bush's foreign policy adviser, Condoleezza Rice, wrote that the containment of Iraq and North Korea *was* effective policy. Writing in *Foreign Affairs* during the

2000 presidential campaign, Rice echoed George Kennan's advice about containing the Soviet Union: "One thing is clear: the United States must approach regimes like North Korea resolutely and decisively. The Clinton administration has failed here, sometimes threatening to use force and then backing down, as it often has with Iraq." Yet Rice made it clear that there was *no* need for urgent action regarding these undesirable regimes: "These regimes are living on borrowed time, so there need be no sense of panic about them. Rather, the first line of defense should be a clear and classical statement of deterrence—if they do acquire WMD [weapons of mass destruction], their weapons will be unusable because any attempt to use them will bring national obliteration."[48] Once the Bush administration took power, this view of patient containment was discarded in favor of an active policy of regime change.

Once in office and especially after 9/11, the Bush administration argued that containment of Iraq was not sufficient and that urgent action was required to deal with the imminent Iraqi threat. The administration made a different argument regarding the threat of a nuclear-armed North Korea. This case has been discussed earlier, so it will not be considered at length again. Suffice it to say that the Bush administration proposed what it called the "tailored containment" of North Korea. Tailored containment, as described by the administration, was more akin to what Kennan had proposed. The administration claimed that each case was different and warranted different methods; in the case of Iraq, military action was greatly and urgently needed, and in the case of North Korea, tailored containment involving more nuanced political and economic pressures would need to be applied.[49] Thus, the Bush administration would invade and occupy Iraq while doing nothing of substance to stop North Korea from joining the ranks of the nuclear-armed states.

Defensive Defense

Although our discussion has been about the use of military force, we still are on the topic of *defense* and *deterrence* rather than on the offensive use of force. It is, though, in some sense hard to dispute the old axiom that what appear as defensive measures to some appear as offensive and therefore threatening measures to others. This is part of the dilemma in the security dilemma. Sometimes countries embrace this ambiguity to enhance the danger of underestimating them, and sometimes countries attempt to dispel this ambiguity by adopting policies that are overtly transparent and nonthreatening.

A revision to French nuclear policy after the 9/11 attacks demonstrates the difficulties with determining what level of force capability and what kind of use-of-force policies form an effective deterrent without threatening others more than is necessary. The threat must be there or there would be no deterrent value, but how much force capability and what kind would provide a sense of security in one's deterrent? French nuclear policy was revised after 9/11 to include an option for nuclear strikes on rogue regimes and regional powers.[50] This was seen as a necessary adjustment to a world in which major power conflict was less likely than an attack on one's vital interests by a smaller opponent. The expansion of possible targets from other major powers to regional powers and rogues might lead one to conclude that French nuclear policy was expanded and thus even more threatening to others. Yet this revisioning only continued a 1990s-based policy of not targeting any particular enemy, whether larger or smaller. The use of a nonspecific nuclear deterrence policy arguably might be less provocative than one that identifies potential enemies by targeting them.

In order to demonstrate that its nuclear arsenal was only for deterrence and defense, France went "much further than other nuclear powers in terms of irreversible unilateral disarmament gestures. France destroyed all its land-based systems and reduced its overall number of launchers by 50 percent."[51] French policy also included the idea of a "final warning," or *ultime avertissement*. "The idea is to demonstrate French resolve with a single, limited strike on military targets. If an adversary persisted, the final warning would be followed by a massive strike."[52] This final strike without a doubt would employ nuclear weapons, as France had long rejected a "no-first-use" policy.

Did the French nuclear policy constitute a widening or a narrowing of the instances in which France might use nuclear weapons? The ambiguity was probably intentional, as ambiguity can bolster a deterrent threat. But French nuclear policy seems to demonstrate the earlier point about how difficult it is to distinguish a truly defensive posture from an offensive one (the first being widely justified and acceptable, the other ambiguous and threatening) and the even earlier point that harnessing military force designed to destroy life and property to protect life and property is a precarious balancing act. From a realist perspective, we might add to this the problem of how one might disarm unilaterally or draw down one's military capabilities without leaving one vulnerable to a power grab or coercive diplomacy by another state. Perhaps we might understand French nuclear policy as a hybrid between realist views and what we will in short order consider to be purely defensive views: French nuclear policy was designed to be minimal in that the French reduced their nuclear arsenal in unprecedented ways, and it was designed to be nonprovocative in that no specific country was targeted, yet it was designed to be used against large and small threats and to mean business as demonstrated in a "final warning" nuclear strike.

Despite the unusualness of French nuclear policy, it was still embedded in a realist frame and still dependent on the threat of punishment to deter attacks on France or its interests. There is an alternative notion of defense that would reject any kind of nuclear deterrent precisely because it is embedded in realism and is too provocative. This alternative view is that a state should deploy a military force that is "manifestly defensive" or, as Geoffrey Wiseman explains, a military force that "is defensive, and is seen by one and all to be so, not just in stated overall purpose, but also in its inherent characteristics."[53] Such a defensive posture would be intended to serve as a "shield" rather than a "sword"[54] and ideally would not be a shield that could serve as cover for the wielding of a sword.

Defensive defense, nonprovocative defense, and nonoffensive defense are related terms suggesting "a conventional approach to [defense] aimed at creating an environment that [favors] defensive strategies and operations rather than offensive options. According to this view, offensiveness can be derived from the structure of a military and [defense] forces should therefore have defensive structures and capabilities that are not threatening to other countries."[55] Johan Galtung proposes that we

> locate the definition of the offensive/defensive distinction in geographical space: *can the weapon system be effectively used abroad, or can it only be used at home?* If it can be used abroad then it is offensive, particularly if that "abroad" includes countries with which one is in conflict. If it can only be used at home then the system is defensive, being operational only when an attack has taken place.[56]

Wiseman tells us that "a central assumption of non-provocative defense concepts is that manifestly defensive capabilities provide reassurance to others about intentions."[57] Reassuring others is hardly the stuff of realism and the security dilemma. Instead, Wiseman contends that advocates of nonprovocative defense attempt to "reverse the deterioration process" associated with the realist security dilemma.[58] This reversal is accomplished by employing defensive military postures that eliminate the possibility of inadvertent or unintentional security dilemmas.[59] Evert Jordaan and Abel Esterhuyse go beyond this and argue that nonoffensive defense is "a way to prevent the security dilemma and an arms race" from beginning in the first place.[60]

In post–World War II global politics, defensive defense arose in response to the absurdities of the Cold War and nuclear deterrence. Alternative defense notions arose with the development of peace research studies (rather than security studies), especially in Scandinavian countries.[61] These alternative defense notions were incorporated into Swedish Prime Minister Olof Palme's advocacy of common security—or security *with* other states rather than against other states.[62] This alternative defense movement attempted "to balance realist and idealist perspectives on security by combining the aims of self-reliance, self-preservation, and the existence of anarchy with collective security and interdependence."

Alternative defense concepts that are "manifestly defensive" encourage national leaders to be self-aware and self-reflective about how one's own actions are perceived internationally.[63] Because it is so difficult for others to assess "subjective motivations" and because it is possible to use ostensibly defensive weapons for offensive purposes, national leaders need to configure their resources in defensive modes that would make reconfiguration impossible or so time consuming that would-be targets would be alerted long in advance of any attack. Transparency in the deployment of actual, material defensive forces would be the key to reassuring others. To Galtung, the ideal defensive defense strategy would involve immobile defensive systems having only a local impact area or, less ideally, short-range systems with a limited impact area. Long-range systems with extensive potential impact areas would qualify only as offensive systems.[64] Additionally, defensive defense puts heavy emphasis on nonprofessional, generally conscript armies and militias that would go to war only reluctantly and then only to defend national territory.[65]

In a practical sense, Japan and Germany in the post–World War II era were required to assume defensive defense postures as part of the terms of surrender and occupation. Nonprovocative defense postures may be particularly well suited for the postwar reintegration of losing states, especially from the standpoint of former targeted/victimized states. In some sense, the sanctions regime imposed on Iraq after the 1991 Gulf War can be understood as imposing a defensive defense posture on Iraq.

By way of a more elaborate example and one that does not involve a defeated enemy, Wiseman describes Switzerland's "deterrence by denial," through which it would "deter attack by setting a high price for invasion":[66]

In theory, the Swiss concept of "general defence" involves the entire population. There is no professional army; arms, ammunition, and uniforms are kept in homes; and a well-trained militia force capable of mobilizing some 680,000 troops (comprising men 20 to 50 years of age) is trained to fight within the country's borders . . .

In the event of an external armed attack, the armed forces would assume the major role in defending the country. . . . Should large parts of Switzerland become occupied, citizens would carry out activities ranging from guerrilla warfare to sabotage and civil disobedience. *No form of retaliation or punitive action against the adversary's population is planned.* Switzerland would rely heavily on passive defences, such as obstacles against tanks, anti-aircraft missiles, and early-warning radar systems.

Undoubtedly, these military preparations are manifestly defensive. Switzerland seeks only to defend its territory, it does not threaten others, and will not fight unless attacked.[67]

There are some problems with the notions of nonprovocative defense. One might question whether a state in a dangerous neighborhood—such as South Asia—ought to risk a defensive defense posture. Perhaps only states that are especially important to all parties to a potential dispute—such as Switzerland during World War II—or conversely countries that tend to be peripheral to the central issues of world politics might be successful in adopting defensive defense strategies. Additionally, in this age in which nonstate actors more so than states pose critical security threats, it may be nearly impossible to invoke civil defense strategies that can effectively deter by denial or dissuasion; the goal of nonstate actors is not to invade and occupy but to do significant harm to a target state.

Another thorny issue arises in that we live in an age marked by intrastate rather than interstate conflict. As Wiseman suggests, a defensive strategy that depends on arming and mobilizing a population for homeland defense may well be suicidal for any given government under conditions of probable and impending civil ruptures, conflict, and war. We can turn this around as well; Galtung warns,

> *A policy of defensive defense is not offensive against an outside adversary, but could be highly offensive against an inside adversary.* The types of weapons that are described . . . as being defensive are defensive because they cannot reach outside national borders in any significant manner. But they can certainly hit inside those borders, otherwise they would not have any capability at all. And they would not necessarily distinguish between external and internal foes of the regime. As a matter of fact, they are exactly the type of weapons that a repressive government might use against insurgent forces, whether their claims are justifiable or not.[68]

Finally, despite Jordaan and Esterhuyse's claim that defensive defense augments collective security,[69] the claim seems without merit unless one lived in a world populated by states committed to nonprovocative defense. Galtung admits that "*defensive defense presupposes a high level of national self-reliance in defense matters.* If weapon systems are not supposed to be quick, long range, and mobile, then they cannot be transported from one country to another in order to help that other country (rather than attacking it) either."[70] This has implications for military alliances as well as for international security arrangements like the United Nations that depend on member states' offensive military capabilities. Galtung proposes that the undermining of military alliances is a long-term good: "Clearly, a country which is used to relying on allies, and particularly on a superpower ally, will not mobilize all its defense resources." But "if one really means what one says, that freedom is worth a fight, then that fight has to be done by nobody else than oneself."[71] But what happens in those cases when insurgents or governments turn defensive resources against their internal foes? Who comes to the aid of civilians caught in the crossfire or civilians caught in the genocidal plans of a monstrous government? Even in an idealized world in which states harbored no aggressive intentions toward one another and demonstrated this by deploying only defensive, nonprovocative defense systems, international and human security still may be imperiled by deadly internal arguments over who composes the state and nation.

The Central Intelligence Agency's (CIA) National Intelligence Council (NIC) is a twenty-five-year-old institution whose mission is to draw on governmental and nongovernmental expertise to think strategically about present global problems and future global trends. The NIC makes "over-the-horizon" estimates about security trends, issuing regular National Intelligence Estimates as well as special reports such as *Global Trends 2015: A Dialogue about the Future with Nongovernment Experts*[1] and *Mapping the Global Future: Report of the National Intelligence Council's 2020 Project*.[2] These latter two reports indicate that the balance of power in South Asia will tip sharply in India's favor over the next decades, with Pakistan collapsing into near–failed state status. Relevant excerpts are provided verbatim here.

Excerpts from *Global Trends 2015*
South Asia Regional Trends

- India will be the unrivaled regional power with a large military—including naval and nuclear capabilities—and a dynamic and growing economy. The widening India-Pakistan gap—destabilizing in its own right—will be accompanied by deep political, economic, and social disparities within both states.
- Pakistan will be more fractious, isolated, and dependent on international financial assistance.[3]

India in 2015. Indian democracy will remain strong, albeit more factionalized by the secular-Hindu nationalist debate, growing differentials among regions and the increase in competitive party politics. India's economy, long repressed by the heavy hand of regulation, is likely to achieve sustained growth to the degree reforms are implemented . . .

Despite rapid economic growth, more than half a billion Indians will remain in dire poverty. Harnessing technology to improve agriculture will be India's main challenge in alleviating poverty in 2015. The widening gulf between "have" and "have-not" regions and disagreements over the pace and nature of reforms will be a source of domestic strife . . .[4]

Pakistan in 2015. Pakistan . . . will not recover easily from decades of political and economic mismanagement, divisive politics, lawlessness, corruption and ethnic friction. Nascent democratic reforms will produce little change in the face of opposition from an entrenched political elite and radical Islamic parties. Further domestic decline would benefit Islamic political activists, who may significantly increase their role in national politics and alter the makeup and cohesion of the military—once Pakistan's most capable institution. In a climate of continuing domestic turmoil, the central government's control probably will be reduced to the Punjabi heartland and the economic hub of Karachi.[5]

Excerpts from *Mapping the Global Future*
[India and China are projected to be major "rising powers" by 2020.]

Rising Powers: Tinder for Conflict?

The likelihood of great power conflict escalating into total war in the next 15 years is lower than at any time in the past century, unlike during previous centuries when local conflicts sparked world wars . . .

This does not eliminate the possibility of great power conflict, however. The absence of effective conflict resolution mechanisms in some regions, the rise of nationalism in some states, and the raw emotions on both sides of key issues increase the chances for miscalculation.

India and Pakistan appear to understand the likely prices to be paid by triggering a conflict. But nationalistic feelings run high and are not likely to abate. Under plausible scenarios Pakistan might use nuclear weapons to counter success by the larger Indian conventional forces, particularly given Pakistan's lack of strategic depth.[6]

Notes

1. Central Intelligence Agency, National Intelligence Council, *Global Trends 2015: A Dialogue about the Future with Nongovernment Experts*, December 2000, http://www.cia.gov/nic/NIC_globaltrend2015.html (accessed July 1, 2005).

2. Central Intelligence Agency, National Intelligence Council, *Mapping the Global Future: Report of the National Intelligence Council's 2020 Project*, December 2004, http://www.cia.gov/nic/NIC_globaltrend2020.html (accessed July 1, 2005).

3. Central Intelligence Agency, National Intelligence Council, *Global Trends 2015*, 64.

4. Central Intelligence Agency, National Intelligence Council, *Global Trends 2015*, 66.

5. Central Intelligence Agency, National Intelligence Council, *Global Trends 2015*, 66.

6. Central Intelligence Agency, National Intelligence Council, *Mapping the Global Future*, 98.

6

Going on the Offensive

In chapter 2, I noted Charles Tilly's important observation that states made war and that war made the states. Successful political authorities managed to eliminate internal and external rivals while securing access to sufficient resources necessary to maintain protection against any potential challenger.[1] War serves a fundamental purpose in the creation and maintenance of states, or, in another observer's words, "without war no state could be. All those we know of arose through war, and the protection of their members by armed force remains their primary and essential task."[2] More than survival, war brings greatness; Tilly remarks, "Victorious violence and armed repression, after all, shaped every major European state."[3]

Political theorists and statesmen over the centuries since Westphalia have done more than just note the utilitarian nature of war for the state. War, some have asserted, advances human civilization. Herbert Spencer, a nineteenth-century English sociologist, proclaimed,

Warfare among men, like warfare among animals, has had a large share in raising their organizations to a higher stage. . . .

. . . The killing-off of relatively feeble tribes, or tribes relatively wanting in endurance, or courage, or sagacity, or power of co-operation, must have tended ever to maintain, and occasionally to increase, the amounts of life-preserving powers possessed by men.

. . . we everywhere find that union of small societies by a conquering society is a step in civilization.[4]

115

Spencer's contemporary, German nationalist and advocate of German colonialism Heinrich von Treitschke, similarly was held in the sway of social Darwinism when he wrote in *Politics*, "The great strides which [civilization] makes against barbarism and unreason are only made by the sword." Yet Treitschke saw war as going beyond survival of the fittest: "Between civilized nations also war is the form of litigation by which states make their claims valid. The arguments brought forward in these terrible law suits of the nations compel as to argument in civil suits can ever do." And, by virtue of war, civilized nations "learn to know and respect each other's peculiar qualities." Further, war bestows on states—and by derivation their citizens—glory: "The grandeur of war lies in the utter annihilation of puny man in the great conception of the state, and it brings out the full magnificence of the sacrifice of fellow-countrymen for one another."[5] Ultimately, because of the glory that war confers on states, citizens, and civilization, Treitschke rejects peace—especially perpetual peace—as "not only impossible but immoral."[6]

Treitschke's use of "heroes" to mean those who die so that the state may survive resonates in post-9/11 American rhetoric. The victims of the 9/11 attacks on the United States were hailed as "heroes" who, unbeknownst at the time to anyone but the terrorists, were on the "front line" in the war on terror. A hero, according to the *American Heritage Dictionary*, is "a man, often of divine ancestry, who is endowed with great courage and strength, celebrated for his bold exploits, and favored by the gods. . . . A person noted for feats of courage and nobility of purpose, especially one who risked or sacrificed his or her life." In our current international system in which sovereignty resides in each reified state, the "divine ancestry" of the modern hero is manifested in his or her citizenship, a citizenship for which the individual may sacrifice all and thus be duly celebrated. The victims of the 9/11 attack as well as the emergency personnel who lost their lives attempting to rescue victims were hailed as heroes since they died not because of who they were individually but because of whom they represented—their state.

Since 9/11, it has been well understood in American politics that *not* to honor the "heroes" of the 9/11 attacks and the wars in Afghanistan and Iraq would be political folly, so much had they become identified as symbols of the greatness and righteousness of the country wrongly attacked. This, too, would be understood by political observers from earlier times. For instance, Treitschke proclaimed,

Most undoubtedly war is the one remedy for an ailing nation. Social selfishness and party hatreds must be dumb before the call of the state when its existence is at stake. Forgetting himself, the individual must only remember that he is part of the whole, and realize the unimportance of his own life compared with the common weal.[7]

Thus, war creates and maintains the glorified state, and war is glorified for the ways in which it contributes to the grandeur of the state and to the forwarding of civilization. Citizens, too, by virtue of their relationship to the glorified state, can move beyond their "puny" existence and be part of something divine.

Following on this view, peace inhibits the course of civilization and thus is suspect. As Treitschke warned, the promotion of "perpetual peace" was "immoral." Peacemakers interrupt the natural and edifying process that is war. A century after Treitschke, Edward Luttwak launched a diatribe against UN peacekeeping and humanitarian efforts in civil wars:

> An unpleasant truth often overlooked is that although war is a great evil, it does have a great virtue: it can resolve political conflicts and lead to peace. This can happen when all belligerents become exhausted or when one wins decisively. Either way the key is that the fighting must continue until a resolution is reached. War brings peace only after passing a culminating phase of violence.[8]

By intervening in civil conflicts in the name of "frivolous motives" such as humanitarianism, Luttwak declares, the United Nations only caused more suffering and damage. "If the United Nations helped the strong defeat the weak faster and more decisively, it would actually enhance the peacemaking potential of war."[9] Luttwak concludes that "too many wars nowadays become endemic conflicts that never end because the transformative effects of both decisive victory and exhaustion are blocked by outside intervention."[10] Genocidal civil wars, by Luttwak's hard and cold realist logic, must be allowed to move to their "natural" conclusion in order to advance final political solutions and thereby move the society in question forward. Presumably interstate wars premised on some kind of "clash of civilizations"[11] foundation must also move posthaste to their natural conclusions in which one civilization succumbs to the might of the other, thereby advancing the whole of humanity. War, then, is not just a response borne from self-defense but a movement toward greatness and even evolutionary—at least in the views of some!

The Bush Doctrine

The Bush doctrine enacted in the 2003 invasion of Iraq was claimed to be a direct renunciation of containment and deterrence, and it portrayed preventive war as preemptive self-defense. The Bush administration began establishing its new reading of self-defense and preemption soon after the 9/11 terrorist attacks. The secretary of defense remarked in October 2001,

> There is no question but that the United States of America has every right, as every country does, of self-defense, and the problem with terrorism is that

there is no way to defend against the terrorists at every place and every time against every conceivable technique. Therefore, the only way to deal with the terrorist network is to take the battle to them. That is in fact what we're doing. That is in effect self-defense of a preemptive nature.[12]

Well after the military toppling of the Taliban in Afghanistan, Bush gave a speech in June 2002 at the West Point military academy in which he dismissed deterrence and containment:

For much of the last century, America's defense relied on the Cold War doctrines of deterrence and containment. In some cases, those strategies still apply. But new threats also require new thinking. Deterrence—the promise of massive retaliation against nations—means nothing against shadowy terrorist networks with no nation or citizens to defend. Containment is not possible when unbalanced dictators with weapons of mass destruction can deliver those weapons on missiles or secretly provide them to terrorist allies.[13]

Then, in the September 2002 National Security Strategy of the United States of America, the Bush administration claimed that international jurisprudence and the recognized principle of self-defense in a murky time of global terrorism allowed for an adaptation of the notion of imminent threat:

For centuries, international law recognized that nations need not suffer an attack before they can lawfully take action to defend themselves against forces that present an imminent danger of attack. Legal scholars and international jurists often conditioned the legitimacy of preemption on the existence of an imminent threat—most often a visible mobilization of armies, navies, and air forces preparing to attack.

We must adapt the concept of imminent threat to the capabilities and objectives of today's adversaries. Rogue states and terrorists do not seek to attack us using conventional means. They know such attacks would fail. Instead, they rely on acts of terror and, potentially, the use of weapons of mass destruction—weapons that can be easily concealed, delivered covertly, and used without warning. . . .

The United States has long maintained the option of preemptive actions to counter a sufficient threat to our national security. The greater the threat, the greater is the risk of inaction—and the more compelling the case for taking anticipatory action to defend ourselves, even if uncertainty remains as to the time and place of the enemy's attack. To forestall or prevent such hostile acts by our adversaries, the United States will, if necessary, act preemptively.[14]

The Bush doctrine established by these statements was expanded in the second inaugural address of January 2005. With this expansion, "ending tyranny" in the world became a vital security interest of the United States:

We have seen our vulnerability—and we have seen its deepest source. For as long as whole regions of the world simmer in resentment and tyranny, prone to ideologies that feed hatred and excuse murder, violence will gather, and multiply in destructive power, and cross the most defended borders, and raise a mortal threat. There is only one force of history that can break the reign of hatred and resentment, and expose the pretensions of tyrants, and reward the hopes of the decent and tolerant, and that is the force of human freedom.

We are led, by events and common sense, to one conclusion: The survival of liberty in our land increasingly depends on the success of liberty in other lands. The best hope for peace in our world is the expansion of freedom in all the world.[15]

By this logic, even contained tyrannical governments posed a national security threat and thus could no longer be tolerated. As will be discussed later in this chapter, little of this Bush doctrine amounted to an altogether new justification for military intervention. But what was new was the apparent refutation of containment and deterrence and the stretching of self-defense to mean both preemptive and preventive war.

Despite statements to the contrary, the Bush doctrine in practice appeared at key junctures to be a repackaging of containment. Consider the case of North Korea and nuclear weapons previously discussed in chapter 4. The Bush administration went from declaring that it would not allow North Korea to obtain nuclear weapons to declaring that the *proliferation* of nuclear weapons materials from North Korea would not be tolerated. That is, the stated policy switched from preemption to containment and deterrence (albeit deterrence with an unspecified and uncertain threat of punishment).

Even this Bush preemptive nonproliferation policy was dealt a serious blow by the Bush administration itself shortly after the policy was elaborated in late 2002. The Bush administration warned that the United States would act preemptively to stop the use of weapons of mass destruction (WMD) and would consider using nuclear weapons to do so. Presumably, if the administration would not hesitate to use nuclear weapons to stop the use of the same, it would also proactively stop WMD proliferation. On the very same day that this policy was announced, news came that the Spanish navy, acting on instructions from the U.S. government, had intercepted a ship in the Arabian Sea carrying Scud missiles from North Korea. The Spanish navy fired warning shots at the freighter to get it to stop, a potentially dangerous act by the Spanish and in times past a prelude to war. Yet the very next day, the U.S. government released the freighter and missiles. The Scuds had been purchased from North Korea by Yemen, and the White House spokesperson said that "there is no provision under international law prohibiting Yemen from accepting delivery of missiles from North Korea."[16] The government of Yemen, however, had pledged not to buy Scuds from North Korea when Yemen became an ally in the war on terror eighteen months before.[17] (The harbor of Aden, Yemen, was the site of the October 2000 bombing of the USS *Cole*, and the Yemeni government had blocked a thorough investigation by the Federal Bureau of Investigation [FBI] after the fact.) Nonetheless, the White House declared that the United States had no international authority to stop a "state-to-state" commercial transaction from the "evil" rogue North Korea to the new U.S. "friend" Yemen, and the Scuds were released to their buyer.[18]

What was clear in this case was that Spain was ready to assist in a *multilateral* preemptive nonproliferation policy that would serve broader international interests, but the Bush administration wanted to tailor the policy to the specific case. A preemption policy pushed on others when it suited major power interests was not so bold a move in the history of the state system. A multilateral preemption initiative might well have been bold and forward thinking and might well have generated multinational participation.[19] Such a multilateral preemption initiative would need ground rules that all parties would understand and act within, eliminating the fear that one party might revise the rules as it goes.

If the Bush doctrine was consistent on any point, it was that the administration retained the absolute right to revise the rules and terms of the "game" as it desired. Consider the issue of whether Saddam Hussein's Iraq was contained sufficiently prior to the 2003 war. Richard Betts asserts that Iraq had been well contained for more than a decade: "Going to war in 1991, the [first] Bush administration warned Saddam of dire consequences if he used WMD during the war. Despite humiliating defeat, Saddam held those weapons back. Nor has Iraq attacked any of its neighbors since American deterrence has been made clear over the past decade."[20]

British Prime Minister Tony Blair's top foreign policy and security advisers had reached the same conclusion about the successful containment of Hussein a full year before the March 2003 invasion. In secret memos released in May 2005 and acknowledged by the Blair government as authentic, it was revealed that Blair had agreed in April 2002 to assist the Bush administration in a war to enact regime change in Iraq. A memo written in July 2002 after a meeting of Blair, his security advisers, and the British attorney general stated that the American and British governments agreed that a justification would need to be invented for the war since "it seemed clear that Bush had made up his mind to take military action, even if the timing was not yet decided. *But the case was thin. Saddam was not threatening his [neighbors], and his WMD capability was less than that of Libya, North Korea or Iran.*"[21] The same memo noted that "the US had already begun 'spikes of activity' to put pressure on the regime" many months before the U.S. Congress and UN Security Council were presented with the "imminent threat" of the Iraq regime. The "spikes of activity" were conducted in order to push the Iraqi regime into doing something that would legitimize an invasion.

"Preemptive self-defense" as demonstrated by the regime change in Iraq is better understood as self-interested military intervention repackaged under a new name. But, in fact, the packaging had already been tested. In 1983, the Organization of Eastern Caribbean States (OECS) claimed the right to launch a "preemptive defensive strike" against Grenada as justification for a U.S. military intervention.[22] The "preemptive defensive strike" was justified by the OECS on many grounds: well-founded fears of "further loss of life," "general deterioration of public order," suppression of Grenadians, and fears that the new Grenadian regime would wield disproportionate military strength relative to its neighbors. The goal of the U.S. invasion of Grenada was to remove a Soviet-leaning junta. Distancing itself from the OECS claim, the U.S. government announced that its intervention was justified to protect U.S. nationals in Grenada. The OECS claim of "preemptive self-defense" was not embraced—everyone understood that the self-interests of the United States and OECS members prompted the intervention.

Preemptive and Preventive War

To a large degree, whether a state engages in preemptive or preventive war or whether a state launches a war of sheer aggression, the justification for such violence will typically come down to self-defense or defense of one's vital interests, although the targeted state and some third parties may argue otherwise. Michael Glennon suggests that "aggression and self-defense are opposite sides of the same coin."[23] Betts agrees: "Whether a given attack was aggression or self-defense depends on which side is making the characterization. Victims always cite enemy attacks as aggressive, perpetrators always cite them as preventive or preemptive. With few exceptions, governments making war believe that they are acting defensively and legitimately."[24]

Preemption or preemptive war is explained by Betts to be

unobjectionable in principle, since it is only an act of anticipatory self-defense in a war effectively initiated by the enemy. If the term is used accurately, rather than in the sloppy or disingenuous manner in which the Bush administration has used it to justify preventive war against Iraq, preemption assumes detection of enemy mobilization of forces to attack, which represents the start of the war. Beating the enemy to the draw by striking before he launches his attack is reactive, even if it involves firing the first shot. Striking first may be the only way to avoid the consequences of being struck first in the very near future.[25]

Preemption, Betts tells us, is "legitimate in principle and sometimes advisable in practice."

In the context of international jurisprudence and accepted state practices, Neta Crawford delineates four necessary conditions that must be met in order to conduct a legitimate preemptive strike or war:

> First, the party contemplating preemption would have a narrow conception of the "self" to be defended in circumstances of self-defense. Preemption is not justified to protect imperial interests or assets taken in a war of aggression. Second, there would have to be strong evidence that war was inevitable and likely in the immediate future. Immediate threats are those which can be made manifest within days or weeks unless action is taken to thwart them. This requires clear intelligence showing that a potential aggressor has both the capability and the intention to do harm in the near future. Capability alone is not a justification. Third, preemption should be likely to succeed in reducing the threat. Specifically, there should be a high likelihood that the source of the military threat can be found and the damage that it was about to do can be greatly reduced or eliminated by a preemptive attack. If preemption is likely to fail, it should not be undertaken. Fourth, military force must be necessary; no other measures can have time to work or be likely to work.[26]

Chris Brown agrees that preemption is justifiable in terms of self-defense. "States, it is presumed, do not have an unqualified right to use force in international relations, but they do have the right to defend themselves—a right established in customary international law and reaffirmed in the UN Charter—and, crucially, are under no obligation to allow an aggressor to strike first." Yet this right is indisputable only when "there is an imminent threat of an unprovoked aggression."[27]

When the Bush administration made claims that it needed to conduct regime change in Iraq before a mushroom cloud appeared over cities in the United States, it was making a claim of "an imminent threat of unprovoked aggression." The claim, we now know, was manufactured in order to conduct regime change and give the British government some political and legal justification for assisting the Bush administration in the invasion. The main way in which the Iraqi regime was said to threaten the security of the United States was through the transfer of WMD to terrorists who would deploy the weapons in the United States. The claim was that the threat was more or less immediate—that is, imminent—and thus time was of the essence. The administration started making this claim in the fall of 2002, although, as discussed previously, the Bush and Blair governments had agreed to invade Iraq five months earlier, and thus the claim of imminence is problematic. Moreover, as Glennon argues, even the claim that the United States was threatened by the possible transfer of WMD from Iraq to terrorists would not be a sufficient claim in international law to justify military actions in self-defense, whether preemptively or after an attack. The International Court of Justice ruled in the case of *Nicaragua v. United States of America* that providing weapons and support to terrorists or other nonstate actors does not constitute an "armed attack."[28] Thus,

> The implications for the war against terrorism are clear. Use of force against the Taliban government of Afghanistan was . . . unlawful. . . . Indeed, the entire approach of the United States in fighting terrorism—refusing to distinguish between terrorists and those who harbor them, which has come to be called the "Bush Doctrine"—is outlawed by this precept to the extent that it precludes any use of force against states that only passively provide a safe harbor for terrorists and avoid substantial involvement in the terrorists' activities.[29]

What would constitute a legitimate preemptive war if the U.S. war against Iraq was not? Betts offers the case of the Israeli attack on Egypt and Syria in 1967 as the "most promising" of real-world cases to fit the category. "The closure of the Strait of Tiran and political rhetoric at the time made the circumstantial evidence that the Arabs were preparing to attack Israel as good as such evidence ever gets."[30]

If the U.S. war on Iraq that began in March 2003 was not a preemptive war for self-defense, what was it? Domestic critics of the Bush administration have called the war an "elective" war much like elective surgery that is chosen not because one's life and health are in jeopardy but because of the benefits that might accrue from such a procedure. The war has also been called a *preventive* war. Randall Schweller defines preventive war as "those wars that are motivated by the fear that one's military power and potential are declining relative to that of a rising adversary. . . . [S]tates wage preventive wars for either offensive or defensive reasons: to take advantage of a closing window of opportunity or to prevent the opening of a window of vulnerability."[31] Charles Kegley and Gregory Raymond state that "a *preventive* military attack entails the use of force to eliminate any possible future strike, even when there is no reason to believe that aggression is planned or the capability to launch such an attack is operational."[32] Betts would add that "the rationale for preventive war is that conflict with the adversary is so deep and unremitting that war is ultimately inevitable, on worse terms than on present, as the enemy grows stronger over time."[33] These explanations of preventive war mesh with reports that Bush administration officials had long sought to "finish" the "unfinished business" of the 1991 Gulf War by removing Saddam Hussein from power. Despite claims by Bush foreign policy adviser Condoleezza Rice in the 2000 presidential campaign that Saddam Hussein was successfully contained and that time was against him, other Bush administration officials saw a window of opportunity open with the 9/11 terrorist attacks and launched a war of opportunity rather than one of self-defense.

The Bush doctrine said that preemption must be fitted to a time of shadowy terrorist groups seeking to do harm to the United States; that is, preemption in an age of global terrorism requires what previously was called prevention. Some analysts would disagree with this use of "preemption" while agreeing that the intended foreign policy behavior is necessary. Brown laments that we live in an

> imperfect world. Suppose we lived in a world with a fully developed legal framework governing the use of force in international relations and outlawing its use as an instrument of foreign policy, and in which there were an international body charged with the maintenance of peace and security that possessed legitimate and effective decisionmaking procedures and the capacity to enforce its judgments. In such a world, the distinction between preemption and prevention would be clear-cut and of critical importance. Preventive war would be totally illegitimate because if one state believed that developments in another might threaten its security, it could refer the matter to the international body, where it would be investigated and dealt with appropriately . . .
>
> The problem is that we do not live in this world.[34]

Brown admits it would be good to live in a world "where the kind of existential insecurity of the present world no longer existed." But, given that we do not and given that "predatory" states exist, it "may sometimes be necessary for nonpredatory states to act unilaterally or outside the official institutional structure."[35] He does warn, though, with a prudent eye cast on the Bush doctrine, that "states should not allow themselves to pursue the chimera of absolute security." This is because to try "to eliminate all such threats is to commit to an endless series of wars to end all wars."

In 2006, the Bush administration did not appear *necessarily* to be intent on an "endless series of wars to end all wars." Notwithstanding the second inaugural boast that the United States would seek to end all tyranny in the world, the Bush administration appeared selective about when its doctrine would or would not lead to military intervention. Selectivity in using military intervention and intervention based on the claim of self-defense are nothing new in world affairs.

Military Intervention

Self-interested military intervention in the domestic affairs of other states is an age-old practice. The Treaty of Westphalia did not put a stop to military intervention even though the treaty put emphasis on respecting state sovereignty. The justifications for intervention were understood to be limited by the treaty, however. The Thirty Years' War had begun over religious disagreements that prompted countries to engage in military "humanitarian interventions" to protect coconfessants in other countries. The treaty that ended the war established the principles of sovereign equality and nonintervention, but nonintervention was conditional. The treaty prohibited military intervention for modifying religious practices, but states were permitted to intervene "to promote their national security, protect their independence, and preserve established international law."[36]

National security and national interests often have been translated into *regime* security and *regime* interests rather than securing the people or nation and popular interests. When the first government premised on popular sovereignty appeared in Europe—revolutionary France—conservative European governments cited national security reasons for military intervention against the French. British politician Edmund Burke proclaimed in 1796 that there was a "right to intervene against a public menace" such as that embodied in the French Revolution. Burke warned that the type of government being instituted in France would in time be *imposed* on neighboring countries or that, at the very least, France's neighbors would live forever in enmity with the public menace. Burke asserted,

> There is a *law of the neighbourhood* which does not leave a man perfectly master on his own ground. When a neighbour sees a *new erection*, in the nature of a nuisance, set up at his door, he has a right to represent it to the judge; who, on his part, has a right to order the work to be stayed; or, if established, to be removed. . . . No *innovation* is permitted that may redound, even secondarily, to the prejudice of a neighbour.[37]

The lack of a judge in the neighborhood of states meant that each state had a right to act itself as judge to prevent the threatening innovation. "What in civil society is a ground of action, in politic society is a ground of war."[38] Evan Luard notes,

> This kind of argument—that states had the right to intervene against a revolutionary regime elsewhere (closely parallel to the arguments to be used 150 years later to justify US intervention against Cuba, the Dominican Republic and Nicaragua)—was widely used by conservative statesmen after 1815 to justify intervention, unilateral or collective, to put down revolution in other states.[39]

As the nineteenth century wore on, the governments of Europe became more friendly to notions of popular sovereignty (for Europeans at least). Military intervention became justified in terms of a government's responsibility to its own citizens. Governments declared a right to defend their nationals *abroad*. In a speech to the British Parliament in

1850, Lord Palmerston justified British military intervention in Greece in this manner:

> I say then, that if our subjects abroad have complaints against individuals, or against the government of a foreign country, if the courts of law of that country can afford them redress, then, no doubt to those courts of justice the British subject ought in the first instance to apply; and it is only on a denial of justice, or upon decisions manifestly unjust, that the British government should be called upon to interfere.[40]

This statement sounds similar to one made over a hundred years later in 1960 by the Belgian representative to the United Nations explaining Belgian military intervention in Congo: "I should like to make our present position clear. We sent troops; they intervened to the extent necessary to fulfil our sacred duty to protect the lives and honour of our nationals."[41]

On the founding of the United Nations in 1945, the claim of the right to intervene to protect one's nationals became the primary justification for military intervention, well ahead of the sometimes harder to prove claim of self-defense. As discussed in chapter 8, the United Nations was founded to uphold the principles of sovereign equality and nonintervention while creating an international order to prevent interstate war. Sovereign equality and nonintervention arguably became more important for newly independent states as they joined the United Nations than for more established states.[42] Military intervention still occurred despite the UN system, but its practitioners took pains to explain their actions on the basis of their responsibility to protect their own citizens and sometimes to protect other foreign nationals.

A few examples are in order here. These examples derive from the work of Thomas Weiss, Don Hubert, and a team of international researchers who examined ten cases of military intervention conducted for humanitarian purposes from 1945 to 1989.[43] In all ten cases, the intervening countries declared a right to defend foreign nationals (the humanitarian intervention claim) or self-defense as their justification. The unilateral Belgian intervention in Congo in 1960 and the U.S.-Belgian intervention in Stanleyville, Congo, in 1964 were justified in terms of the rescue of foreign nationals, although these countries also intervened to shore up Western-friendly governments in the face of mounting rebel gains. The 1964 intervention occurred under the cover of an invitation from the prime minister, who had first tried to defend his government using white mercenaries hired from South Africa and Rhodesia.[44] After rebels took foreigners hostage, the Americans and French decided to launch a rescue attempt, and *then* they were invited in by the prime minister. This intervention stopped Organization of African Unity negotiations over the hostages and resulted in massive killing of both Congolese and hostages. Similarly, French and Belgian intervention in Shaba province, Zaire (the renamed

Congo), in 1978 was conducted under the claim of rescuing foreigners from rebel violence and on the invitation of the government. (Refer back to extended discussion box 2.2 for more about the former Congo.)

Three of the cases Weiss and Hubert studied—the Indian intervention in East Pakistan in 1971, the Vietnamese intervention in Cambodia in 1978, and the Tanzanian intervention in Uganda in 1979—were justifiable as humanitarian interventions in the current understanding of the term. In each of these cases, widespread mass murders were ended by unilateral military intervention and the toppling of the offending regimes. Yet humanitarian claims on behalf of local people in distress were not made, nor would such claims have been acceptable to the international community:

> Although the invocation of humanitarian claims in the most egregious of the episodes would have been appropriate—in East Pakistan's mass murders in 1971, in Idi Amin's Uganda throughout the 1970s, and in Pol Pot's Cambodia in the late 1970s—intervening states chose to frame the legitimacy of their respective interventions on the grounds of self-defence. Furthermore, few other states raised the issue in international debates. Certainly the strongest contemporary advocates—NATO [North Atlantic Treaty Organization] members—categorically rejected the existence of a norm of humanitarian intervention. In fact, these countries continued to recognize the Khmer Rouge as the representative of Cambodia for another decade.[45]

These three cases are worth brief exploration here.

In mid- to late 1971, the Pakistani army committed massive human rights violations, mass murder, and genocide against the Bengali people of East Pakistan. The violence caused ten million refugees to flee to India. India had been supporting Bengali rebels, offering them safe haven and air support. In retaliation for this support, Pakistan attacked Indian air force positions along the border in early December, prompting a full Indian military intervention. In debates at the United Nations, India claimed that it acted out of self-defense—defending itself against the Pakistani attack on Indian airfields and against "refugee aggression."[46] Few countries accepted the self-defense claim in the UN debates, "and not a single country argued that India had a right to intervene militarily in order to rescue the beleaguered people of East Pakistan. Although India had not expressly invoked a right to intervene for humanitarian reasons, the countries participating in the debate were well aware of claims of mass murder, and even of genocide, in East Pakistan."[47] With few exceptions, UN members ignored the egregious human rights violations and emphasized the principle of nonintervention as the fundamental building block of the United Nations and the international system.

When Vietnam intervened in Cambodia in 1978, it had already been engaged in a low-level border war with the Pol Pot regime since 1975.

Vietnamese intervention ended the "killing fields" of the genocidal Cambodian regime. Although Vietnam did not claim a humanitarian justification for its intervention—it claimed self-defense—the issue of humanitarian intervention was debated in the United Nations. Western countries argued that even massive human rights violations would not justify military intervention. The Norwegian representative declared that despite its own previous protests to the Pol Pot government about human rights abuses, "the domestic policies of that Government cannot—we repeat, cannot—justify the actions of Vietnam over the last days and weeks." The French representative echoed this: "The notion that because a regime is detestable foreign intervention is justified and forcible overthrow is legitimate is extremely dangerous."[48]

Finally, when the homicidal Idi Amin regime of Uganda was overthrown by Tanzanian military intervention in 1979, the Tanzanian government made no claims about protecting the Ugandan people. Instead, Tanzania claimed self-defense, a claim that was supported by Amin's attempt to militarily annex part of Tanzania. Little or no condemnation of Tanzania resulted from its intervention, and no state spoke in relief on behalf of the Ugandan people.[49]

It is important to reiterate that in the Weiss-Hubert study of cases from 1945 to 1989, no intervening state ever argued that its intervention was justified to save a "population in distress." In every case, the intervening state had vested interests in reinforcing the power of a friendly government or in replacing an unfriendly government. Moreover, the interveners employed substantial offensive military capabilities that were well matched to their task and moved quickly to use force to obtain their objectives. Self-interest guided these military interventions, and this self-interest was cast in terms that all states could appreciate as within the rights of states.

In the 1990s, much of this changed dramatically. Military intervention on behalf of populations in distress (regardless of nationality) became common in the post–Cold War era. In chapter 9, I examine this change and the humanitarian interventions undertaken by the United Nations or approved by the United Nations. We will see that although the humanitarian intentions were genuine in the interventions of the 1990s, these interventions were far less successful than some of the earlier ones that made no such humanitarian claim. It may well be that states find it easier to commit to and execute military intervention when they know how a situation threatens their own national interests.

Having made this last point, self-interest in and of itself is not a solid template for military intervention. Do states *successfully* promote their own interests when they choose to intervene militarily in the affairs of other states? In the ten cases Weiss and Hubert studied, the answer was yes, but they never claimed to study the whole universe of cases of intervention. Some infamous military interventions from this period come to mind:

> *Vietnam*, the quagmire from which the United States could not extricate itself for more than a decade; *Afghanistan*, which became a "bleeding wound" (the term was Mikhail Gorbachev's) for the Soviet Union; *Lebanon*, where Israel suffered its first military defeat . . . and *Sri Lanka*, where India sent its peace-keeping forces, only to have them become another party to a brutal war.[50]

These cases suggest that military intervention in promotion of any justification—the defense of foreign nationals, the defense of populations in distress, or even promoting something like the Bush doctrine of preemptive self-defense—may backfire and become protracted and ultimately poisonous to the longer-term interests of the intervening state.

Charles Kupchan argues that in Vietnam (for the United States), Afghanistan (for the Soviet Union), Lebanon (for Israel and in part for Syria), in Angola (for Cuba and South Africa), and Sri Lanka (for India), the intervening states made erroneous assumptions about the political situations into which they launched their troops and then, when the situation on the ground was not as assumed, they made critical errors in the application of force.[51] These starting assumptions were that the "balance of resolve" would favor the intervener, that "the local ally would serve as a reliable political/military partner," and that "the intervention would not fundamentally alter the political landscape in the target state, *except as intended* by the intervener."[52]

Because the intervening states assumed they could stay in control of the situations created by their interventions, they underestimated and/or were dismissive of the agency and power of their opponents. Kupchan explains the failures in judgment that followed this underestimation:

> None of the interveners was intent on physical destruction of the enemy. The goal was to neutralize the adversary through superior force, thereby convincing him that to continue the struggle was futile. In the meantime, the intervener's local ally would consolidate its military and political position and, eventually, be able to establish control over the country with only indirect assistance from outside. The core issue was essentially one of resolve. The intervener's military might and staying power would crush the adversary's will. The balance of resolve would shift to the local ally and gradual disengagement would take place.[53]

In each of the cases named, there were no facts to support these judgments, and events on the ground proved how wrong these judgments were.

In the case of the U.S. invasion of Iraq in March 2003, we see some of the same misjudgments. The Bush administration assumed that it would

enjoy widespread local support for its actions and have reliable local partners in the form of Iraqi expatriate groups. The administration seemed to
assume that any enemies in Iraq could be neutralized by simply replacing
the top one or two leaders of each government agency (of the existing
Saddam Hussein government) with favored Iraqis. Events on the ground
changed this expectation when the Hussein government totally collapsed
as the invasion commenced. The U.S. occupation authority then compounded this calamity by firing all persons associated with the former
ruling political party rather than recalling the dispersed authorities (especially the military and police) toward the goal of quickly restoring law,
order, and government services. This policy was later repudiated in part,
but by then lawlessness had taken hold, an insurgency began that could
not be brought under control, and even basic government services were
not restored to prewar levels as of mid-2006.

In Kupchan's analysis, the interveners seemed to understand going in
that the intervention would require substantial military commitment, but
they suffered from a failure to understand the political nature of the situation. The "intelligence communities demonstrated a glaring inability to
gather accurate and reliable information about political, as opposed to
military, variables."[54] In the case of the Iraq war, this played out with
some difference. Before the invasion, the U.S. Army chief of staff testified
before the Senate Armed Services Committee that the postinvasion occupation would take a substantial commitment of "several hundred thou-
sand soldiers." Nonmilitary Pentagon officials declared that the general
had "misspoke[n]" and that no large military commitment would be
needed.[55] Thus, in this case the political planners overruled the military
planners and underestimated the size of the military commitment
needed. However, the Bush administration did make the mistake
Kupchan identifies of placing inordinate value on bad and self-interested
intelligence from the Iraqi expatriate community. From "evidence" of
WMD that formed the primary justification for the intervention to the
notion expressed by the U.S. vice president that U.S. forces would be
"greeted as liberators," military planning became hostage to unreliable
intelligence and expectations.

In the cases reviewed by Kupchan, as erroneous assumptions based on
flawed intelligence led to uncertain, poorly understood and shifting political goals,

military objectives became more amorphous and less narrowly specified. In
some cases, initial military operations were frustrated by the adversary. As a
result of these initial setbacks, the intervener, rather than focusing on the protection of key cities or strategic points, tended to redefine its mission as
destroying the will of the adversary, convincing him that victory was not
attainable. This more ambitious objective often played an important role in

convincing the intervening state to switch from defensive to offensive tactics and to increase its commitment of military personnel. In combination with the rising importance of reputational goals [particularly projecting an image of resolve], this dynamic provided a key source of escalatory pressure.[56]

More than three years after the initial intervention in Iraq, the Bush administration defined the core issue to be that of resolve; "we cannot afford to fail" became a refrain of administration officials. The administration declared in the face of decreasing American public support for the war that the U.S. forces would stay to help the new Iraqi government as long as was necessary. The president said in August 2005 that "as Iraqis stand up, we'll stand down," and repeated this throughout the next year.[57] The goal of U.S. forces in Iraq was sometimes said to be fighting the war on terror on the new front line in Iraq, and sometimes said to be that of training the Iraqi military to defend the state and people against terrorists. The former goal involved military offensives utilizing overwhelming force, whereas the latter involved American forces standing behind the new Iraqi army and then withdrawing over time to protected positions away from the main conflict zones:

> To some these might seem like conflicting force postures, a conflict made worse by . . . the difficulty the Americans [had] in distinguishing between the 320,000 members of the Iraqi Army and the police, and the thousands of other armed irregulars now stalking the land. Some of these irregulars . . . were members of Kurdish and Shiite militias; some private security forces recruited by ministers; still others, bodyguards to other prominent Iraqis.[58]

John Burns calls this and the American uncertainty about *who* might be trusted local partners the "shadowlands" of Iraq that existed more than thirty months after the United States invaded. American commanders put their own spin on the president's mantra that reflected their unease with the shifting goals of their mission: "Iraqi units will only stand up when they see American units begin to stand down."[59]

Perhaps one reason the Bush administration got bogged down in Iraq was the changing nature of warfare itself and an attitudinal and institutional resistance by policymakers to fully accommodate that change.

"New Wars"

Two trends seemed to have shaped recent views on warfare in Western capitals if nowhere else. The first trend involves the recognition of the transformation of war. Rarely are wars fought now between organized armies representing legal states; instead, wars involve states battling against nonstate actors (a phenomenon long recognized in non-Western capitals, to be sure). The second trend—also predominantly in the West—involves a merger of changing attitudes about fighting wars with a "revolution" in military strategy. Taken together, these two trends clarify as well as confuse some aspects of the fight against terrorism and outside military intervention in civil conflicts.

Martin van Crevald distinguishes between what he calls "modern" war and the majority of wars in the current international era—which we will call "new wars." Modern wars are those waged between modern states. Modern states are characterized by clear "division[s] of labor" between their government, armed forces and citizenry.[60] The technology deployed in such modern wars is immense and can be successfully wielded only by similarly immense, "bureaucratically-managed armed forces."[61] Further, such technological warfare comes with "enormous logistic demands. . . . [T]he vast majority of supplies required in modern war are not those which sustain the lives of soldiers. Instead they are those which are consumed or expended by machines: in other words spare parts, ammunition, fuel, engineering materials, and the like."[62] These logistical demands, in turn, require strong communication and supply lines. The objective of modern warfare, then, is to attack and destroy the enemy's lines of communication and supply before the enemy does the same to yours.

With this portrait of "modern" war in mind, Crevald asserts that most wars since 1945 could not be called "modern." By Crevald's calculations, from 1945 through 1999 approximately one hundred wars occurred, but fewer than twenty involved states on both sides.[63] Instead, the majority of wars involved combatants that were not regular armies; that could not deploy large, high-tech–based weaponry; and that were "very hard to cut off from their virtually non-existent bases."[64] Besides the operational differences between "modern" wars and these others, the political stakes have been different as well. Crevald contends that there has "scarcely been a single case where any international border has moved" by "modern" war since 1945, whereas nonstate wars have "led to political change all over the globe."[65] The overall conclusion Crevald draws from this is that "both organisationally and in terms of the equipment at their disposal the armed forces of the world will have to adjust themselves to this situation by changing military doctrine, largely jettisoning heavy military equipment, and becoming more like the police."[66]

John Mueller would make this conclusion more pointed. Mueller notes that much "of what remains of war, sometimes labeled 'new war,' 'ethnic conflict,' or, most grandly, 'clashes of civilization,' is more nearly opportunistic predation waged by packs—often remarkably small ones—of criminals, bandits, and thugs."[67] Because these "bullies" are not "particularly interested in engaging a formidable opponent," managing or policing such wars does not require large modern military organizations.

Instead, "a sufficiently large, impressively armed, and well-disciplined policing force can be effective in pacifying those conflicts which are thug-dominated."[68] Ultimately, the best cure for such warfare is the promotion of good, stable, democratic governments that can prevent the formation of such packs of thugs in the first place.

American military doctrine has embraced the idea that "new wars" will be fought largely against nonstate actors in population centers in which combatants intermingle with noncombatants.[69] To fight this new kind of war, U.S. forces require "adaptive dominance" or the ability "to defeat changing enemy patterns of operation faster than the enemy himself can exploit them."[70] Adaptive dominance is a corollary of the idea of asymmetrical warfare in which one attempts to identify one's own vulnerabilities to creative enemy attacks and to generate plans for "attacking or responding to an enemy action, in a manner at variance with the prevailing operational conditions and often avoiding a force on force engagement."[71]

Countering enemies in these new wars, according to both American and British military thought, requires rapid and "decisive theater superiority." In this, "the vital objective is not just deployment velocity, but rather an operational momentum that never relinquishes the initiative once it is seized."[72] When fighting a nonstate enemy under "new war" conditions, the established army should adopt "maneouver warfare" techniques aimed at "shattering the enemy's overall cohesion and will to fight"[73] just as the enemy attempts to attack "the will and cohesion of the stronger player, without the need to achieve military success."[74] The key to this rapid, decisive effort is to recognize that since a "weak protagonist usually has a greater incentive to engage in nonconventional asymmetric warfare, and is likely to gain greater benefits than its stronger opponent," the stronger opponent (here, a state) should turn the tables on the nonstate actor, using its own strategy against it.

Employing an asymmetric war strategy against a weaker, nonstate opponent is easier said than done, given that modern state militaries are, as suggested earlier, immense, highly bureaucratic, logistic-oriented, technology- and resource-hungry organizations that are resistant to widespread doctrinal and organizational changes. Moreover, the possibility that states may yet fight other states in so-called modern wars means that militaries cannot be reconfigured totally for fighting "new wars." Thus, we see a conundrum that is made all the more difficult by a concurrent alteration in attitudes among Western populations about war fighting itself.

Western leaders believe that Western publics are casualty averse. Whether this is the case is less important than that this belief guides decisions to use force. Because of this belief, war-fighting theories in the West since the end of the Cold War have been characterized by four distinctive

qualifiers, according to Colin McInnes. All these qualifiers are premised
on the absolute need to keep public opinion on the side of the war effort.
First, one's own casualties must be kept to a minimum. Second, wars
should be fought by professional, all-volunteer militaries. Third, wars
must be fought quickly. Finally, collateral damage must be kept to a min-
imum.⁷⁵ McInnes explains the dynamics at work:

> This sudden return to the just war niceties of non-combatant immunity is not
> to be solely explained by humanitarian or moral concerns. Rather it is because
> since we—the normal citizens of the West, going about our everyday busi-
> ness—are not directly affected by the war, then citizens of the enemy state
> should not be unduly affected either by making them targets. . . . The protag-
> onists in war are not societies but individuals or groups. Thus NATO was at
> pains in the war over Kosovo to emphasize that the Yugoslav people were not
> its enemy, but rather that their President was; it was not the Iraqi people who
> were demonized in the 1990–91 Gulf War, but Saddam Hussein.⁷⁶

To keep the support of publics who have no appetite for the hard realities of war, Western states execute "manoeuvrist strategies" employing air
force and information technology and attempt thereby to engage in "cost-
free" war.⁷⁷ This approach, which McInnes calls "spectator sport warfare," emphasizes "attacks not upon the enemy's combat power, but upon
its willingness to fight and upon its operational cohesion, or what is sometimes called 'centre of gravity.'"⁷⁸ What this means, in practical terms, is a
military campaign that uses air power in an attempt to decapitate the
operational leadership of the enemy—its command, control, and communications centers—without creating damage that would appear on television to be disruptive to the life of the people in the targeted state. The elec-
trical grid and water systems should stay intact, hospitals should not be
attacked, roads and bridges for the most part should remain passable and
usable—collateral damage of all sorts must be limited. In the initial stages
of such an operation, one's own troops remain in remote positions protected from harm so as to be able to e-mail loved ones back home at the
end of the workday.

This "spectator sport warfare" was lauded by Donald Rumsfeld as the
kind of "transformation" of the military he envisioned—and the Pentagon resisted—prior to the 9/11 attacks. Such warfare turns on the strategic placement of special operation forces and the manipulation of high-
tech capabilities. In an article in *Foreign Affairs* after the overthrow of the
Taliban but before the 2003 Iraq war, Rumsfeld wrote romantically about
the special forces in Afghanistan who "sported beards and traditional
scarves and rode horses trained to run into machine gun fire" as they
called in coordinates for far-off cruise missiles using global positioning
devices.⁷⁹ The toppling of the Taliban was proof to Rumsfeld that a war

could be won without committing significant ground forces or running into public exhaustion with the war effort.

The problem with this kind of war fighting should be easy to identify by considering post-Taliban Afghanistan or postinvasion Iraq. The centers fell, to be sure; the Taliban was thrown out of effective control in Afghanistan, and Saddam Hussein's government in Iraq was overthrown. But defeating the centers did not end the war in either place, as insurgencies sprang up in the place of old foes. "Spectator sport warfare" works well against an organized enemy—that is, against a "modern" state, to use Crevald's idea—that wishes to minimize its own losses and so capitulates when faced with mounting destruction. A prime example of this is the capitulation of Yugoslavia to NATO demands in response to the NATO air war during the Kosovo crisis of 1998. But wars of this sort— "modern" wars—are far less likely in the current international system than are wars against nonstate opponents.

Nonstate opponents, particularly insurgencies and terrorist groups, do not tend to have centers of gravity that can be effectively targeted. Nonstate enemies do not have established lines of communication that can be breached and destroyed. Nonstate enemies set their own timetables, making it difficult for state militaries to sweep in with "decisive theater superiority" that "never relinquishes the initiative once it is seized."[80] Effective wars against nonstate opponents may not be possible using "cost-free" spectator sport warfare that maximizes military technologies and minimizes human costs. Perhaps nonstate enemies must be confronted in what British doctrine depicts as "war without rules where the emphasis is on terror and the target is hearts and minds, employing improvised technologies and involving police and security agencies."[81]

As the nature of war changes, the ways of fighting war also must change. Repackaging old ideas based on the unilateral pursuit of national security may not be adequate to the new charge. Narrowly conceived national security strategies may not ensure national security for most states. Indeed, this idea started gaining ground *at the start of the twentieth century* as national leaders and analysts began to conclude that their world was too connected by globalization to make unilateral national security efforts practicable. As I discuss in the next chapter, long-standing notions of the absolute right of states have conflicted with new thinking about collective efforts to manage security. The resulting compromise is discussed in the remaining chapters of this book.

7

International Security

In December 2004, the UN secretary-general's High-level Panel on Threats, Challenges and Change issued a report titled *A More Secure World: Our Shared Responsibility*. In one passage, the panel gave this explanation for why states should work together to maintain a system that ensures international security:

> No State, no matter how powerful, can by its own efforts alone make itself invulnerable to today's threats. Every State requires the cooperation of other States to make itself secure. It is in every State's interest, accordingly, to cooperate with other States to address their most pressing threats, because doing so will maximize the chances of reciprocal cooperation to address its own threat priorities.[1]

As we have seen in previous chapters, the Australian government perceived a security threat posed by boat people or undocumented migrants attempting to claim safe haven in Australia. This security threat was perceived to be increased after the 9/11 terrorist attacks on the United States, particularly after the Australian government joined the U.S.-led global war on terror. The changed international context intensified fears over who the boat people were and what their intentions might be. In order to manage this heightened security risk, Australia declared in late 2004 that it would establish a 1,000-nautical-mile maritime security zone. As explained in chapter 4, this policy designed to deal with Australian insecurity created insecurities for neighboring states.

Australia's policy did more than set into play the spiraling insecurities and actions and reactions we associate with the security dilemma. The policy also would violate international law, specifically the United Nations Convention of the Law of the Sea (LOS). The LOS was first signed in 1982 and entered into force in November 1994. Australia was the sixty-fifth country to accede to the treaty, doing so in October 1994; Indonesia acceded nearly a decade earlier in 1986, New Zealand in 1996, and Papua New Guinea in 1997. Thus, Australia and most of the countries directly affected by the new Australian policy were members of a convention that prohibited Australia from implementing the declared maritime security zone.

Several passages of the LOS are relevant here. First, the Convention states that sovereignty extends twelve nautical miles into the state's territorial waters. However,

> the Convention retains for naval and merchant ships the right of "innocent passage" through the territorial seas of a coastal State. This means, for example, that a Japanese ship, picking up oil from a Gulf State, would not have to make a 3,000-mile detour in order to avoid the territorial sea of Indonesia, provided passage is not detrimental to Indonesia and does not threaten its security or violate its laws.
>
> In addition to their right to enforce any law within their territorial seas, coastal States are also empowered to implement certain rights in an area beyond the territorial sea, extending for 24 nautical miles from their shores, for the purpose of preventing certain violations and enforcing police powers. This area, known as the "contiguous zone," may be used by a coast guard or its naval equivalent to pursue and, if necessary, arrest and detain suspected drug smugglers, illegal immigrants and customs or tax evaders violating the laws of the coastal State within its territory or the territorial sea.[2]

The Convention also allows for a 200-nautical-mile exclusive economic zone giving states sovereign rights over natural resources and economic activities. Clearly a 1,000-nautical-mile security zone would violate the Convention's allowance for a twenty-four-nautical-mile "contiguous zone," and Indonesia and New Zealand protested the violation of their exclusive economic zones. The Convention does allow for the temporary suspension of innocent passage in specified areas of a state's territorial sea "if such suspension is essential for the protection of its security, including weapons exercises,"[3] although this provision would not seem to allow the sweeping and indefinite security zone claimed by Australia.

After protests, the Australian government reconsidered and then proposed a new plan called the Australian Maritime Identification System. The new plan called for information sharing by ships coming within 500 nautical miles of Australian territory but only on a "wholly voluntary basis" and based on "co-operative international arrangements, particularly with neighbouring countries, and in accordance with international and domestic law."[4]

If Australia was so concerned about potential terrorists entering Australia or attacking Australian offshore oil interests, why would it back off from its 1,000-nautical-mile security zone? One answer is the near impossibility of Australia managing such an enormous zone on its own using just its own resources and personnel. Australia would need the cooperation of its neighbors, and cooperation would not be forthcoming if Australia were to scorn the international agreements already in place. Rather than evoking necessary cooperation, Australia's 1,000-mile zone would evoke hostility and perhaps retribution. To preserve orderly and cooperative relations with neighboring states and guard against provoking hostile reactions, Australia needed to honor previous international agreements that limited its range of maneuver. By so limiting itself, Australia would be able to elicit international cooperation to deal with its perceived security threat. This case explains in a nutshell why states enter into agreements to protect international security.

Before I unpack this last statement, it is useful to point out that although Australia decided that the best course of action was to honor its obligations to other states incurred by its involvement in international conventions such as the LOS, Australia felt no such obligation to the Afghan boat people, as discussed in chapter 1. When Australian naval vessels blocked the Norwegian freighter from delivering the rescued Afghan boat people to Australian territory, the Australian government failed to honor its commitment under various international agreements, including the 1951 Convention on the Status of Refugees. In the order of things that are important and privileged in the international system, states will more or less honor the interests of other states for fear of the consequences if they do not. Who would promote and protect the interests of the Afghan boat people against Australian actions? The answer to this is demonstrated in the absence of international outrage over Australia's forced displacement of the boat people to other states.

To paraphrase the High-level Panel quoted at the start of this chapter, Australia could not on its own make itself invulnerable to the threat posed by undocumented migrants and would-be terrorists. Australia was dependent on the assistance of other states and so had to demonstrate its own good neighborliness and cooperative nature.

A Focus on Power and Order in Interstate Relations

International security in the first instance refers to a system of protecting international order to provide protection for states. In chapter 10, I will consider a widening of the concept of international security to include human security, but our discussion of international security must stay for now with this state-centric focus. The *Penguin Dictionary of International*

Relations defines international order as "patterns of activities or the set of arrangements that characterizes the mutual behavior of states." This order "has a number of formal attributes—political, diplomatic, legal, economic, military—which provide method and regularity to international relations."[5]

Prior to the twentieth century, international order was managed primarily by the balance-of-power idea, which is discussed in chapter 4. The great power balance was for a short time organized into a more or less formal arrangement called the Concert of Europe in the early nineteenth century. The Concert ostensibly was designed to prevent European war, but it is better understood as an organized effort by conservative governments to prevent revolutionary liberalism from spreading to their own territories.

In the European balance-of-power system, war was a constitutive element in both creating the order and credentialing the countries at the top. Dorothy Jones explains that the Japanese attack on Russia at the beginning of the twentieth century was motivated by such an understanding of the relationship between war, great power standing, and the international order. Japan sought to enter the "tight little club" of great powers centered in Europe. Through careful observation of European politics, Japanese leaders concluded that "what counted in the eyes of the powers that mattered" was force. "Japanese leaders drew the obvious conclusion that force was not only an acceptable means to great power standing, but an effective one."[6] Jones continues,

> The Japanese took the world as they found it when they emerged from centuries of isolation, and the tactics they adopted to achieve their goals are a telling commentary on the kind of place it was. It was a world of warlord states. Their very existence rested on force, and their relations with each other were shaped by well-deserved suspicion. In London, Paris, Rome, Vienna, Washington, St. Petersburg, and Tokyo, there was a perpetual casting up of the accounts of power and a compulsion to act as if these were seen to be out of balance.[7]

To use a realist understanding of the world order, the great powers established through force the rules of their relationships with one another, and from this flowed the structure of the international system and the rules of the game for all other peoples, whether sovereign states or dependencies.

Some of the great powers did try from time to time to limit their use of force in international relations. For example, writing in the early eighteenth century (a hundred years before the Concert of Europe), French politician and writer Abbé de Saint-Pierre proposed "A Project for Settling an Everlasting Peace in Europe." His idea was to create a "European Society" of internally sovereign states committed to not using force in their relations with one another. "No Sovereign shall take up Arms or commit any Hostility, but against him who shall be declared an Enemy to the

European Society," Saint-Pierre proposed. Disputes between states would be taken to an international senate for mediation or for arbitration. The society of states would possess a right to declare war for a variety of reasons: "The Sovereign who shall take up Arms before the Union has declared War, or who shall refuse to execute a Regulation of the Society, or a Judgement of the Senate, shall be declared an Enemy to the Society, and it shall make War upon him."[8] Saint-Pierre's project for a "European Union" was not adopted, but the idea that states would refrain from using force against each other yet also keep their ranks in line by threatening the collective use of force would form the basis for international security arrangements in the twentieth century.

The twentieth century saw the beginning of *universal* institutionalized agreements among great and small powers regarding the use of force in international affairs. As in previous times, twentieth-century great powers used their might to construct a world order that kept them privileged and protected their status, but this order would seem to constrain the great powers as well. John Stoessinger writes that international relations have been characterized by the "ever-present tension between the struggle for power and the struggle for order."[9] The first half of the twentieth century was in particular a time of great power struggles for power and order—World War I was a struggle for power that resulted in the League of Nations order, and World War II was a power struggle that resulted in the UN order. Until the mid-twentieth century, great powers still used great power war to sort out the order of international relations while also attempting to regulate when wars might be fought. After the United Nations came into being, great power wars ended (for a variety of reasons), but great powers reserved the right to use war and force to preserve the UN system and principles.

It is important to keep in mind this instrumental purpose of the international order created during the twentieth century—this order served the interests of those who had become great powers roughly by the start of the century. In chapter 2 we considered the relationship between war making and state building. The argument was that European and North American great powers used war to consolidate their states against external and internal threats. Violence and warfare were "natural" to the building of strong states and great powers. Over the course of the late nineteenth and early twentieth centuries, the existing great powers sought to prevent other states from challenging their status. Toward this end, they constructed and imposed international norms that prohibited other states from using the methods they had used to become great powers.

Ian Lustick explains how this worked in one region of the world:

> In the Middle East . . . and in the Arab Middle East in particular, rulers of territories, or candidates for rulership, found themselves not only overwhelmed

by the tremendous power of individual European or North American states (especially Britain, France, Italy, and the United States) but subjected to an elaborate array of international institutions and norms (represented by the system of Concerts and Congresses of the nineteenth century and the League of Nations and the United Nations in the twentieth century).[10]

This "elaborate array of international institutions and norms" stressed antibelligerency and collective punishment for any use of warfare that threatened to expand the power of those who had not yet achieved great power status. "Existing (European and North American) great powers repeatedly and decisively intervened to prevent successfully fought wars from being used by Middle Eastern state builders as a means of doing what their European and North American predecessors had done."[11] The reason for these great power interventions was to stop the accumulation of any power that would challenge their own position in the international system; the *explanation* given for the interventions was to uphold the principles of the international system.

The rules and institutions of international order by the twentieth century were the instruments of those states that could both impose a global order and maintain it to their own advantage. The great powers (or some of them, more precisely) were committed to the use of force to maintain the order that they had forged through the use of force. Yet they claimed that they would use force only to construct and maintain a better, more secure world order. For example, in setting forth his famous "Fourteen Points" as a basis for a new League of Nations, Woodrow Wilson proclaimed that Americans

> [had] entered [World War I] because violations of right had occurred which touched us to the quick and made the life of our own people impossible unless they were corrected and the world secured once and for all against their recurrence. What we demand in this war, therefore, is nothing peculiar to ourselves. It is that the world be made fit and safe to live in; and particularly that it be made safe for every peace-loving nation which, like our own, wishes to live its own life, determine its own institutions, be assured of justice and fair dealings by the other people of the world as against force and selfish aggression.[12]

Wilson's "fit and safe" world would be one in which states respected the sovereign rights of one another, engaged in open and transparent international relations, removed barriers to trade and naval navigation, and reduced armaments. Toward this end, Wilson proposed that "a general association of nations must be formed under specific covenants for the purpose of affording mutual guarantees of political independence and territorial integrity to great and small states alike."[13] Finally, Wilson declared, "For such arrangements and covenants we are willing to fight and to continue to fight until they are achieved; but only because we . . .

desire a just and stable peace such as can be secured only by removing the chief provocations to war, which this program does remove."[14] Thus, to create an international security system that ended the provocations of interstate war, Wilson proposed that America was willing to continue to fight interstate war.

After the second global struggle for power—World War II—the United Nations was founded "to save succeeding generations from the scourge of war, which twice in our lifetime has brought untold sorrow to mankind." Toward this end, the founding member states committed "to ensure, by the acceptance of principles and the institution of methods, that armed force shall not be used, save in the common interest."[15] As I will take up in detail in the next chapter, the UN Charter gives the Security Council the authority to launch a war in the common interests. More recently, as we will see, the Security Council has approved wars not fought under UN command to stop the use of war and violence. The UN order would not tolerate the use of war except war intended to uphold the UN order. The UN order, of course, was and is an order that rewards the great power victors of World War II. The UN international security system protects a particular great power order that was constructed by the last global struggle for power.

Constructing Global Security Organizations

The twentieth century was noteworthy for many things, good and bad, arguably the greatest of which (in terms of overall impact) was and remains globalization. The century began and ended in periods of globalization with the interim years witnessing global wars and global institution building designed both to protect against and to ensure globalization's impact. Globalization—"the process of increasing integration of the world in terms of economics, politics, communications, social relations, and culture"[16]—created the necessity and the mechanisms for the construction of global security organizations, such as the ill-fated League of Nations and the United Nations. Great power accords or concerts would not be sufficient to manage the new world order.

The old order that privileged states and military power was not left behind. The century started, after all, with World War I—the war to end all wars. At the Paris peace talks after that war, Jones reminds us, the same old power game was afoot:

> Peace? That was certainly the goal of the delegates at Paris [who met to discuss the terms of the end of World War I]. And justice, too. But this justice and this peace were through and for the states of the international system—armed as ever, suspicious as ever, and only temporarily frightened by the consequences of their own warlordish behavior.[17]

Yet at the same time, the old order's rules were found to be inadequate to the new era. Jones proposes that even the terms of the debate had shifted:

> The context of the conference and the experiences of the participants were so different from any earlier period that words such as conflict, justice, rights, and peace had a meaning peculiar to the twentieth century. The greatest change with which people were struggling was the rapid increase in scope and intensity of the relationships between the states of the international system. . . .
>
> Implicit in all discussions of world affairs in this period was the question, "What does it mean to be international?"[18]

Writing in 1916 and thinking about the potential shape of global affairs after the world war ended, Leonard Woolf gave this compelling description of the impact of globalization on how states and people existed in this new age:

> The world is so closely knit together now that it is no longer possible for a nation to run amok on one frontier while her [sic] neighbour on the other is hardly aware of it. We are so linked to our neighbours by the gold and silver wires of commerce and finance—not to speak of telegraph wires and steel rails—that a breeze between the Foreign Offices of Monrovia and Adis Ababa would be felt the same day in every Foreign Office from Pekin [sic] to Washington, and every war threatens to become a world war. And the closer the interconnections of international life become, the more necessary becomes this principle to save international society from dissolution. And one must face the fact that what stands in the way of acceptance of this principle in the regulation of international affairs is the diplomatic, governmental and, to a lesser extent, popular view of the independence and sovereignty of States.[19]

Woolf's description of the world emphasizes growth and process. This new age did not just appear suddenly but instead resulted from long-occurring trends that had finally coalesced. These trends included an enormous growth in international law, which itself resulted from the increasingly common expectation that interstate relations, especially interstate trade, should be standardized by rules. Thus, an international organization dedicated to the prevention of war *was not utopian* but a natural and necessary outgrowth of intensifying trends and obvious needs.[20] This idea remained throughout the twentieth century and merits reiterating. International institutions, including the United Nations, were not the result of utopian visions but instead were practical necessities for managing the vastness and dangers of globalization.

J. A. Hobson, a contemporary of Woolf's, also urged the creation of a new league of states to prevent future wars such as World War I. This new league, for Hobson, could not simply be an alliance among the winning powers of World War I, as this would only continue the old, unworkable ways:

> A few nations forming such a League would not differ substantially from the other nominally defensive alliances with which the pages of history are filled. Their purely defensive character would be suspected by outside Powers, who would tend to draw together into an opposing alliance, thus reconstituting once more the Balance of Power with all its perils and competing armaments.[21]

Moreover, this new league should not leave out any major power since "an absolute preponderance of military and naval strength" was needed inside the league to guarantee its proper operation. Striking a "rigorously defensive attitude," the league would consider attacks on any of its members an attack on the league itself and take appropriate steps in retaliation and defense.[22] This idea would later be incorporated into the UN Security Council as we will see in the next chapter.

Hobson's desire, like those of many of his contemporaries, was for a new system that worked better at managing international power relations than did the known balance-of-power system. This new system would be based on the theory of collective security. "Collective security" refers to a universal system in which members consider international peace to be primary and indivisible. An act of aggression anywhere in the world is considered an action against the whole or against the peace. Aggressors would be confronted with an "overwhelming preponderance of power"[23] in the form of collective punishment. This collective punishment would be implemented automatically and by obligation. The threat of this collective punishment would deter would-be aggressors and protect the peace. Both collective security and balance-of-power theories were based on what Inis Claude called the "paradox of 'war for peace,'" in which "the fulfillment of the urge for peace is to be achieved by the possession of capacity to fight and the assertion of the will to fight."[24] Importantly, the preponderance of power in a collective security system would be available "to everyone for defensive purposes, but to nobody for aggressive purposes."[25] Thus, non–great powers would be "emancipated" from great power rivalries, and no state would be permitted to become "so preponderantly powerful that it can trespass with impunity upon the basic interests of other states."[26]

Advocates of collective security did not propose to ignore or downgrade state power in international relations. In Claude's words,

> Balance of power and collective security have the merit of maintaining a steady focus on the *state* as the object of central concern. They reflect awareness of the fact that the problem of international order can be accurately defined only in terms of the necessity of developing methods for controlling

the exercise of power by these constituent entities of the world system. They are addressed, in short, to the reality of the multistate system.[27]

After World War I, the League of Nations was formed to manage international power relations in a globalized world. The League will not be discussed in much detail here. Suffice it to say that it was not universal in its membership, and it was not committed fully to honoring the sovereign rights of all nations—colonized peoples were denied their right to self-government and were not represented in the League. Further, the League did not bind in all the great powers; the United States remained removed and distant. Finally, the League did not ensure the sovereign rights and integrity of even its members, and soon its failure was apparent in World War II. After World War II, another effort would be made by the great powers to construct an institutionalized international security system through the United Nations. As I will discuss in the next chapter, the UN system embodies both collective security and balance-of-power aspects. I will also discuss the relative success of this hybrid effort in ensuring international security. But first we need to continue considering why states seeking security would pursue a strategy that binds their fate to other states rather than simply pursuing a unilateral national security strategy.

Why States Would Bind Themselves

In the aftermath of first one and then another world war, the world's states moved to create an order that would eliminate the possibility of yet another global war. As I have stated, this order would serve the interests of great powers but also serve the interests of all states in time. What seemed clear to the architects of the twentieth-century international institutions was that states could more efficiently and effectively pursue national security by adopting an "international security strategy."[28]

We can start here with the same realist-based view of states as self-interested, self-righteous, absolutist entities. As the realists remind us, states pursuing their own security set in motion chains of events in which other states perceive potential hostilities gathering against them. Barry Buzan explains that when a state pursues a national security strategy, it "cannot escape from the interactive consequences of its own effect on the system."[29] Both Buzan and Claude agree that the amassing of nuclear weapons during the Cold War by the superpowers and then by other states intensifies the dangers of these "interactive consequences," and, as Claude notes, this makes the "problem of the management of power in international relations" the "central issue of our time."[30]

A central proposition here is that unilateral action may not make a state more secure but may instead make it less secure. Buzan suggests that by adopting an "international security strategy," a state's security policy can focus

> on the sources and causes of threats, the purpose being not to block or offset the threats [a national security strategy], but to reduce or eliminate them by political action. The early history of the European Community, for example, represents an international security strategy aimed at solving the rivalry between France and Germany. Similarly, the Conference on Security and Cooperation in Europe (CSCE) [was] an attempt to reduce the level of threat between East and West, and ASEAN [Association of Southeast Asian Nations] a mechanism for reducing threats among the non-communist states of Southeast Asia.[31]

An international security strategy, for Buzan, offers advantages over a more narrowly conceived self-interested national security strategy. In the first instance, an international security strategy addresses global and regional insecurities preventively, saving states the resources that they would otherwise expend in fighting wars to defend their interests. Second, resources not invested in arms acquisitions also do not fuel arms races, and thus the overall level of international competition and tension is lowered. Finally, an international security strategy is available to all states, whereas only the most powerful states can (or could) pursue a national security strategy with any realistic possibility of success. An international security strategy "offers options other than association with a great power to the majority of lesser states whose resources do not permit them to pursue a comprehensive national security strategy of their own."[32] Thus, adopting an international security strategy can serve to restore some degree of sovereign choice to the smaller or weaker powers.

Despite the apparent benefits of pursuing international security to achieve national security, old habits are hard to break. The UN system begun in 1945 was marked by tensions between the old habit of pursuing national security and the need for a working international security system. This tension characterizes the sixty-plus-year history of the United Nations, as I discuss in the next chapter.

8

The United Nations and International Security

The year 2005 marked the sixtieth anniversary of the San Francisco Conference, at which fifty states met to put the finishing touches on the details of the postwar, global order–maintaining institution known as the United Nations. The origins of the UN Charter are found in several proclamations issued during World War II. These proclamations, taken together, declared a desire for peace, the right of states to exist free from the threat of aggression, the need to respect the sovereign rights of all states, and the need to create a *system* that would discourage states' use of armed force. These proclamations also signaled that as early as 1941 certain great powers were already planning the postwar order.

The first was the June 1941 "Declaration of St. James's Palace," in which fourteen states (free and occupied by Nazi Germany) stated that "the only true basis of enduring peace is the willing cooperation of free peoples in a world in which, relieved of the menace of aggression, all may enjoy economic and social security. . . . It is our intention to work together, and with other free peoples, both in war and peace, to this end."[1] The second proclamation foundational to the UN system was the "Atlantic Charter," issued in August 1941 by U.S. President Franklin Delano Roosevelt and British Prime Minister Winston Churchill. In this, the two countries indicated that they looked forward to restoring a peace that would defend the sovereignty and freedom of all people and that they would "collaborate" to bring about economic and social security for all. The Charter also used words that would be echoed in the UN Charter yet to come. The two

149

countries declared that "all of the nations of the world, for realistic as well as spiritual reasons, must come to the abandonment of the use of force."[2]

The final elements of the soon-to-be established United Nations came in a third document. The "United Nations Declaration," signed January 1, 1942, by the United States, Great Britain, the Soviet Union, and China and joined the next day by twenty-two other states, "pledged the signatory governments to the maximum war effort and bound them against making a separate peace." Eventually, twenty-one other states would sign the declaration before the end of the war. According to the UN website, "Three years later, when preparations were being made for the San Francisco Conference, only those states which had, by March 1945, declared war on Germany and Japan and subscribed to the United Nations Declaration, were invited to take part."[3] Thus, the United Nations would be founded by the winning side of a global war as a means for structuring and managing the postwar order.

The UN Charter created an international security system that would openly support a realpolitik great power spoils-of-war system as well as promote a more idealistic commitment to establishing universal rules governing the use of force. As explained by Inis Claude,

> The creation of the United Nations in 1945 represented an explicit effort to determine the general outlines, and provide the institutional components, of the postwar system of international relations, even though the precise nature of the situation within which that system would have to operate was by no means clearly predictable. On the whole, statesmen exhibited a commitment to the ideal of a planned, a consciously designed, structure of international relations; they opted against leaving the field to the free interplay of states, to undisciplined and uncoordinated maneuvering, to improvisation of arrangements for dealing with crises as they might arise; they saw themselves as system-builders.
>
> In this sense, it might be said that the founders of the United Nations rejected the balance of power system. However, they did not clearly envisage and totally commit themselves to the erection of an alternative system. They were strongly influenced by the ideology of collective security, and they wrote a Charter which bore the imprint of that ideology in many respects. They endorsed the basic proposition that aggression anywhere is everybody's business, and stipulated that all states share responsibility for safeguarding the common interest in peace and order. They held out the promise of a limited version of collective security, a scheme in which the great powers would take the lead, whenever they were unanimously disposed to do so, in suppressing aggression by lesser states. But they pulled back from the notion of collective security when contemplating the problem of dealing with aggression launched or supported by the great powers; in these most critical cases, they discarded the hope of effectuating collective security, and rejected the risks which they believed the effort to effectuate it would entail. In this fundamentally important respect, then, they refrained from making the United Nations a design for a collective security system.[4]

The UN system contained six principal organs, each of which had a role to play in preserving the new international security system. These organs were the Security Council, the General Assembly, the Secretariat, the Economic and Social Council, the Trusteeship Council, and the International Court of Justice. The International Court of Justice would help establish a body of international law that would bring regularity and predictability to interstate legal affairs. The Trusteeship Council (now essentially defunct) would oversee the end of colonial rule and the potentially violent transition from dependent territory or colony to sovereign state. The Economic and Social Council would provide a variety of programs and agencies tasked with eliminating the socio-welfare causes of violent conflict and war. The Secretariat would provide an international civil service dedicated to the execution of the UN's agenda, blind to national differences. The General Assembly would provide a democratic one-country, one-vote forum in which the many issues confronting the world's peoples would be openly discussed and in which the member states would exercise democratic oversight over the other organs. Finally, the Security Council would be the primary organ of the United Nations, tasked with maintaining and restoring international peace and security. The Council's design demonstrated both the UN founders' affection for collective security as well as their conservative embrace of great power politics.

The Security Council as a Rigid Great Power System

As might be expected after a war, the most powerful members of the winning side of World War II gave themselves a privileged position in the new UN system and ensured by the UN Charter that their status would not be challenged by rising great powers. In the previous chapter, I discussed how the theory of collective security stresses the importance of binding the preponderance of military power in the world within the organization. In a true collective security system, this preponderant power would be available defensively to all states large and small and would not be instrumental to the aggressive purposes of any single state. Great powers and small powers alike would be subject to the threat of collective punishment for acts of aggression.

Although the UN Charter obliges states to abstain from the use of military force except in the common good, and Chapter VII obliges states to assist in the preservation of international peace and security, the Charter effectively does not restrict the great powers from using armed force. By Article 23 of the Charter, the Security Council is composed of fifteen members: ten nonpermanent members holding two-year nonconsecutive terms and the "Big Five," or permanent members: the United States, Great Britain, France, Russia, and China. The permanent members were given the responsibility to maintain the new order militarily as well as the privilege of the veto to control the order's shape. The veto power is the ability of any one of the permanent members to stop an action of substance on war and peace even if that action is supported by the majority of the other members of the Security Council. The veto power makes it unimaginable that the Council would approve any resolution condemning the use of force by any of the permanent five. In the history of adopted Council resolutions, it is rare to find even a mention that any of five ever used force against another state. For example, in the long history of the U.S. war in Vietnam, U.S. actions in Vietnam were not the subject of a single Security Council resolution.[5] For more examples of when the Security Council avoided adopting resolutions condemning the use of armed force by the permanent five, see extended discussion box 8.1.

In late 2002 and early 2003, as the United States and ally Great Britain began to make a case for forced regime change in Iraq, the Americans and British tried to obtain Security Council support for their proposed action. Although the issue was debated in the Council, no formal vote on the war was ever taken because of the certainty that Russia, France, and/or China would veto the resolution and because of the uncertainty of even a "moral" majority in favor of the proposed military action. More to the present point, the Security Council did not vote to *condemn* the intervention as an act of aggression and/or the unlawful use of force since such a vote would be subject to a U.S. and/or British veto.[6] Given the nature of the great power arrangement codified into the Charter, no one reasonably could expect the Security Council to try to stop the United States and Great Britain.

Writing forty years before the 2003 invasion of Iraq, Claude noted how the United Nations failed to restrain the great powers *and* how it was never designed to restrain them. The real value in the United Nations was its ability to cause the great powers to be self-limiting:

> The best hope for the United Nations is not that it may be able to develop a military establishment which will enable it to exercise coercive control over great powers, but that it may be able to continue the development of its capability to serve the interests of the great powers—and of the rest of the world—by helping them to contain their conflicts, to limit their competition, and to stabilize their relationships.[7]

How much the great powers have exercised self-control because of the stabilizing role of the UN framework is arguable. However, it is the case that none of the Big Five have walked entirely away from the United Nations even when they objected to particular actions or inactions. For instance, the Soviets and French opposed UN peacekeeping during much of its "first generation," but they never vetoed any peacekeeping resolutions. (Peacekeeping is examined in chapter 9.) After the People's Republic of China assumed the China seat in the United Nations, it also opposed peacekeeping in principle but never used the veto against it. In the 1990s, when the Security Council authorized many Chapter VII peace enforcement operations, China abstained twenty-seven times but never vetoed authorizations, "thus registering its disagreement but not blocking action."[8]

The Big Five veto power extends to the General Assembly as well. By Article 108, Charter amendments must be adopted by a two-thirds vote of the General Assembly with the concurrence of the permanent members of the Security Council. This means that a resolution to amend the Charter would fail if 190 members voted for the resolution and one of the permanent five voted against it. One of the most contentious of possible UN Charter amendments has involved the recomposition of the Security Council permanent membership. Many UN member states have called for the democratization of the Security Council; this recomposition might entail better regional membership, or reflect better the kinds of contributions members make to the organization, and/or end the Big Five veto. In 2005 a many-fronted initiative was engaged to increase the permanent membership of the Council. This movement was supported by many and sabotaged by many; it was sabotaged by countries large and small reacting to the possibility that someone else might gain permanent membership. Thus, Pakistan was strongly opposed to Council reform if India were to be one of the new permanent members. Of course, Pakistan's opposition to India or any other would-be permanent member would not sink a candidacy—but opposition from any of the Big Five could. And so although Japan had for many years made the second-highest financial contributions to the United Nations, its possible rise in status was opposed vehemently by veto-wielding China and by the China-conscious United States.

The veto casts into stone the power distribution of 1945 (or even earlier). Both this institutionalizing of great power status and the fact that the veto would give the permanent five the ability to act in ways inconsistent with a collective security ideal were seen as the costs of forming a United Nations. As the UN website explains, the veto was both controversial and inevitable at the San Francisco Conference in 1945:

> Above all, the right of each of the "Big Five" to exercise a "veto" on action by the powerful Security Council provoked long and heated debate. At one stage the conflict of opinion on this question threatened to break up the conference. The smaller powers feared that when one of the "Big Five" menaced the peace, the Security Council would be powerless to act, while in the event of a clash between two powers not permanent members of the Security Council, the "Big Five" could act arbitrarily. They strove therefore to have the power of the "veto" reduced. But the great powers unanimously insisted on this provision as vital, and emphasized that the main responsibility for

maintaining world peace would fall most heavily on them. Eventually the smaller powers conceded the point in the interest of setting up the world organization.[9]

The UN Charter and International Peace and Security

The UN Charter contains two chapters devoted to dispute settlement: Chapter VI covers the pacific settlement of disputes, and Chapter VII details what actions the Security Council may take in response to threats to international peace and security up to and including the use of armed force.

Chapter VI, Article 33, starts with what seems to be an imperative that

> parties to any dispute, the continuance of which is likely to endanger the maintenance of international peace and security, shall, first of all, seek a solution by negotiation, enquiry, mediation, conciliation, arbitration, judicial settlement, resort to regional agencies or arrangements, or other peaceful means of their own choice.

There is no penalty to states for failure to seek peaceful resolution. Although the secretary-general is not mentioned in Chapter VI, it is usually the Secretariat that is tasked by the Security Council with Chapter VI duties. Peacekeeping that does not involve Chapter VII authority to use "all means necessary" generally is said to fall conceptually between Chapters VI and VII, as will be elaborated on in chapter 9.

Chapter VII contains the muscle of the UN system and offers limits on national and collective self-defense. The first provision of Chapter VII, Article 39, states that it is the Security Council that determines whether "any threat to the peace, breach of the peace, or act of aggression" has occurred. Should such an act be identified, Article 41 allows the Security Council to restore the international status quo through authorizing measures short of the use of force, such as economic sanctions or the disruption of communications and diplomatic relations. Article 42 states that "should the Security Council consider that measures provided for in Article 41 would be inadequate or have proved to be inadequate, it may take such action by air, sea, or land forces as may be necessary to maintain or restore international peace and security."

Article 43 instructs states to undertake to assist the Security Council's measures by providing assistance including maintaining ready armed forces. Air forces also should be kept on the ready, according to Article 45. By Articles 45, 46, and 47, a Military Staff Committee composed of the chiefs of staff of the militaries of the permanent members should coordinate with and otherwise assist the Security Council in enforcing mandates. Article 50 allows third-party states to consult the Security

Council when Chapter VII authorizations create special economic problems for them.

Finally, Article 51 specifies both when states may take actions in self-defense and when states should turn over their defense to the Security Council. Article 51 states,

> Nothing in the present Charter shall impair the inherent right of individual or collective self-defence if an armed attack occurs against a Member of the United Nations, until the Security Council has taken measures necessary to maintain international peace and security. Measures taken by Members in the exercise of this right of self-defence shall be immediately reported to the Security Council and shall not in any way affect the authority and responsibility of the Security Council under the present Charter to take at any time such action as it deems necessary in order to maintain or restore international peace and security.

Article 51 requires some elaboration. First, a state has an "inherent" right to immediate self-defense of itself or its ally (or allies). This right, however, is limited to situations when "an armed attack occurs." Thus, preventive self-defense would be out of line with Article 51 because by definition prevention would occur well before an attack took shape. Preemption, too, would be out of step with this article because although the time frame is shortened, when compared to prevention, preemption is designed to stop an impending attack, not counter it.

Further, a state has the "inherent right" of self-defense but only "until the Security Council has taken measures necessary to maintain international peace and security." Michael Glennon contends that this "extinguishes" the so-called inherent right of self-defense because this right exists only until the Security Council takes over.[10] However, if a state *could* depend on the Security Council to authorize assistance, it would not have to face aggression or the threat of aggression alone. A state would be relieved of the burdens of defending itself and compelling the attacker to make restitution for war damages. This, in turn, would mean that states would be relieved of the burden of heavy defense spending. This was one reason the U.S. State Department supported the new United Nations.[11] Indeed, Jonathan Soffer tells us that most of the early members of the United Nations looked forward to cutting their defense budgets once the United Nations became fully functional.[12] Thus, although Article 51 puts limits on self-defense, in the larger scheme of things where states make difficult trade-offs in pursuit of national security, Article 51's cost to absolute sovereignty might be worth the benefits of an effective collective enforcement system that would defend states and relieve them of the burden of large defense spending.

By the second sentence in Article 51, a state acting in self-defense must immediately report the measures it takes and, by standard interpretation of this phrase but not by its explicit language, limit its measures to those considered proportional.[13] Also in the second sentence, any measures taken in self-defense do not affect the authority of the Council to take "such action as it deems necessary." Beyond the previously mentioned issue concerning *whether* the Council would act, this raises the hypothetical situation of a state taking actions in immediate self-defense that are deemed to be disproportional and thus those very acts would be perceived as threats to international peace and security. The Council might then order measures against the state that was originally attacked. Yet, in the best possible world, states would feel secure under the umbrella of the Council and thus would feel compelled to use proportional force only in order to quickly return to the status quo.

To make Chapter VII work, the preponderant military power of the community would need to be harnessed and commanded. On the one hand, this would require political willingness to work together for the common good—something that has not always been present or forthcoming, as I will discuss shortly. On the other hand, harnessing and commanding the world's military would require practical decision making about who would contribute what, when, and where, and who would control the military forces that resulted from those contributions. As mentioned previously, armed force contributions to the United Nations are discussed in Articles 43 and 45 of the Charter; command and control issues are discussed in Articles 45, 46, and 47.

By Articles 43 and 45, members are instructed to conclude agreements with the Security Council regarding armed and air forces ready and on call for Chapter VII operations. Early negotiations over the UN system suggested that member states understood Articles 43 and 45 to require the creation of standing UN forces. According to Soffer, the United States was at the lead in this interpretation, pushing hard for a large UN force: "The Americans wanted a huge force of twenty land divisions, thirty-eight hundred aircraft, three battleships, fifteen cruisers, six carriers, and eighty-four destroyers, and they were prepared to make the bulk of the naval and air contributions."[14] The permanent members were in disagreement over what size forces were necessary; none of the others embraced the American vision for such a large force. There was also disagreement over what kind of contributions would be made by the permanent five—would they contribute equally to the UN forces, or would they make comparable contributions? Equal contributions would result in a much smaller force than the United States proposed; comparable contributions would draw on each country's relative strengths but also would have the practical effect of making some states contribute more troops than others.[15]

Without accord among the permanent members, the issue of whether there should be a standing UN force was resolved by default—there is none, there has been none. Instead, drawing on Articles 43 and 45, the Security Council instructs the secretary-general to negotiate separate agreements with members about what forces they could make available to the United Nations when asked to do so. Countries still maintain the right to say no to particular requests, reading no obligation into these standby agreements. The resulting problems with this arrangement have been demonstrated in numerous UN peacekeeping operations—operations that ought to require (in theory) far less of a military force than would a collective security action. Richard Longworth describes how this system is no system at all using the example of the 1994 Rwandan genocide and catastrophic failure of the UN member states to respond. "Nineteen nations had joined the standby force [to assist peacekeeping in Rwanda] when the Rwandan crisis broke out, but after hearing that U.N. troops from Belgium were being macheted on the streets of Kigale, all 19 reneged."[16] Despite standby force agreements, UN officials go begging for military contributions whenever a new operation is authorized or an existing operation needs expansion. Begging takes time, and situations can degrade rapidly while member states are considering UN requests.

A related problem involves the training and preparedness of troops available on a standby basis. Force commanders could safely assume that a *standing* force would be trained for the many specialized tasks that might be entailed in UN operations—from rapid reaction forces to civilian policing. Further, a standing force presumably would be equipped with the weapons, vehicles, communications devices, food, water, shelter, and all the other necessities of an effective military force. Conversely, experience from UN peacekeeping operations has shown that the level of training and discipline of standby contingents varies greatly by country. Countries send their troops into UN peacekeeping operations with vastly different material possessions and needs. The lack of a standing UN force that is already trained and equipped contributes to situations in which peacekeeping force commanders must divert their attention and resources from the task at hand and turn instead to the training and equipping work that should have been performed in advance of the mission. By way of example, consider the description by Roméo Dallaire, the UN force commander in Rwanda, of how the lack of a sufficient number of UN troops in Rwanda was complicated by the presence of poorly trained and equipped troops:

> I had known the Bangladeshis would have little to no equipment or support, but I had hoped they would be well-led and well-trained. I was keen to get them on the ground. . . .
>
>   But when the Bangladeshis got off the planes in Kiglai airport in mid-December, they had nothing but their personal weapons and their kit, and expected the UN to supply everything else they needed—from their first

meal in the field to the canvas over their heads. The added logistical burden of caring for this force was a plague on the mission. . . .

We commenced a rigorous training plan, half-heartedly implemented on the Bangladeshis' part. They harried me and their immediate superiors in the sector HQ on a daily basis with requests for everything from soap to ammunition, vehicles to sandbags. The Bangladeshis had agreed to first deploy their infantry battalion and then send the other units they had promised (an engineer company, a control platoon) in phase two. This is what I had planned for and what I needed from them. But these four hundred soldiers were a mixed bag of each element, and officer-heavy to boot. A four-hundred-man unit would usually be commanded by a lieutenant colonel, if not a major. The Bangladeshis were commanded by a full colonel, with no fewer than six lieutenant colonels, dozens of majors and an unaccountable number of captains and lieutenants under him. I needed riflemen on the ground, not officers in the mess or headquarters.[17]

By not finding common ground on the matter of standing UN forces, the permanent five set the stage for an ineffective, inefficient system of standby arrangements for UN military operations. The founding members of the United Nations understood how critical a standing force would be to the new international security system, yet they failed to agree on the most basic details of such a force, leaving the Secretariat the almost impossible task of cobbling together standby forces. This failure of the UN members—especially the Big Five—was colossal.

Failure also marked discussions about how a UN force would be commanded. Chapter VII provides for the creation of a Military Staff Committee (MSC) composed of the chiefs of staff of the permanent members or their representatives (Article 47, paragraph 2). Working together and using consensus decision making, the MSC would be responsible for the "strategic direction of any armed forces placed at the disposal of the Security Council" (Article 47, paragraph 3). Strong disagreements among the permanent members about how the MSC would execute its duties doomed it from the start. The strongest proponent of a large standing UN force—the United States—opposed an operative MSC. During the early years of World War II, the American president had favored an Anglo-American entente to maintain postwar order.[18] British negotiators endorsed this idea by suggesting an MSC for the new United Nations that would "be a continuation of the successful American-British Combined Chiefs of Staff, which operated during World War II."[19] Soffer writes that the British negotiators wanted the MSC to be "high powered," but by the San Francisco Conference the American negotiators had backed away from giving any substantial role to the MSC in preserving postwar peace and security.[20] Among the other permanent members, the French had supported both a strong standing UN force and a powerful MSC, while the Soviets "ignored the MSC almost entirely."[21]

No agreement was reached on the MSC, and thus it never managed to take shape or play a role in any UN Chapter VII operations. As we will discuss shortly, there have been only two times in which collective security has been approximated in the history of the United Nations—in the 1950–1953 Korean War and the 1991 Gulf War—but in these cases the lead nation pushing for Chapter VII action *opposed* the use of the MSC. The United States preferred in both cases to put its own military in command of the multinational forces, intentionally sidestepping the MSC in order to avoid multilateral decision making. In Korea, the American position was that the MSC had to be sidelined in order to avoid the Soviet veto.[22] In the 1991 Gulf War, the Soviets strongly endorsed activating the MSC,[23] but the first Bush administration was not inclined to share command and control with any other country. Eventually, in 2005, a World Summit of UN member states recommended the elimination of the MSC.[24]

Collective Security: From Korea to the 1991 Gulf War

We have said that the UN system did not establish a fully functional collective security organization but instead created a modified great power system that was greatly influenced by the collective security ideal. Chapter VII of the Charter provides the mechanism by which a UN collective security resolution would be approved and implemented. First, the Security Council would note that an act of aggression had occurred and would name the state(s) that breached the peace. All the permanent members would need to agree on this determination, as would a majority of the Council as a whole. The aggressor would be ordered to stop its hostile actions and return to the preaggression status quo. If the aggressor failed to comply with this order, the Council could impose economic and diplomatic sanctions to compel compliance. If these failed—or if there was insufficient time for these sanctions to work—the Council could order member states to use all means necessary—which would include armed force—to restore international peace and security. The permanent five would coordinate the military logistics through the MSC and provide the majority of the military requirements for the successful conduct of this UN war. Other states would contribute as both volunteered and requested by the MSC and Security Council.

Analysts disagree about which later cases might be labeled "collective security," but all agree that the first instance in which UN collective security was invoked involved the North Korean invasion of South Korea. In June 1950, the communist forces of North Korea launched an invasion across the thirty-eighth parallel, which formed the internationally recognized border between the divided Korean nation. The Security Council met on June 25, 1950, and declared that the invasion was a breach of international peace. In Resolution 82 (June 25, 1950), the Council ordered an immediate cessation of hostilities and called for the withdrawal of North Korean forces. Two days later, the Council declared "that the authorities in North Korea have neither ceased hostilities nor withdrawn their armed forces to the 38th parallel, and that urgent military measures are required to restore international peace and security" (Resolution 83, June 27, 1950). Toward that end, the Council recommended that members "furnish such assistance to the Republic of Korea [South Korea] as may be necessary to repel the armed attack and to restore international peace and security in the area." The Korean War, thereby, was authorized by the UN Security Council.

The vote in the Council was seven in favor and one opposed (Yugoslavia). At that time, the Council numbered eleven states, five permanent and six rotating. Nonpermanent members Egypt and India did not participate in the vote and the Soviet Union was absent when it was taken. The Soviet Union had been boycotting Council sessions to signal its political opposition to the seating of the Republic of China (Taiwan) rather than the communist People's Republic of China in the China permanent seat. When Resolutions 82 and 83 were adopted, the Soviet ambassador was not there to cast votes. The practice of the Council was that absences did not count in the affirmative or the negative. Had the Soviet ambassador been present, it is most likely that he would have vetoed Resolution 82 rather than name fellow communist country North Korea as an aggressor. With the Soviet veto, the resolution would have died, and the United Nations might well have had no official stand on the war raging on the Korean peninsula.

Instead, the war was authorized and the Council authorized the United States to command the UN forces in Korea. The Soviet Union returned to Council sessions and used its veto power to stop further substantive discussions of the war. In response, the United States used its strong majority support in the General Assembly to pass a resolution that would give the United States a continuous UN stamp of approval for its war efforts in Korea. From this point on, great power agreement on naming an aggressor would be impossible to obtain until the Council creatively interpreted Chapter VII for the 1991 Gulf War.

Discussions of the Korean War were moved to the General Assembly by the Uniting for Peace Resolution (General Assembly Resolution 377 [V], November 3, 1950). According to the UN Charter, the General Assembly cannot discuss any matter under consideration in the Security Council. The Security Council is named as the proper authority for discussing matters of international peace and security. The Council, however, had been deadlocked by the Soviet veto, while the United States wanted to maintain UN endorsement for its operations in Korea. The General Assembly, easily dominated by U.S. friends and allies in its early years, passed the

Uniting for Peace Resolution. The resolution declares that a "failure of the Security Council to discharge its responsibilities on behalf of all the Member States . . . does not relieve Member States of their obligations or the United Nations of its responsibility under the Charter to maintain international peace and security." Thus, the General Assembly resolved that whenever a "lack of unanimity of the permanent members" causes the Council to fail to exercise its Charter duties, an emergency session of the General Assembly can be called to consider the matter that has caused Council deadlock. This session can be called when requested by *any* seven Council members or by a majority of the General Assembly members. The veto does not apply here. For example, in Resolution 120 (November 4, 1956), the Security Council voted ten to one—the Soviet Union voted no— to call an emergency session of the General Assembly regarding the "grave situation [that] has been created by the use of Soviet military forces to suppress the efforts of the Hungarian people to reassert their rights." Under Uniting for Peace, the Assembly can make nonbinding recommendations to members regarding the issue at hand.

The Uniting for Peace Resolution has been invoked ten times, resulting in ten emergency General Assembly sessions since the Korean War. For a list of these ten emergency sessions and their subjects, see extended discussion box 8.2. In 2002–2003, a group of states and nongovernmental organizations opposed to the imminent American-British military intervention in Iraq floated plans to enact the Uniting for Peace Resolution before the invasion. By the draft proposal, this resolution would have declared "that military action against Iraq without a Security Council resolution authorizing such action is contrary to the UN Charter and customary international law."[25] What would have been the value in invoking the Uniting for Peace Resolution against the United States and Britain? On the one hand, the General Assembly has no enforcement authority; thus, this resolution would amount only to a recommendation. On the other hand, such a resolution would carry great moral and public opinion weight. The United States understood the importance of this in 1950 and used the General Assembly to promote its interests in the Korean conflict. Such a statement coming from the General Assembly in late 2002 or early 2003 might have been a strong counter to U.S. plans regarding Iraq.

Not until forty years after the start of the Korean War would the Security Council authorize another Chapter VII operation. The instance that revived UN collective enforcement action was the 1990 Iraqi invasion of Kuwait. The context that allowed UN collective enforcement action was the end of the Cold War and the preoccupation of Soviet authorities with holding their country together. In the years between the 1950 Korean War authorization and the November 1990 Gulf War authorization, the Security Council authorized peacekeeping operations that intentionally and expressly were not like collective security actions. I take up peacekeeping in the next chapter. The end of the Cold War shifted expectations about what the United Nations might accomplish, and member states, including the Big Five, seemed to have developed some political willingness to act cooperatively on matters of peace and security.

On August 2, 1990, Iraq invaded Kuwait. The countries had been engaged in open dispute regarding sovereignty over oil reserves and the terms of repayment of loans made by Kuwait to Iraq during the Iraq-Iran War of the previous decade. On the day of the invasion, the Security Council met and voted fourteen to none (Yemen abstaining) to condemn the invasion, demand "that Iraq withdraw immediately and unconditionally all its forces to the positions in which they were located on 1 August 1990," and call on both Iraq and Kuwait "to begin immediately intensive negotiations for the resolution of their differences" (Resolution 660, August 2, 1990). In this resolution, the Council specifically invoked Article 40, in which the Council can call on parties in a dispute to comply with provisional measures designed to prevent aggravation of the situation at hand.

Four days later, the Council voted thirteen to none (Yemen and Cuba abstaining) under Chapter VII authority to impose economic and diplomatic sanctions on Iraq for failure to comply with its earlier resolution (Resolution 661, August 6, 1990). In Resolution 661, the Council noted that Kuwaiti government officials had signaled their readiness to comply with the earlier Council call to negotiate but that Iraq had not. In response to Resolution 661, Iraq announced it would annex Kuwait, leading the Council to denounce the annexation and to call on all states and international organizations not to recognize it (Resolution 662, August 9, 1990).

The voting behavior of the Big Five suggests that they were in agreement about these Council actions up until this point. The next step in the face of Iraqi noncompliance—and in light of this apparent great power accord—might have been a vote in favor of a Chapter VII, Article 42, collective security resolution authorizing a war. This war, following Articles 46 and 47, would have been conducted by the MSC, making primary use of the military might of the permanent members. This is not how events transpired. First, let's consider the wording of the war authorization and then consider the great power politics involved.

Resolution 678 (November 29, 1990) noted the continued Iraqi refusal to comply with the then multiple Council resolutions regarding its invasion and occupation of Kuwait. Acting under Chapter VII, the Council authorized

Member States co-operating with the Government of Kuwait, unless Iraq on or before 15 January 1991 fully implements . . . the above-mentioned resolutions, to use all necessary means to uphold and implement resolution 660 (1990) and all subsequent relevant resolutions and to restore international peace and security in the area.

The Council then requested all states to provide "appropriate support" for whatever steps were to be taken and that the "concerned" states should inform the Council regularly about their activities pursuant to this authorization. Thus, although Resolution 678 did authorize the use of armed force, the authority to do so was granted to any states interested in cooperating with Kuwait. The Council did not call on *all* members to collectively restore the peace. No requirements were put on anyone, particularly the permanent Council members, to act. But states *choosing* to use "all necessary means" would not be in violation of the UN Charter or international law. Further, these states would coordinate their actions with one another but not under UN Security Council or MSC command and control. Because the resolution avoided universal requirements and authorized a non–UN-commanded war, its outcome—the Gulf War of 1991—should be understood not as a collective security enforcement action but simply as an enforcement action. Resolution 678 passed with twelve yes votes, two no votes (Cuba and Yemen), and China abstaining.

It would be appropriate to think about Resolution 678 as an agreement among great powers on how to manage the world order. The United States wanted Council approval to use force and wanted to use that force on its own terms. Steve Yetiv contends that although Security Council approval was sought, the first Bush administration was prepared to go to war without it and even without U.S. congressional approval. Yetiv writes that "contrary to popular concessions, the overall political approach was a classic case of coercive diplomacy. Washington led and said, 'Do you want to be with us?'"[26] Perhaps this was the message to the non great powers, as suggested by Thomas Friedman:

> With America's place in the world, not to mention Mr. Bush's political future, riding on the outcome of the gulf crisis, the Administration never hesitated to let other nations know that their support for this resolution was vital to Washington, which would remember its friends, and its foes. Minutes after the Yemeni [delegate] joined the Cubans in voting against the resolution at the Security Council . . . , a senior American diplomat was instructed to tell him: "That was the most expensive no vote you ever cast"—meaning it would result in an end to America's more than $70 million in foreign aid to Yemen.[27]

But the message to the veto-wielding members of the Security Council was perhaps more like this: "We intend to go to war; tell us what would make this okay with you."

Ever since it replaced the Republic of China in the United Nations in 1971, the People's Republic of China generally was opposed to UN peacekeeping as unlawful intervention in the domestic affairs of sovereign states. UN peacekeeping does not compare to Resolution 678 in terms of the implications for Iraqi sovereignty, yet China apparently never really threatened to block 678. Instead, when the vote was taken, China abstained, registering neither approval nor disapproval of the resolution. Was there a quid pro quo or some accommodation made between the United States and China resulting in China's accordance with U.S. interests? Then Chinese foreign minister Qian Qichen said there was—Chinese officials expected the foreign minister to be met at the White House in return for the abstention.[28] There was great significance in this. High-level diplomatic exchanges had been barred by the Bush administration ever since the Chinese government forcefully suppressed pro-democracy protests in Tiananmen Square in June 1989—just eighteen months before the Gulf War resolution.[29] On the same day that Resolution 688 was passed, China received its first loan from the Asian Development Bank since June 1989,[30] and two days after the resolution was passed, the Chinese foreign minister was welcomed back to the White House explicitly because the United States and China had found "common ground" in standing up to Iraq's aggression.[31]

Were accommodations made between the Soviets and Americans? The Bush administration and the Gorbachev government seemed to have reached accord about the use of force against Iraq despite news reports that Soviet military advisers were actively working in Iraq months after the Kuwaiti invasion.[32] The U.S. administration persuaded "Saudi Arabia to give $1 billion in aid to help the Soviets through the winter" in order to foster Soviet support for Resolution 678.[33] Then, in the last days before the January 15, 1991, deadline for Iraq to withdraw from Kuwait or face war, Soviet troops launched an attack on a Lithuanian broadcasting center, killing thirteen and wounding more than 160.[34] This attack culminated almost a year of Soviet repression of a nonviolent Lithuanian independence movement. The Bush administration had been less than insistent in opposing this crackdown. The Soviet use of force in January 1991 received only a statement about Bush administration concern, signaling to the pro-independence members of the Lithuanian parliament that they were on their own.[35] Meanwhile, media reports at the time indicated that the U.S. administration believed that disarray in the Soviet government was to blame for the crackdown in Lithuania, not Gorbachev. In return for this quiet support, the Soviet leader did not block the Gulf War through any last-minute diplomatic efforts or deals with Iraq.

Even as the two most likely opponents to the Gulf War were accommodated by the United States, the European Community states (particularly Britain and France) were receiving assurances that the Bush administration would use force only to liberate Kuwait, not attack Iraq itself.[36] Taken together, the road to war was paved through a series of great power agreements that coalesced in Security Council Resolution 678 and the subsequent UN-authorized Gulf War. These great power agreements resulted from accord over how to manage the international order in the face of the

Iraqi invasion of Kuwait and kept great power management duties (in this case, war) within the UN framework. Moreover, none of the great powers felt their own interests threatened by the Gulf War resolution, or, if they did, the tangible payoff for cooperation was greater than the payoff for blocking the war resolution.

The Gulf War episode demonstrated what Claude had hoped for the United Nations some forty years before. Claude had hoped the United Nations might "be able to continue the development of its capability to serve the interests of the great powers—and of the rest of the world—by helping them to contain their conflicts, to limit their competition, and to stabilize their relationships."[37] Claude continued,

> The greatest potential contribution of the United Nations in our time to the management of international power relationships lies not in implementing collective security or instituting world government, but in helping to improve and stabilize the working of the balance of power system, which is, for better or for worse, the operative mechanism of contemporary international politics. The immediate task, in short, is to make the world safe for the balance of power system, and the balance system safe for the world.[38]

Between the Korean War and the November 1990 Gulf War resolution, the Security Council failed to pass a single collective enforcement resolution. Great power disagreement over Korea deadlocked the Council. In 1956, a crisis in the Sinai peninsula put into question the ability of the UN great power system to manage the balance in a way that was safe for great powers, for the world, and for the new global organization. Working within the UN framework, some visionaries found a way to protect the balance and protect the United Nations. This is the story of UN peacekeeping, our next topic of discussion.

In the history of the Security Council, the permanent members rarely find themselves mentioned, much less criticized for their use of force against another country or party. The following cases demonstrate this point.

Suez Crisis, 1956

On October 13, 1956, the Security Council passed Resolution 118 indicating that "exploratory conversations on the Suez question" were under way between the secretary-general and the foreign ministers of Egypt, France, and the United Kingdom. This resolution also offered guidelines for resolving the crisis brewing over Egypt's nationalization of the Suez Canal Company. Before talks could come to fruition, Israel, the United Kingdom, and France had attacked Egypt, prompting Resolution 199 on October 31, 1956. This resolution called for an emergency special session of the General Assembly under the Uniting for Peace Resolution because "a grave situation has been created by action undertaken against Egypt." The grave situation and its perpetrators were not named in the resolution. See chapter 9 for more on this case.

Hungary, 1956

In Resolution 120 on November 4, 1956, the Security Council did a rare thing and noted the use of force by a member of the permanent five. The Council's language was particularly strong: "A grave situation has been created by the use of Soviet military forces to suppress the efforts of the Hungarian people to reassert their rights." Then the Council called for a General Assembly emergency session under Uniting for Peace. The vote in the eleven-member Council was ten votes in favor and one vote—the Soviet Union—against. Any Uniting for Peace Resolution is not subject to the veto of the permanent members.

Laos, 1959

The only resolution voted on by the Security Council in the entire year of 1959 was titled the "Question Relating to Laos." In Resolution 132 on September 7, 1959, the Council did not explain the question or the circumstances but did appoint a committee consisting of Argentina, Italy, Japan, and Tunisia to "examine the statements made before the

Security Council concerning Laos." The vote was ten in favor, and the Soviet Union opposed. No follow-up resolutions occurred on this topic.

What might have been the question relating to Laos? According to William Keylor, in the late 1950s Soviet premier "Khrushchev appeared intent on seizing every available opportunity to challenge the West." Thus, "in Laos, a landlocked kingdom in Southeast Asia formerly attached to the French Indochinese empire, the Soviet Union sent massive military supplies to the pro-Communist guerrilla movement that challenged the authority of the right-wing government forces that were being trained and equipped by the United States."[1] This description of events and the fact that the committee appointed by the Council to investigate the "question" consisted of pro-American countries suggest why no follow-up resolutions were considered on this topic.

Cambodia, 1964

In Resolution 189 on June 4, 1964, the Council took up the "complaint concerning acts of aggression against the territory and civilian population of Cambodia." In this resolution, the Council deplored "the incidents caused by the penetration of the units of the Army of the Republic of Viet-Nam into Cambodian territory" and called for "just and fair compensation" to be made to Cambodia. The Council did not condemn South Vietnam but noted instead that "apologies and regrets" were tendered by it to Cambodia for "incidents which . . . occurred on Cambodian territory" and for the "existing situation" on the border between the countries. The United States was not mentioned at all in this resolution despite the fact that there were already more than 15,000 U.S. military "advisers" in South Vietnam. That number and the nature of U.S. involvement would soon expand dramatically. This resolution was adopted unanimously by the Council.

No other resolution involving the U.S. war in Southeast Asia would be voted on by the Security Council. The next time Vietnam was mentioned in a Security Council resolution was in Resolution 413, July 20, 1977, in which the Council recommended Vietnam for membership in the United Nations. This occurred four years after the U.S. withdrawal and two years after the communist forces of North Vietnam defeated the government of the South, unifying the country.

Afghanistan, 1980

On January 9, 1980, the Security Council took up Resolution 462 titled "International Peace and Security." This resolution contained no indication of the events prompting its adoption. The resolution noted that "the lack of unanimity of its permanent members at the 2190th meeting has prevented it from exercising its primary responsibility for the maintenance of international peace and security," and thus an emergency special session of the General Assembly was called. The Council by this time numbered fifteen; twelve voted in favor of the resolution, Zambia abstained, and the Soviet Union and the German Democratic Republic (East Germany) voted against it.

The event behind this resolution was the Soviet Union's invasion of Afghanistan in December 1979. No other Council resolution would take up the Soviet war in Afghanistan either directly or indirectly. In Resolution 622, October 31, 1988, and in Resolution 647, January 11, 1990, the Council noted that there were agreements on the "settlement of the situation relating to Afghanistan." The only countries mentioned in these resolutions were Afghanistan and Pakistan.

Falkland Islands/Islas Malvinas, 1982

On April 2, 1982, Argentina invaded the Falkland Islands, or Islas Malvinas, a self-governing territory under the sovereign control of Great Britain. Argentina was asserting a long-standing sovereignty claim by the invasion. In Resolution 502 on April 3, 1982, the Council noted the invasion by Argentine forces and that this amounted to a "breach of the peace in the region." The Council called for immediate cessation of hostilities, for the withdrawal of Argentine forces, and for Great Britain to find a diplomatic solution to the crisis.

Rather than seek a diplomatic end to the crisis, Great Britain sent a naval task force to the area to engage the invading Argentine forces. Heavy fighting resulted, and by June, Great Britain had asserted control once again over the Falklands. The Council noted this war between Argentina and Great Britain in Resolution 505 of May 26, 1982, but did not condemn it in any way. Instead, in a unanimous decision, the Council ordered the secretary-general "to enter into contact immediately with the parties with a view to negotiating mutually acceptable terms for a cease-fire."

Note

1. William R. Keylor, *The Twentieth-Century World: An International History* (New York: Oxford University Press, 1996), 306.

The following list is derived from the Dag Hammarskjöld Library of the United Nations.[1] The first and second General Assembly emergency sessions were essentially concurrent on the topics of the Suez and Hungarian crises, respectively. All but one of these emergency sessions were held on the basis of the Uniting for Peace Resolution passed on November 3, 1950, A/RES/377 (V).

- 1st Emergency Special Session: Suez, November 7–10, 1956
- 2nd Emergency Special Session: Hungary, November 4–10, 1956
- 3rd Emergency Special Session: Lebanon, August 8–12, 1958
- 4th Emergency Special Session: Democratic Republic of the Congo, September 17–19, 1960
- 5th Emergency Special Session: Middle East, June 17–September 18, 1967 (not convened under Uniting for Peace but by a letter from the Soviet Union invoking rule 20 of General Assembly rules of procedure, A/6717)
- 6th Emergency Special Session: Afghanistan, January 10–14, 1980
- 7th Emergency Special Session: Palestine, July 22–29, 1980; April 20–28, June 25–26, August 16–19, September 24, 1982
- 8th Emergency Special Session: Namibia, September 3–14, 1981
- 9th Emergency Special Session: Occupied Arab Territories (Golan Heights), January 29–February 5, 1982
- 10th Emergency Special Session: Occupied East Jerusalem, Palestine Territory, April 24–25, July 15, November 13, 1997; March 17, 1998; February 8–9, 1999; October 18 and 20, 2000; December 20, 2001; May 7, August 5, 2002; October 20–21, December 8, 2003; July 16 and 20, 2004

Note

1. UN-I-QUE (UN Info Quest) R03055, http://lib-unique.un.org/lib/unique.nsf/Link/R03055 (accessed June 23, 2005).

9

Keeping the Peace

The rancor over the U.S.-led military invasion of Iraq in 2003 is but the latest installment in the troubled story of the Middle East, a story that continually has bedeviled the United Nations and member states' relations. The first Arab-Israeli war began on May 15, 1948, the day after Israel declared its independence in defiance of UN plans for the partition of Palestine into separate Jewish and Arab states. The Security Council called for a cease-fire and in June 1948 sent in a small group of military observers to supervise, investigate, and report on issues surrounding the cease-fire. The group of observers was called the UN Truce Supervision Organization (UNTSO).[1] The UNTSO precedent led the next year to the deployment of another small military observer group, the UN Military Observation Group in India and Pakistan (UNMOGIP), to supervise a cease-fire in Jammu and Kashmir between India and Pakistan.[2] These military observer missions might be understood as the eyes and ears of the Security Council—but eyes and ears with military expertise useful for detecting any military action that might disrupt the cease-fire and require stronger Council intervention. UNTSO played a practical and a conceptual role in the next Middle East crisis to erupt.

In October 1956, two major events put the Security Council great power balance into question. The first involved efforts by a liberal government in Hungary to establish its political independence from the Soviet Union and to sever its military ties with the newly created Warsaw Pact. This revolution was crushed by Soviet tanks. The Soviet military kept a heavy hand in Hungarian politics thereafter to ensure Hungary's continued membership in and contribution to the Soviet bloc. The second was the October 29 attack on Egypt by Israel with the collusion and cooperation of Great Britain and France. Both events created deadlock in the Council, and both became the subject of emergency General Assembly sessions. One resulted in the further consolidation of a great power's sphere of influence, and the other resulted first in potential great power war and then in the creation of the first UN peacekeeping force. The two events no doubt were linked in the minds of top decision makers with the politics of each impacting to some degree the resolution of the other.[3]

The Soviet use of force to stop Hungarian independence efforts was the subject of UN Security Council Resolution 120 (November 4, 1956). This resolution resulted in an emergency General Assembly session (the second emergency session; see extended discussion box 8.2 in chapter 8), but nothing done within the UN framework undid the Soviet military consolidation of its control over Hungary.

The Israeli-British-French attack on Egypt at the end of October 1956 disrupted UN activities aimed at defusing low-level conflict between Egypt and Israel and resolving political and economic disputes over the Suez Canal between Egypt, Britain, and France. In the previous year, Egypt had supported Palestinian fedayeen raids into Israel, and Israel had responded with force.[4] UNTSO observers and the secretary-general worked to calm the sides down in order to preserve the 1948 cease-fire. Meanwhile, the United States withdrew a previous offer of financial support to Egypt for the building of the Aswan Dam. The dam was critical for Egyptian economic development; in response to the withdrawn U.S. offer, President Gamal Abdel Nasser nationalized the Suez Canal Company in order to fund Aswan.

The British and French brought a complaint against Egypt to the Security Council. The Council set out principles to guide resolution over claims to ownership of the canal, principles that acknowledged Egypt's sovereignty (Resolution 118, October 13, 1956). In the meantime, British, French, and Israeli officials had been conspiring to reclaim the canal and establish a military buffer zone for Israel in the Sinai peninsula. In a scene of old-style gunboat diplomacy, this is what occurred as described by the UN Department of Peacekeeping Operations:

> The Israeli forces crossed the border on the morning of 29 October. In the early hours of 30 October, the Chief of Staff of UNTSO, Major-General E. L. M. Burns (Canada), called for a ceasefire and requested Israel to pull its forces back to its side of the border. In the afternoon of the same day, the British and French Governments addressed a joint ultimatum to Egypt and Israel calling on both sides to cease hostilities within 12 hours and to withdraw their forces to a distance of 10 miles on each side of the Suez Canal. They also requested

Egypt to allow Anglo-French forces to be stationed temporarily on the Canal at Port Said, Ismailia and Suez for the purpose of separating the belligerents and ensuring the safety of shipping. The ultimatum was accepted by Israel whose troops in any case were still far from the Suez Canal, but it was rejected by Egypt. On 31 October, France and the United Kingdom launched an air attack against targets in Egypt, which was followed shortly by a landing of their troops near Port Said at the northern end of the Canal.[5]

In an odd twist in the early Cold War, the Americans and Soviets joined to condemn the British, French, and Israeli actions. The Soviets, recall, were massively involved in stopping the Hungarian revolution in this very same month. In the Security Council, the British and French vetoed American and Soviet resolutions demanding a cease-fire and return to pre–October 29 positions. By Resolution 119 (October 31, 1956), the Council noted that a "lack of unanimity of its permanent members . . . has prevented it from exercising its primary responsibility for the maintenance of international peace and security." It therefore approved a Uniting for Peace Resolution sending the matter to the General Assembly for discussion. The resolution enacting an emergency General Assembly session on the matter of Hungary noted quite boldly that the Soviet forces were to blame; the corresponding resolution on the Suez crisis simply noted that "a grave situation has been created by an action undertaken against Egypt," but no perpetrators of that action were named.

Not naming the perpetrators became key to defusing this crisis. The Security Council great powers were split but not in the typical four-to-one split of the United States, the Republic of China (Taiwan), Great Britain, and France versus the Soviet Union. This split had the Americans and Soviets versus the British and French over the obvious military attack on and invasion of Egyptian territory. While the United States tacitly acknowledged the Soviet Union's right to police its own sphere of influence (Hungary), it agreed with the Soviet Union that the British and French had no such claim or right in the Middle East. Yet the British and French were not to be humiliated by this situation. Instead, some politically neutral egress point would be created to restore the preinvasion balance.

UN Secretary-General Dag Hammarskjöld and Canadian Foreign Minister Lester Pearson are credited with imagining a way out of this great power impasse. Their idea was to establish a neutral UN peacekeeping force in the area. In General Assembly Resolution 998 (ES-1, November 4, 1956), the secretary-general was asked to submit "a plan for the setting up, with the consent of the nations concerned, of an emergency international United Nations Force to secure and supervise the cessation of hostilities." Several ideas about peacekeeping could be discerned in this resolution. First, the secretary-general would be tasked with setting up the plan; second, the plan would need the consent of those involved; third, the plan would involve a military force deployed in an emergency situation; finally, the force would supervise a cease-fire.

In General Assembly Resolution 1000 (ES-1), passed the following day, more details about peacekeeping emerged. First, the Assembly declared that the force would be under UN command. Second, the chief of the command was instructed to recruit officers for the force "who shall be nations of countries other than those having permanent membership in the Security Council."

In General Assembly Resolution 1001 (ES-1), passed on November 7, the Assembly approved a set of guidelines for the force developed by the secretary-general. First, the force commander would be appointed by and responsible to the General Assembly or Security Council. The force commander's "authority should be so defined as to make him fully independent of the policies of any one nation," thus reflecting basic principles on which the United Nations was established.[6] Second, not only the officers but the entire force should be recruited from member states other than the permanent five to avoid any appearance of bias or great power political involvement. Third, the force was to supervise a cease-fire and expressly should not "influence the military balance in the current conflict, and thereby the political balance affecting efforts to settle the conflict."[7] Fourth, the force could not be deployed until all the disputants had agreed to it and honored the terms of the cease-fire. Fifth, the force could not be deployed without the consent of Egypt since the force would be deployed to Egyptian territory and the sovereign rights of Egypt could not be abridged. Finally,

> The Force obviously should have no rights other than those necessary for the execution of its functions, in cooperation with local authorities. It would be more than an observer corps, but in no way a military force temporarily controlling the territory in which it was stationed; nor should the Force have functions exceeding those necessary to secure peaceful conditions, on the assumption that the parties to the conflict would take all necessary steps for compliance with the recommendations of the General Assembly.[8]

By this, the force would need to carry weapons only for self-defense since it was not an occupation force and was present with the goodwill and good compliance of all the disputants.

The UN Emergency Force (UNEF I) was so constituted and deployed as the first official UN peacekeeping operation. Peacekeeping fulfilled the mission of the United Nations to restore international peace and security in situations in which combatants had agreed already to seek a peaceful resolution of their disagreements. At times, combatants might need to be persuaded by the Security Council to come to the negotiating table, but the payoff for combatants would be far better than the political and military costs of being named as an aggressor by the world body (*if* the Council could agree that aggression had occurred).

In the Suez crisis, it would have been politically impossible for the Security Council to name the British and French as aggressors. The Council was designed to maintain these states' great power privileges and, as discussed previously, to exempt them from the same threat of collective punishment to which other states were subject. The problem at hand, however, was that the faith of *all* UN members in the basic correctness of the UN system had to be maintained, and this meant that practical measures were needed to overlook the great powers' aggression (without seeming too obvious) and to ease their way back into the great power consultations over managing the crisis. The peacekeeping solution presented the United Nations with a mechanism through which the British and French (and Israelis) could bow out of the confrontation without incurring any costs for starting it. Peace could be restored, and the UN system would remain intact, thereby ensuring international stability.

UN Peacekeeping

The essential practice of peacekeeping was established with UNEF I. Because peacekeeping was a creative response to great power stalemate over Suez, there was and is not a clear doctrinal or Charter foundation for it. Instead, peacekeeping is sometimes said to fall under Chapter VI, Pacific Settlement of Disputes, and sometimes under Chapter VII, Action with Respect to Threats to the Peace, Breaches of the Peace, and Acts of Aggression; sometimes analysts refer to the fictional in-between dimension of "Chapter VI½."

Following the first peacekeeping operation, traditional peacekeeping was understood in principle to include the following elements:

- Each operation is approved by the Security Council or General Assembly and tasked to the secretary-general for implementation.
- Each operation is under the command and control of a force commander appointed by the secretary-general and answerable to the United Nations.
- A cease-fire or truce is agreed to by the disputants in advance of the deployment of the peacekeeping force.
- The consent of local authorities is secured prior to the deployment in order to respect the sovereignty of member states. Consent also signifies that the locals will act in compliance with the peacekeepers.
- The mission consists of supervising a cease-fire and reporting violations thereof to local and UN officials. In more complex peacekeeping, peacekeepers are tasked with facilitating peace talks, voluntary

    disarmament, supervising arms embargoes, assisting in the provision of humanitarian relief, securing environments for elections, and many other tasks.
- The peacekeeping force is neutral regarding all the combatants, naming no party as an "aggressor" and taking no military action against particular parties.
- The peacekeeping force is neutral regarding the contributors, avoiding the use of officers and troops from the permanent five and other interested countries (such as former colonial powers).
- Finally, because of all the previously mentioned points, peacekeepers carry sidearms only for self-defense purposes. In more complex operations, peacekeepers might employ heavier weapons but also only for defensive purposes.

For each of these aspects of traditional peacekeeping, there are many examples when the practice of peacekeeping did not match the theory. Many times, deviations from peacekeeping principles resulted from ambiguities in local conditions and inadequate mandates. Other deviations resulted from the lack of genuine will on the part of disputants to comply with cease-fire and other political agreements. Many exceptions to the principles, too, resulted from states' reluctance to allow the UN force commander any real control over their troops. I'll discuss a few examples shortly.

For most of the Cold War period (1945–1989), peacekeeping operations were limited in number and usually in size and mandate (with the exception of the UN Operation in Congo, 1960–1964). During the Cold War, only eighteen peacekeeping operations were approved and deployed. These included ten smaller military observer missions and eight peacekeeping forces. Almost half of these operations (eight) were deployed in the Middle East, four in Asia, three in Africa, two in the Americas, and one in Europe. Table 9.1 presents a list of past and current operations by region. The lack of any significant number of peacekeeping missions in Europe and the Americas in this period could be attributed to the Cold War blocs policing their own spheres of influence. Certainly there was no lack of war in Central America during this era, but the wars there were both characterized as internal (and thus outside the gambit of the United Nations) and/or involved some form of U.S. intervention. The "overlay" of Cold War politics in which local and regional wars took on the guise of proxy wars fought on behalf of or with the support and involvement of the superpowers[9] tended to limit UN peacekeeping.

Where UN peacekeeping was fairly active (the Middle East), great power interests tended to coalesce in favor of stabilizing the region that possessed so much of the world's energy supplies. This is not to suggest that the Cold War was not at play in the Middle East (it was), but the

Table 9.1 Past and Current UN Peacekeeping Operations

Africa

Past	Current as of Mid-2006
ONUC—UN Operation in the Congo, 1960–1964	MINURSO—UN Mission for the Referendum in Western Sahara, 1991–
UNAVEM I—UN Angola Verification Mission I, 1988–1991	MONUC—UN Organization Mission in the Democratic Republic of the Congo, 1999–
UNTAG—UN Transition Assistance Group in Namibia, 1989–1990	UNMEE—UN Mission in Ethiopia and Eritrea, 2000–
UNAVEM II—UN Angola Verification Mission II, 1991–1995	UNMIL—UN Mission in Liberia, 2003–
UNOSOM I—UN Operation in Somalia I, 1992–1993	UNOCI—UN Operation in Côte d'Ivoire, 2004–
ONUMOZ—UN Operation in Mozambique, 1992–1994	ONUB—UN Operation in Burundi, 2004–
UNOSOM II—UN Operation in Somalia II, 1993–1995	UNMIS—UN Mission in the Sudan, 2005–
UNAMIR—UN Assistance Mission for Rwanda, 1993–1996	
UNOMUR—UN Observer Mission Uganda-Rwanda, 1993–1994	
UNOMIL—UN Observer Mission in Liberia, 1993–1997	
UNASOG—UN Aouzou Strip Observer Group, May–June 1994	
UNAVEM III—UN Angola Verification Mission III, 1995–1997	
MONUA—Observer Mission in Angola, 1997–1999	
UNOMSIL—UN Observer Mission in Sierra Leone, 1998–1999	
MINURCA—UN Mission in the Central African Republic, 1998–2000	
UNAMSIL—UN Mission in Sierra Leone, 1999–2005	

Table 9.1 *(continued)*

Americas

Past

Current as of Mid-2006

DOMREP—Mission of the Representative of the Secretary-General in Dominican Republic, 1965–1966

MINUSTAH—UN Stabilization Mission in Haiti, 2004–

ONUCA—UN Observer Group in Central America, 1989–1992

ONUSAL—UN Observer Mission in El Salvador, 1991–1995

UNMIH—UN Mission in Haiti, 1993–1996

UNSMIH—UN Support Mission in Haiti, 1996–1997

MIPONUH—UN Civilian Police Mission in Haiti, 1997–2000

MINUGUA—UN Verification Mission in Guatemala, January–May 1997

UNTMIH—UN Transition Mission in Haiti, August–November 1997

Asia

Past

Current as of Mid-2006

UNSF—UN Security Force in West New Guinea, 1962–1963

UNMOGIP—UN Military Observer Group in India and Pakistan, 1949–

UNIPOM—UN India-Pakistan Observation Mission, 1965–1966

UNGOMAP—UN Good Offices Mission in Afghanistan and Pakistan, 1988–1990

UNAMIC—UN Advance Mission in Cambodia, 1991–1992

UNTAC—UN Transitional Authority in Cambodia, 1992–1993

UNMOT—UN Mission of Observers in Tajikistan, 1994–2000

UNTAET—UN Transitional Administration in East Timor, 1999–2002

UNMISET—UN Mission of Support in East Timor, 2002–2005

Table 9.1 (continued)

Europe	
Past	*Current as of Mid-2006*
UNPROFOR—UN Protection Force in former Yugoslavia, 1992–1995	UNFICYP—UN Peacekeeping Force in Cyprus, 1964–
UNCRO—UN Confidence Restoration Operation in Croatia, 1995–1996	UNOMIG—UN Observer Mission in Georgia, 1993–
UNMIBH—UN Mission in Bosnia and Herzegovina, 1995–2002	UNMIK—UN Interim Administration Mission in Kosovo, 1999–
UNPREDEP—UN Preventive Deployment Force in Macedonia, 1995–1999	
UNMOP—UN Mission of Observers in Prevlaka, 1996–2002	
UNTAES—UN Transitional Authority in East Slavonia, Baranja, and Western Sirmium, 1996–1998	
UNPSG—UN Civilian Police Support Group, January–October 1998	

Middle East	
Past	*Current as of Mid-2006*
UNEF I—UN Emergency Force I, 1956–1967	UNTSO—UN Truce Supervision Organization, 1948–
UNOGIL—UN Observation Group in Lebanon, June–December 1958	UNDOF—UN Disengagement Observer Force, 1974–
UNYOM—UN Yemen Observation Mission, 1963–1964	UNIFIL—UN Interim Force in Lebanon, 1978–
UNEF II—UN Emergency Force II, 1973–1979	
UNIIMOG—UN Iran-Iraq Military Observer Group, 1988–1991	
UNIKOM—UN Iraq-Kuwait Observation Mission 1991–2003	

Source: UN Department of Peacekeeping Operations, http://www.un.org/Depts/dpko/dpko/index.asp (accessed June 23, 2006).

Soviet Union did not veto UN peacekeeping in the region even though peacekeeping tended to be dominated by the United States and its military allies. When we examine the pattern of who participated most frequently in UN peacekeeping from 1948 to 1989, this Western domination is apparent. The top fifteen contributors to UN peacekeeping operations at this time in rank order (with number of operations participated in listed in parentheses) were Canada (seventeen), Sweden (fifteen), Ireland (thirteen), Finland (twelve), Norway (twelve), Denmark (eleven), India (eleven), Italy (eleven), Australia (nine), the United States (nine), Austria (eight), Ghana (eight), Brazil (seven), the Netherlands (seven), and New Zealand (seven).[10] This list includes the United States and five of its North Atlantic Treaty Organization (NATO) allies (Canada, Norway, Denmark, Italy, and the Netherlands), along with three non-NATO European countries that enjoyed de facto NATO protection during the Cold War (Sweden, Ireland, and Austria), and three other U.S. military allies (Australia, New Zealand, and Brazil). With two-thirds of the top peacekeeping contributors being Western military allies, the Soviet Union's decision *not* to veto UN peacekeeping can be understood as tacit great power accord that UN peacekeeping was a useful tool for stabilizing international power relations. The Soviet Union, like France, did not want to pay for this stabilization, nor did it wish to participate in it, but it stood to benefit from these stabilization actions.

At the close of the Cold War, there was some real enthusiasm and optimism among UN member states for making the United Nations at last a bold tool for managing and sorting out power relations. Growing great power accord in this period allowed for the first UN-sanctioned war since Korea, as discussed previously. Great power accord also opened the door to more and more ambitious UN peacekeeping efforts and to UN-sanctioned peace enforcement operations (to be examined shortly).

Recall that in the Cold War period there were eighteen UN peacekeeping operations. Five of these older missions remained active through 2006. From 1990 through mid-2006, forty-two new operations were launched. The geographical distribution of these new missions was remarkably different from the Middle East–concentrated earlier missions. In this new era, twenty new operations were launched in Africa, nine in Europe, seven in the Americas, five in Asia, and only one in the Middle East.

This geographical change was matched by a significant increase in the number of states contributing in some way to peacekeeping operations. For example, in mid-2005, 103 states (slightly more than half of UN members) participated in sixteen active UN peacekeeping operations. European countries as a group dominated eleven of these operations by number of participating countries.[11] Despite this European presence in peacekeeping, other states—particularly the states of South Asia—were the premier troop contributors as of 2005, following a trend developing through the decade. This amazing growth in the number of missions and the number of states contributing to these missions created a momentum that carried the United Nations into situations that were ill suited to peacekeeping.

The 1990s—Combining Peacekeeping with Peace Enforcement

Beyond the major enforcement action of the Gulf War of 1991 discussed in the previous chapter, two other UN-sanctioned missions created enthusiasm among UN member states for positive post–Cold War international intervention. The first was Operation Provide Comfort (OPC), an enforcement operation undertaken in 1991 by some members of the Gulf War coalition: the United States, Austria, Belgium, Canada, France, Germany, Italy, Luxembourg, the Netherlands, Portugal, Spain, and Great Britain. The goal of OPC was to stop a humanitarian disaster in northern Iraq after the conclusion of the Gulf War. The next case was a "second-generation," or "complex peacekeeping," operation, the UN Transitional Authority in Cambodia (UNTAC), which functioned from 1992 to 1993 with mixed results. I will discuss these in turn because of the precedent each set.

As the government of Saddam Hussein was surrendering to the UN-sanctioned multinational coalition in March 1991, U.S. President George H. W. Bush urged the Kurds and Shi'ia of Iraq to rise up and overthrow the Hussein regime. Thomas Weiss writes that Hussein had kept troops in reserve for this possibility.[12] The uprisings and subsequent repression resulted in tens of thousands of deaths and then massive flows of people attempting to flee Iraq through different routes across international borders. Those refugees who made it into Iran were welcomed and given safe haven, although international aid and attention were scarce. The would-be refugees who fled north to Turkey were stopped at the border by the Turkish army. "Human rights abuses by Turkish border guards and the life-threatening winter conditions of the border-mountain region led to an increasing death rate—between 400 and 1,000 per day."[13]

Because this crisis came on the heels of the 1991 Gulf War, there were still hundreds of thousands of foreign troops in the area. The national leaders of key members of the Gulf War coalition were disposed to use their available troops in what would soon be called a humanitarian intervention. The goal would be to stop the immediate suffering of Kurds on the Turkish border and to create conditions that would provide future security for Kurds in Iraq. (Aspects of this case also are discussed in chapter 6.)

On April 5, 1991, the Security Council passed Resolution 688, in which the Council first honored the provisions of Article 2, paragraph 7, of the Charter and then expressed grave concern over "the repression of the

Iraqi civilian population in many parts of Iraq, including most recently in Kurdish-populated areas, which led to a massive flow of refugees towards and across international frontiers and to cross-border incursions which threaten international peace and security in the region." In this latter statement, the Council established its authority to act. In the former statement, the Council (probably not intentionally) reminded everyone of the ambiguities in the overall mandate of the United Nations. Article 2, paragraph 7, states,

> Nothing contained in the present Charter shall authorize the United Nations to intervene in matters which are essentially within the domestic jurisdiction of any state or shall require the Members to submit such matters to settlement under the present Charter; but this principle shall not prejudice the application of enforcement measures under Chapter VII.[14]

How a government chooses to govern its own territory was and is a matter of domestic jurisdiction. The United Nations is dedicated to protecting the sovereign rights of its member states. Article 2 both reaffirms these ideas and suggests that there are limitations on them—limitations created by spillover problems for other states.

In Resolution 688, the Council condemned the repression of the Iraqi people, declared that this had created problems for international peace and security in the region, called on the Iraqi government to stop the repression and to allow humanitarian organizations immediate access to all parts of Iraq, and appealed to member states to contribute to the humanitarian relief efforts. In most contexts, this resolution would seem a weak admonishment of Iraq and a weak appeal to the international community. But in this situation in which a large multinational military force was poised, ready, and willing to step in, this resolution was heard as approval for a massive humanitarian intervention.

American military planners and humanitarian relief organizations determined that the best way to help the Kurds stranded on the Turkish border was to move them off the mountains and back to their hometowns and villages. To do this safely, Iraqi forces would need to be denied the ability to threaten the Kurds both on the way home and once resettled there:

> The solution was the creation of a security zone in northern Iraq to be patrolled by Allied aircraft, which in turn would form the basis to enforce the no-fly zone in June, which interdicted Iraqi flights above the thirty-sixth parallel. In August 1992, another no-fly zone was created in southern Iraq, below the thirty-second parallel, to protect the Shiites.[15]

Acting under the authority of a resolution that did not say much of anything, the multinational coalition responded massively and successfully to the Kurdish humanitarian crisis. In so doing they also created a mechanism (the no-fly zone) for ensuring longer-term Kurdish security and effective autonomy from the Iraqi government. This operation and the 1991 Gulf War itself established precedents for a creative interpretation of Chapter VII to come in due time—that of peace enforcement operations approved by the Council but commanded by a lead nation and executed by a coalition of the willing.

In Cambodia, the United Nations launched a second-generation, or complex peace support, operation that combined peacekeeping and peace building, setting another precedent for the post–Cold War era. A four-party Cambodian civil war was brought to an end in October 1991 with the signing of peace accords in Paris. The four parties to the accords—the State of Cambodia; the United National Front for an Independent, Neutral, Peaceful and Cooperative Cambodia; the Khmer People's National Liberation Front; and the Khmer Rouge—agreed to a plan that would involve a massive peacekeeping operation. UNTAC

> was to demobilize 70 percent of the soldiers, take control of the administration of the entire country (including finance, defense, public security, foreign affairs and the media), verify the ceasefire, foster awareness of human rights, supervise the rehabilitation of the country's infrastructure, and create a neutral political environment in which to hold free and fair elections.[16]

Despite its complex mandate, UNTAC was a traditional peacekeeping mission in that no extraordinary Chapter VII authorization to "use all measures necessary" was granted to it. Instead, UNTAC's success, like that of most peacekeeping missions, depended on the willing compliance of local parties. In Security Council Resolution 745 (February 28, 1992), the Council strongly urged

> the Cambodian parties to agree to the complete demobilization of their military forces prior to the end of the process of registration for the elections as well as to the destruction of the weapons and ammunition deposited into the Authority's custody in excess of those, if any, which may be deemed necessary by the Authority for the maintenance of civil order and national defence, or which may be required by the new Cambodian Government.

UNTAC was also traditional peacekeeping in that it was to maintain neutrality regarding all Cambodian parties. This required the peacekeepers and the wider United Nations to treat the Khmer Rouge the same as all the Cambodian parties.[17] The Khmer Rouge was responsible for turning Cambodia into a "killing field" from 1975 to 1978, when the Khmer Rouge ruled the country and killed between 1 and 2 million Cambodians as enemies of the state.

[UNTAC went beyond traditional peacekeeping in its mission, not in its rules of engagement and neutrality.]It was tasked with civil administration and running the first-ever national elections. It also went beyond Cold War–era peacekeeping in its size and expense. At maximum deployment, it numbered 15,991 troops, 3,359 civilian police, 900 international polling station officers, and 50,000 local electoral staff.[18]

[The United Nations offers UNTAC as an example of a successful peace-keeping operation. A national election was freely and fairly conducted with nearly 90 percent of eligible voters participating.] A coalition govern-ment was formed and managed to steer Cambodia toward greater politi-cal stability.[19] Yet for all its success in holding elections, UNTAC failed to disarm and demobilize the combatants. "Even after the peace accord was signed, all sides kept struggling to take as much territory as possible before the U.N. verification system was put in place. By the time verifica-tion was up and running, the Khmer Rouge had refused to cooperate."[20] Once the Khmer Rouge refused to disarm, the other combatants followed suit. Despite this, UNTAC managed to hold the elections and departed Cambodia in 1993 with a coalition government in place. The stage was set for more war, however, and when the peacekeepers departed, a smaller civil war erupted. This war between the coalition government and the Khmer Rouge lasted until 1997, when the Cambodians settled it without international intervention.]

The UN complex peacekeeping mission in Cambodia and the UN-authorized allied enforcement operation in northern Iraq offered models of what the international community might do about intrastate conflicts at the start of a decade that boiled over with such. A new ethic of human-itarian intervention designed to protect populations in distress was endorsed, departing from the earlier tradition of strict nonintervention in the sovereign affairs of UN member states. The relative success of UNTAC gave the United Nations the confidence to deploy large, complex, and multidimensional peacekeeping operations. The success of OPC in north-ern Iraq demonstrated how rapid, massive, short-term military interven-tion could stop a humanitarian crisis when UN members shared the polit-ical will to act.

A pattern took hold during the 1990s in which the Security Council would authorize a complex peacekeeping operation even though there might have been at best a tentative cease-fire and peace on the ground. The peacekeepers would be tasked with complicated mandates but with traditional rules of engagement and never enough personnel or equip-ment. The operation would soon fail or even fail to deploy, as the peace on the ground would prove illusive. Eventually, a powerful country with a particular interest in the conflict would offer to lead a UN-approved peace enforcement mission that would be unencumbered by the tradi-tions and expectations of peacekeeping. This force would create better conditions on the ground for a short time into which a follow-on peace-keeping operation would be launched. With some variation, this pattern was apparent in Somalia, Haiti, Rwanda, Bosnia, Liberia, Sierra Leone, and East Timor and in the twenty-first century in the Democratic Republic of the Congo.[21]

Peace enforcement appeared to be the remedy to the problems inherent to peacekeeping. Both types of operations were given UN Security Council authorization; thus, neither was a violation of international law or the UN Charter. Peacekeeping required the consent and cooperation of parties to the dispute; peace enforcement created its own consent through overwhelming numbers and firepower. Technically, peacekeepers operated under a unified UN command, but in actuality they followed separate, often conflicting directives from their national capitals. Peace enforcement troops conversely operated under the unified command of the dominant contributing state. Peacekeepers could use their weapons only in self-defense; peace enforcement troops had liberal rules of engagement to use all means necessary, including force, to achieve their objectives.

Somalia was the first testing ground for the combination pack of complex peacekeeping and peace enforcement. The central government of Somalia collapsed in 1991, leaving multiple combatants contesting to define and control the state. This state failure did not draw the attention of the Security Council. Instead, a humanitarian disaster of enormous proportions did: state failure and civil war led to the displacement of 29 percent of the entire population at the same time that three waves of famine struck the people of Somalia. The Refugee Policy Group estimated that 90,000 Somalis died in the civil conflict from 1985 to 1994 and that between 300,000 and 350,000 people died from famine by early 1993.[22]

On April 24, 1992, the Security Council passed Resolution 751, in which it noted that the "magnitude of the human suffering caused by the conflict" in Somalia constituted a threat to international peace and security but that the parties to the conflict had signed multiple letters of agreement on a cease-fire. Because of these agreements, a UN Operation in Somalia (UNOSOM) was authorized to facilitate an end to all hostilities, maintain a cease-fire, promote political reconciliation, and help provide "urgent humanitarian assistance." A small group of military observers was to be dispatched to monitor the cease-fire in Mogadishu while the secretary-general worked to achieve agreement among the Somali combatants about the details of deploying UNOSOM.

It took from April until September before UNOSOM could deploy because the Somalis would not agree on the details of its operation. Agreement from each of the dominant armed factions was considered the equivalent of local consent and thus necessary for the deployment of peacekeepers. Ultimately, different factions had different expectations about the peacekeeping operation. In no time, the situation reverted to its earlier status, with open violence and the regular armed robbery of famine relief supplies. Peacekeepers and humanitarian workers alike came under fire. By early December, it was clear that the operation would need to be reconsidered. Responding to a variety of interests, some of which were humanitarian, the U.S. Bush administration proposed launching an enforcement operation to force humanitarian relief into critical areas. In Resolution 794 on December 3, 1992, the Council approved giving Chapter VII authority to an unnamed member state and others to "use all necessary means to establish as soon as possible a secure environment for humanitarian relief operations in Somalia." This UN-approved, U.S.-commanded enforcement action would be known as the United Task Force (UNITAF).

If the enforcement operation in northern Iraq set the precedent, UNITAF established the operating manual. UNITAF deployed up to 38,000 troops (26,000 Americans) for an intentionally short mission. The Council did not require the secretary-general to get the consent of the different factions on the ground—UNITAF and other enforcement operations would create their own consent through numbers, massive military might, and flexible rules of engagement. UNITAF approached all Somalis the same—anyone who cooperated with it would not be harmed, and anyone who impeded the mission would be dealt with using force if necessary. UNITAF established "four no's" to which all factions would be held: no technicals (machine gun–mounted light trucks), no banditry, no roadblocks, and no visible weapons.[23] The Somali factions learned these no's and more or less complied with them as long as UNITAF was present. The most rational choice for combatants was to comply in the short term, hoarding weapons and supplies for that inevitable time when the mission ended and a weaker peacekeeping force replaced it.

The secretary-general understood what the Somali factions understood, and thus he urged UNITAF to do more than just tolerate warehoused weapons. The secretary-general wanted UNITAF to use its superior firepower, discipline, unified command and control, and liberal mandate to forcibly disarm the Somali factions. This was seen as essential to preparing a more secure environment for the follow-on peacekeeping mission that would be able to turn its attention to facilitating humanitarian relief and long-term political reconciliation. But the peace enforcement mission was not under UN command, and the force had no particular reason to execute the wishes of the Security Council, much less the secretary-general. In Somalia, the Bush administration decided that UNITAF should facilitate humanitarian aid but not do anything more, especially anything that might entail some risk taking for American troops. The secretary-general urged disarmament to no avail.

This same disagreement appeared in the U.S.-led peace enforcement mission in Haiti in 1995. The U.S. commanders of the enforcement mission decided that retraining the various militias so they could act as a unified Haitian military force was easier to accomplish than disbanding the militias and starting all over. Both the secretary-general and the restored Haitian president Jean-Bertrand Aristide strongly urged that the militias be disbanded.[24] American policymakers and military commanders won that disagreement as they did in Somalia. A unified command makes execution of a peace enforcement operation more effective; UN command often can be too disjointed for much of anything to be accomplished. But the lead-nation enforcement model leaves decision making and direction of the operation to the lead nation. The lead nation may not have much interest in what happens after the enforcement operation is withdrawn. Ultimately, some of the choices made by the lead nation may set up the follow-on peacekeeping operation to fail.

Because the United States won the argument about disarmament in Somalia, the follow-on UN peacekeeping mission, UNOSOM II, deployed into an environment in which there was no peace to keep. Recognizing this, Security Council Resolution 814 (March 26, 1993) gave UNOSOM II Chapter VII authorization to employ liberal rules of engagement to achieve its mission (although this language is not contained in the resolution). Despite this, national contingents deployed to UNOSOM II decided to read the rules of engagement in their own way, leading to wide variations in activities by the participants (which is, unfortunately, typical of most UN peacekeeping operations). This confusion over the mandate and rules of engagement created chaos for the peacekeepers. The Somali factions saw and took advantage of this chaos.

In early June, a confrontation between the Somali National Alliance (SNA) led by Mohammed Farah Aideed and Pakistani UNOSOM II troops resulted in the killing of twenty-four Pakistanis and the wounding of scores of others. The Security Council then issued Resolution 837 (June 6, 1993) condemning the deaths and reaffirming that the secretary-general could order UNOSOM II to take "all necessary measures against all those responsible for the armed attacks." To U.S. policymakers and military commanders, this was a green light for U.S. troops to take measures to apprehend Aideed and key leaders of the SNA:

> The decision to go after Aideed and his supporters was based primarily on the belief that a deliberate attack against UN peacekeepers could not go unpunished because doing so could have broad repercussions in other ongoing and future UN operations. Not all participating countries were happy with this new direction. Paris and Rome began issuing directions to their contingents that often directly conflicted with orders given them by [the force commander].[25]

From June until early October, the U.S. troops assigned to UNOSOM II made it their business to protect other countries' peacekeepers by going on the offensive against Somalis who had targeted peacekeepers. The infamous "Black Hawk Down" incident on October 3, 1993, in which eighteen American servicemen were killed, resulted from this split mandate. Thereafter, the entire UNOSOM II operation became a self-protection mission until it disbanded the following March.[26]

What happened in Somalia probably *did* influence the poor treatment of peacekeepers in other ongoing and future operations. The UN Protection Force (UNPROFOR) in the former Yugoslavia, deployed from 1992 through 1995, was routinely attacked and impeded by Bosnian Serbian and Croatian forces as well as by the government of Croatia. The UNPROFOR force commander declared that UNPROFOR would maintain its neutrality even in the face of this provocation because he did not want to cross the "Mogadishu line" and get the peacekeepers embroiled in the civil war with disastrous consequences.[27] The disastrous consequences would come in Bosnia regardless of the force commander's decisions. Ultimately, the Security Council authorized NATO to protect the UN peacekeepers, so mistreated were they by the combatants. Even in the face of NATO threats, in the spring of 1994 Bosnian Serb forces took peacekeepers hostage, killed a British peacekeeper, and shot down a British Harrier.[28] The knowledge that NATO was committed to the protection of UNPROFOR only made UNPROFOR troops pawns to be played with by the Bosnian Serb forces. Over the next year, a pattern developed "in which the Western alliance threatened but did not straightforwardly respond to Serbian aggression, because they feared all-out war between the 100,000-strong Serbian forces and the significantly outnumbered UN forces."[29]

Lessons from Somalia were no doubt learned by combatants in Rwanda as well. The Rwandan *génocidaires* learned that peacekeepers would have neither the means nor the mandate to respond forcefully even in self-defense and that Western countries would pull out of an operation rather than suffer Black Hawk Down–like fatalities among their troops. The UN Assistance Mission in Rwanda (UNAMIR) was authorized in October 1993 to facilitate peace accords between the largely Hutu government and the largely Tutsi rebel force, the Rwandan Patriotic Front (RPF). The accords were designed to end civil conflict and establish a transitional, integrated government.

From the start, UNAMIR went begging for proper equipment and for a force of sufficient size and training to accomplish its mandate. In addition, almost from the start, the Rwandan factions, especially the Hutu extremists, tested the peacekeepers and learned that UNAMIR was largely impotent. For the Hutu extremists in the government, this meant they could drag their feet rather than fulfill their commitments to the peace process.[30] For the RPF, this caused a loss of confidence in UNAMIR and the United Nations and solidified the RPF's sense that it would need to militarily defeat the Hutu extremists before peace could be achieved in Rwanda.[31] Making matters worse, the Security Council was unusually impatient with the Rwandans. On April 5, 1994, in Resolution 909, the Council commended the parties on maintaining the cease-fire, yet it still threatened that UNAMIR would be withdrawn if "full and prompt" implementation of all the peace accords had not occurred by the end of July.

The next day, April 6, 1994, an airplane carrying the presidents of Rwanda and Burundi was shot down over the Rwandan capital of Kigali. On this pretense, Hutu extremists started killing moderate Hutu politicians and their families and Tutsis. Right away, Belgian peacekeepers were deliberately tortured and killed and their dead bodies mutilated. "Feeding on the earlier reaction in the United States after the deaths of eighteen marines in Somalia, targeting the Belgian contingent was a deliberate and successful tactic to create conditions for a UN withdrawal."[32]

While a complete withdrawal of UNAMIR troops was not ordered, Belgian forces did pull out. More important, the Security Council stayed completely silent on the genocide for its first two weeks. During these first two weeks, Western countries sent rapid reaction forces into Rwanda to extricate their nationals. This rapid military response demonstrated that the Western powers could launch a swift and effective intervention if they chose to do so—but they did not. Once this military extrication was over, the Security Council took up the matter of Rwanda on April 21. In Resolution 912, the Council expressed its shock over the deaths of the presidents of Rwanda and Burundi and the large-scale violence in Rwanda. The Council then demanded the cessation of hostilities between the government and RPF troops in a deliberate misreading of the situation on the ground as a reignited civil war rather than genocide and then *reduced* UNAMIR from a force of 2,500 to 270.[33]

The UN peacekeeping force commander, General Roméo Dallaire, had been begging for months for his operation to be brought up to full strength (it never was). Dallaire had received good intelligence in the first months of 1994 that the Belgian peacekeepers would be targeted at the start of a genocide campaign aimed at eliminating Tutsis and moderate Hutus. Information from Dallaire's informant and from other sources made it clear that the Hutu government was linked to Hutu extremist groups growing and training throughout the country for this genocide. Adding to this impossible situation was this additional element recounted by Dallaire:

> In one of those ironies of life, as of January 1, the Rwandan [Hutu] regime had a seat on the Security Council—the luck of the rotation that saw member nations take up temporary duties on the council alongside the permanent members. As a result, the [extremist Hutu] Rwandans were now privy to many secure documents concerning the mission in their home country.[34]

These secure documents would include Dallaire's informant's report in which the plan for the genocide was set out with what later turned out to be great precision. Dallaire was ordered to inform the Hutu government of what he had learned and to adhere to UNAMIR's traditional peace-keeping mandate. From April to June, approximately 800,000 Rwandans were killed while the Security Council and the broader international community did nothing. The UN peacekeepers were powerless witnesses to this genocide.

In the 1990s alone, the Security Council authorized thirty-four peace-keeping operations (involving both forces and military observer missions), compared to the eighteen operations launched from 1948 to 1988. Not all of these contained the tragic flaws of the most infamous cases (Somalia, Bosnia, and Rwanda), but the sheer number of operations suggests that many force commanders found themselves ordered to conduct complex peace support operations under traditional mandates in active war zones. The mandates would go well beyond the capacities and capabilities of the limited number of underresourced, hands-tied peacekeeping personnel. In the best cases peacekeepers would find themselves unable to fully execute their missions, and in the worst peacekeepers were powerless observers of atrocities. In the process, the reputation of peacekeepers and peacekeeping became badly tarnished.

We might understand peace enforcement to be a remedy of sorts to the problems inherent in peacekeeping's limited rules of engagement and disconnected command and control. At the same time, peace enforcement brought into the open again the political differences among states and between states and the Secretariat on how best to implement Security Council mandates. Tepid commitments to peacekeeping doom them from the start, but even strong commitments to peace enforcement do not necessarily facilitate common purposes and more effective follow-on peacekeeping and peace building. Both peacekeeping and peace enforcement are creative interpretations of the UN Charter that help UN members get around political differences among members, yet both are still hampered by those same political differences. Complex peacekeeping requires more, not less, commitment on the part of member states. Enforcement requires even more commitment and is premised on far greater agreement among states about their primary purpose than should ever be assumed.

Improving UN Peace Operations

The international community was not satisfied with the events of 1990s and the troubled UN response to the post–Cold War disorder. Some members of the international community started asking whether there might be some way to improve the capacity of the United Nations to respond to complex emergencies. A number of studies by international commissions were undertaken at the end of the decade toward the goal of improving the UN-based system of international security. Two of these are of particular note.

One was the International Commission on Intervention and State Sovereignty formed by the Canadian government and acting external to the United Nations. Its focus was on "the question of when, if ever, it is appropriate for states to take coercive—and in particular military—action, against another state for the purpose of protecting people at risk in that other state."[35] The product of this commission, a report titled *The Responsibility to Protect*, attempts to establish the triggers and methods for coercive action aimed at preventing large-scale loss of human life when states are unable or unwilling to do so. *The Responsibility to Protect* is discussed in more detail in chapter 10.

The other commission of note was the Panel on United Nations Peace Operations, a UN-based panel chaired by Lakhdar Brahimi.[36] The 2000 Brahimi Report concluded to no surprise that during the 1990s, the United Nations failed repeatedly to meet the challenge of the UN Charter "to save succeeding generations from the scourge of war."[37] The report offered a succinct summary of why the United Nations failed and what must be done for the United Nations to succeed in the future:

> Without renewed commitment on the part of Member States, significant institutional change and increased financial support, the United Nations will not be capable of executing the critical peacekeeping and peace-building tasks that the Member States assign to it in coming months and years. There are many tasks which United Nations peacekeeping forces should not be asked to undertake and many places they should not go. But when the United Nations does send its forces to uphold the peace, they must be prepared to confront the lingering forces of war and violence, with the ability and determination to defeat them.[38]

Future peacekeeping, the report proposed, should still be based on the "bedrock principles" of impartiality and the use of force in self-defense only, *but* "rules of engagement should be sufficiently robust and not force United Nations contingents to cede the initiative to their attackers":

> This means, in turn, that the Secretariat must not apply best-case planning assumptions to situations where the local actors have historically exhibited worst-case behaviour. It means that mandates should specify an operation's authority to use force. It means bigger forces, better equipped and more costly but able to be a credible deterrent. In particular, United Nations forces for complex operations should be afforded the field intelligence and other capabilities needed to mount an effective defence against violent challengers.[39]

The Brahimi Report suggested that the Secretariat should be better organized to launch traditional peacekeeping operations within thirty days of a Security Council authorization and complex peacekeeping operations within ninety days. Delayed deployments only delayed the restoration of peace. To facilitate this, the Secretariat was encouraged to develop more reliable standby arrangements with members regarding available and prepared troops, military officers, and civilian police with postconflict experience. The Brahimi Report led to a reorganization of the Secretariat's Department of Peacekeeping Operations and to follow-on discussions on rapid reaction deployments and increasing gender awareness in peace operations.[40]

The Brahimi Report did not reinvent the wheel, so to speak. The report urged the United Nations not to abandon the "bedrock" principles of impartiality and limitedness. From the first official peacekeeping operation in 1956, UN operations were not supposed to "influence the military balance in the current conflict, and thereby the political balance affecting efforts to settle the conflict."[41] A corollary to impartiality was that force could be used only for self-defense and in strictly limited ways; intervention that is designed to avoid influencing the political and military balance in a dispute must have a very light footprint on the ground. Impartiality and limited action also guide UN-endorsed peace enforcement missions. Disputants who do not interfere with the objectives of UN-approved enforcement operations do not have force used against them. Enforcement missions can use "all means necessary" to achieve their objective, but when force is used, it should be proportional to the threat and task and therefore limited.

But there are problems created by this insistence on impartial, limited action in UN-commanded or UN-endorsed operations. Acting in strict compliance with this principle, the United Nations has been reluctant "to distinguish victim from aggressor."[42] The Brahimi Report concluded that nothing "did more to damage the standing and credibility of United Nations peacekeeping" than this. For example, during the peacekeeping operation in Cambodia, UN peacekeepers were required to treat the Khmer Rouge with respect and legitimacy equal to that of all other parties to the cease-fire despite the fact that the Khmer Rouge was known to be responsible for killing 1 to 2 million Cambodians in the late 1970s. Then, when the Khmer Rouge refused to disarm as per the cease-fire agreement, the peacekeeping mandate did not allow UN personnel to exact any punishment for noncompliance.

Impartiality in UNTAC was interpreted to mean that all sides were treated as equal partners in the peace process. This impartiality served the political interests of some permanent Security Council members. For very different reasons, both China and the United States had been supportive of the Khmer Rouge because of the Khmer's hostility toward neighboring Vietnam. Neither the United States nor China had much if any argument with the Khmer Rouge over its use of state terror against Cambodians.

Sometimes the requirement of impartiality plays out in the opposite way. When the Security Council finally spoke out about the violence in Rwanda in late April 1994, the Council criticized all Rwandans for restarting their civil war. Rather than officially recognize that Hutu extremists affiliated with the government were conducting a genocide campaign, the Council hid behind impartiality to lament a fictional version of events in Rwanda that labeled all sides equally guilty and equally wrong. This fiction provided a political excuse for the Council's inaction: if the Rwandans at large were not ready for peace, the United Nations could not help them sort out their differences.

This fictional account of what was happening in Rwanda justified impartial *non*intervention and provided political cover for key Council members. Permanent Council member France was a military and political ally of the Rwandan Hutu government, which sat on the Council at this time. France could use its veto power (or threaten to use its veto) to stop any resolution that might have described accurately the realities of what was happening in Rwanda. Almost three months into the genocide, the Council finally did act by approving a French-led and decidedly partial enforcement mission called Operation Turquoise. The Council's formal approval of Turquoise was not crucial since France intended to intervene with or without Council action. The Council described the French intervention as impartial humanitarian assistance to all Rwandans in need. But French goals for the mission appeared to include protecting the former Hutu government and the *génocidaires* from retaliation by the RPF. The French operation protected Hutu extremists *and* their French-supplied military hardware as they beat a fast course for exile in what was then the country of Zaire. The French enforcement action turned out to be at cross-purposes with the existing UN peacekeeping mission, UNAMIR, impeding rather than assisting the UN force.[43] Operation Turquoise guaranteed that justice would be delayed or denied in Rwanda and guaranteed that longer-term peace in the region would be imperiled.

As stated, the UN Security Council is a rigid great power system that reflects the political interests of its permanent members. Impartiality claims in the case of Cambodia and Rwanda allowed permanent Council members to pursue their own political interests. If this seems morally bankrupt or unjust, then it is useful to recall that the present international system is a state-centric system that runs by rules determined by states. States seek to protect and promote their own interests before those of all others, or at least this is the working assumption. Leaders of states *may* be held to certain standards of morality and justice regarding their own citizens, but in state-state relations, moral judgments are disconnected from political judgments, and "justice" is determined by powerful states.

The political choices made in the Cambodian and Rwandan cases contributed to future wars. When the Khmer Rouge did not disarm and the other Cambodian parties followed suit, the stage was set for the war that erupted after the UN peacekeeping mission left Cambodia. When the French protected the Hutu extremists fleeing Rwanda, they ensured that the Hutus would be able to regroup and contribute to future wars in Zaire. Thus, UN "impartial and limited" intervention in these cases served the interests of particular states but not the interests of long-term peace.

This last point is illustrated with some emphasis by the case of the UN Peacekeeping Force in Cyprus (UNFICYP), which was first deployed in 1964 to maintain separation between the Greek and Turkish Cypriot communities after intercommunal violence. As UN peacekeeping goes, UNFICYP was unable to stop the more serious actions by extremist groups on either side. The peacekeeping force was not tasked with facilitating negotiations between the sides; thus, it was not responsible for the total lack of political progress toward long-term reconciliation of the communities. In 1974, a Greek Cypriot junta overthrew a power-sharing government and pledged to seek the unification of Cyprus with Greece. In response, Turkey launched a military intervention to protect Turkish Cypriots. UNFICYP was present during this invasion but possessed neither the mandate nor the forces necessary to stop it. From 1974 through this writing in 2006, UNFICYP troops maintained one side of the green line separating the two communities, while Turkish troops maintained the other side. Arguably, UNFICYP helped provide a sort of peace in Cyprus, but it was a peace based on stalemate, not a peace based on political settlement.

The stalemate in Cyprus protected the interests of certain Security Council permanent members. The Cyprus problem entangled NATO allies Great Britain, Greece, and Turkey from the start. Britain was the former colonial power in Cyprus. By the terms of Cyprus's independence in 1960, Britain, Greece, and Turkey would guarantee its political independence. In addition, Britain would retain possession of two sovereign naval bases on Cyprus, giving Britain and its Western allies a strategic presence in the Middle East. Attempting to resolve the Cyprus problem might have broken apart NATO. Rather than allow this to happen, the United States promoted UN peacekeeping in Cyprus.[44] Forty years after the deployment of UNFICYP, a 2004 UN-brokered reconciliation plan was approved by the Turkish side and rejected by the Greek side, while the two ethnic communities remained separated by UN peacekeepers and Turkish troops.

Should the United Nations have endorsed political stalemate as it effectively did in Cyprus? UN peacekeeping there only seems to have served intransigence and an unwillingness to cooperate by one side or the other. The UN presence may have allowed the two communities to live side by side since 1964, but partition did not serve long-term reconciliation. Further, the peace on Cyprus—or, more accurately, the absence of war—

might be better attributed to the more than 30,000 Turkish troops amassed since 1974 on the northern side of the green line.

We can use elements of the Cyprus case to propose and explore a counterfactual for Rwanda that exposes another problem with impartial intervention. If we return to early 1994, we might imagine that the Security Council received the reports of the UN force commander with growing concern. In response, the Council might have authorized the peacekeepers to use "all means necessary" to stop violations of the cease-fire and to thwart all activities that might lead to future violence. The *génocidaires* might have been detained before they could launch their campaign or just as the campaign commenced and their weapons and other resources confiscated. The UN peacekeeping presence might have been increased to provide a strong stabilizing force, or the peacekeepers might have been given muscular backup by the well-armed and trained Western rapid reaction forces that came into Rwanda to evacuate foreign nationals. The genocide might have been stopped and hundreds of thousands of people saved.

But there is a dilemma in this counterfactual. More effective intervention in Rwanda in early 1994—even as late as the start of April—might have prevented or stopped the genocide, but it also might have prolonged indefinitely the internal conflict over who ruled Rwanda. A more robust UN force might have stopped the violence, but the operation also would have protected all those who cooperated with it. The argument over who ruled Rwanda was ended when the RPF militarily defeated Hutu government forces *after* the primary thrust of the genocide campaign.

Impartial and limited outside intervention may have saved *hundreds of thousands of human beings*, but it likely would only have postponed the internal war. This suggests that impartial limited intervention of the sort used by the United Nations may not serve lasting peace. As Richard Betts explains,

> Limited intervention may end a war if the intervenor takes sides, tilts the local balance of power, and helps one of the rivals to win—that is, if it is not impartial. Impartial intervention may end a war if the outsiders take complete command of the situation, overawe all the local competitors, and impose a peace settlement—that is, if it is not limited. Trying to have it both ways usually blocks peace by doing enough to keep either belligerent from defeating the other, but not enough to make them stop trying.[45]

Thus, even if UN member states were inclined to act in a way that is universally considered moral (in the Rwandan case this means acting to stop genocide), the way in which the UN would intervene would still pose a moral dilemma.

Wars stop when one side defeats the other(s) or when both or all sides accept a negotiated compromise because they can no longer get much leverage from the use of violence. In most cases, UN-based interventions cannot wield the kind of leverage over all the parties to a dispute to impose a lasting solution on the parties.[46] Stalemate might be the best result of the impartial, limited intervention offered by the United Nations.

Is there some other method by which the United Nations might intervene that would stop conflict once and for all? In chapter 6, we considered Edward Luttwak's realist argument that "if the United Nations helped the strong defeat the weak faster and more decisively, it would actually enhance the peacemaking potential of war."[47] Despite the Westphalian foundations of the present international system, this type of "final solution" should be seen as going too far down the road of condoning wholesale slaughter.

Betts suggests an alternative method that would go beyond the model of peace enforcement developed in the 1990s but would not go as far as Luttwak's suggestion. The international community acting through the United Nations or a strong coalition of the willing could impose peace through an intervention based on "an active, harsh impartiality that overwhelms both sides: an imperial impartiality."[48] Betts cautions that the decision to use such overwhelming force must come with a decision about who wins. This decision about who wins should be made before the intervention is launched. For Betts, the existing conflict should serve as a guide: "If claims or capabilities in the local fracas are not clear enough to make this judgment, then they are not clear enough for intervention to bring peace."[49]

With peace on the ground created by the military victory of one side, the military exhaustion of all sides, or "imperial" intervention, follow-on peacekeeping operations could be used to facilitate postwar reconstruction and rebuilding. In the absence of peace on the ground, "paper settlements"[50] imposed from the outside and upheld by impartial peacekeepers do not help and most certainly cause harm to local people and peacekeepers alike. "Imperial" enforcement operations may create peace but only if the international community first makes the hard decision of what the final endpoint should be—who wins, who loses—and then commits to undertaking a militarily rational, "do-able," and no doubt massive intervention. In the next chapter, I examine how such international intervention might be conducted in order to stop the large-scale loss of life when states cannot or will not.

10

Human Security

In the first chapter of this book and again in chapters 4 and 7, we examined the August 2001 crisis involving Afghan refugees rescued from a sinking boat in the international waters between Australia and Indonesia. A Norwegian freighter had rescued the refugees, and the crew wanted to put the refugees ashore on the nearest land, which turned out to be Australian national territory. Citing grave security concerns and wanting to dissuade future undocumented migrants, the Australian government refused to grant permission for the refugees to be landed. Instead, the Australian navy blocked the freighter to ensure that the refugees could not touch Australian soil. After weeks on the Norwegian freighter, most of the refugees were forcibly removed to Australian naval vessels and taken to the island country of Nauru. A smaller number were granted permission to go to New Zealand.

What became of the Afghan boat people? The more than 400 refugees removed from the Norwegian tanker were later joined by other refugees/boat people rescued from still more unseaworthy vessels in international waters. The majority of these people were shipped to detention camps in Nauru while Australia and other countries considered their claims to refugee status. Most of these people were eventually resettled or returned to their home countries, but more than fifty people were still in detention as of April 2005. UN officials urged Australian officials to accept these men, women, and children as refugees and put an end to their hopeless, indefinite confinement. A spokesperson for the UN High Commission for Refugees suggested that Australia had a *responsibility* to find a permanent solution for these refugees.[1]

Also in chapter 1, we examined the violent suicide of Hanadi Jaradat and the murder of Bruriya Zer-Aviv. Zer-Aviv was eating lunch out with her son, daughter-in-law, and grandchildren when an apparently pregnant Jaradat entered the restaurant and detonated an explosive belt.[2] Jaradat killed herself, Bruriya Zer-Aviv, four members of Zer-Aviv's family, and fourteen others that day. Although Hanadi Jaradat was about to become a lawyer, life in her hometown of Jenin in the occupied West Bank offered her no confidence in her future and no expectations that her people would experience a more secure world. Jaradat's overall sense of insecurity was not of her own making, but she was responsible for what she did in response. Zer-Aviv's insecurity also was not of her own making. Both Jardat and Zer-Aviv belonged to political entities (one a nation that wanted the security of statehood, the other a state wanting security) whose actions and reactions combined and interacted to contribute to the insecurities faced by these women. Jaradat's violent response, especially when aggregated to include all suicide bombers and all violent attacks, threatened the security of the state and people of Israel. The response of the state of Israel threatened the Palestinian people, and so the wheel of violence kept turning.

Human insecurity breeds insecurity at multiple levels—for humans, for states, and for the international community. National efforts to secure the state often create insecurities at the international level and of course at the human level. States are necessary to ensure human security and international security, "but the security provided by states has also come at a terrible price."[3] Few might disagree with these statements, but many would disagree about the implications that might be drawn. An old saying goes that violence begets violence, but debates over security still stumble over questions of *who* should be protected from that violence and *how* as well as whether there exists an obligation or responsibility to protect others—states, neighborhoods of states, and regular people—from the harmful externalities of one's own pursuit of security.

I have said that all states seek to protect three core values: population and territory, political independence and autonomy, and economic well-being. Protecting one's population from threat is in one sense protecting a key resource of the state. Without an able-bodied military and workforce, the state would have no way to amass and secure power. In another sense, protecting one's population has come to take on a different meaning: protecting one's population means protecting the source of legitimacy for states that are constituted on popular sovereignty. Moreover, people have come to agree that there are some inalienable human rights—although there is much debate over *what* these rights might be—that must be secured regardless of how well these rights match up with the utilitarian and power goals of states. The devil is in the details, goes another saying, and *states still are in charge of the details.*

Civilians Come Last—The Geneva Conventions

The pursuit of security seems inevitably to lead to descriptions of wars and strategies of violence aimed at protecting states from wars and violence. States, of course, are collections of people, and so this story of violence is also the story of many, many human lives sacrificed for the goal of preserving states. Despite the grasp of the Westphalian ideas on our state system since 1648, there have been arguments all along that the emphasis on states missed the more primary and ethical goal of securing human beings. But because of Westphalia, we know that the state system understands human security primarily as derivative of and instrumental for state security.

There are modern international agreements whose purpose is to protect humans from the excess of states pursuing security through violence. I'll discuss some of these throughout this chapter. Perhaps the most important of these agreements are the Geneva Conventions and their Additional Protocols. The Geneva Conventions were started by the humanitarian work of a single man who wanted to alleviate human suffering caused by war. States agreed to the Geneva Conventions over time because these were for the most part about protecting their soldiers—a key state asset. The conventions on the treatment of civilians would be drafted last since civilians held less importance than soldiers to the "warlord states."[4]

The ideas behind the Geneva Conventions originated in a single bloody battle over Italian unification in June 1859. The Battle of Solferino involved 300,000 French and Austrian troops. Over the course of one day, 6,000 troops were killed and 40,000 wounded. Caring for the wounded was a French medic named Henry Dunant, who took from the ordeal some ideas about alleviating the suffering of soldiers on the battlefield.[5] Dunant and a handful of other men formed the Geneva Public Welfare Society to put his ideas into practice. At the bidding of this society—later to be called the International Committee of the Red Cross—the Swiss government hosted a conference of governments, organizations, and individuals. The First Geneva Convention was adopted in 1864 as a result of this conference.[6]

There are four Geneva Conventions and two Additional Protocols.[7] Their titles are instructive and worth including here:

- First Geneva Convention (adopted in 1864 and last revised in 1949): Convention (I) for the Amelioration of the Condition of the Wounded and Sick in Armed Forces in the Field

- Second Geneva Convention (adopted in 1949 as a successor to a 1907 treaty): Convention (II) for the Amelioration of the Condition of the Wounded, Sick and Shipwrecked Members of Armed Forces of Sea
- Third Geneva Convention (adopted in 1929 and last revised in 1949): Convention (III) relative to the Treatment of Prisoners of War
- Fourth Geneva Convention (adopted in 1949): Convention (IV) relative to the Protection of Civilian Persons in Time of War
- Protocol I (adopted 1977): Protocol Additional to the Geneva Conventions of 12 August 1949, and relating to the Protection of Victims of International Armed Conflicts
- Protocol II (adopted 1977): Protocol Additional to the Geneva Conventions of 12 August 1949, and relating to the Protection of Victims of Non-International Armed Conflicts

The Fourth Geneva Convention and Additional Protocols concern the protection of civilians in armed conflicts. During wartime, individuals are either civilians or combatants. A combatant is a member of the armed forces of a party to a conflict, whether the forces are under the command of a recognized government or not. Combatants have "the right to participate directly in hostilities," according to Protocol I, Article 43, section 2. The category of "special quasi-combatants"—which might include military subcontractors and perhaps even international terrorists—was rejected in the negotiations of Protocol I.[8] Civilians who take "a direct or active role in hostilities" can be subject to attack. This would apply to civilians accompanying or supporting parties to a conflict, such as military subcontractors.[9]

"A civilian is any person who does not belong to any of the following categories: members of the armed forces, militias or volunteer corps, organized resistance movements, and residents of an occupied territory who spontaneously take up arms."[10] Protocol I, Article 50, section 1, states, "In case of doubt whether a person is a civilian, that person shall be considered to be a civilian." Further, "The presence within the civilian population of individuals who do not come within the definition of civilians does not deprive the population of its civilian character" (Protocol I, Art. 50, sec. 3).

Civilians, civilian objects, and civilian livelihoods cannot be subjected to attack by parties to a conflict; only combatants and military property can be subject to attack. Civilians cannot be used as hostages or human shields or receive differential treatment based on race, religion, nationality, or political allegiance. Civilians cannot be subjected to torture, rape, or enslavement; "outrages upon personal dignity"; collective punishment and reprisals; or deportation; or cannot be attacked with biological or chemical weapons.[11]

The idea that a "civilian" deserves special protection in wartime should be obvious enough, especially in an international system that technically forbids the use of war but that essentially allows for any state action aimed at protecting the state. Despite the Geneva Convention definition of a civilian, however, the concept is difficult to grasp in practical terms. Hanadi Jaradat, the Palestinian suicide bomber discussed earlier, lost protected civilian status when she strapped on her explosive belt, if not sooner. Yet the presence and actions of Israeli occupation forces drove her into the role of combatant. In response to Jaradat's suicide bombing, Israeli authorities destroyed her family's home. Unless all the members of her family were combatants and their home was a military installation, the Israeli authorities violated the Geneva Conventions by this act of reprisal. But Israeli authorities might respond that Jaradat's family and all the families of terrorists serve as a support network for terrorism against Israel. To eradicate terrorist threats to the state and people of Israel, Israeli authorities must treat all Palestinians as enemies. Israeli occupation authorities have not hesitated to act preemptively in the name of national security, rounding up all young Palestinians who meet the "terrorist" profile, although this, too, violates the Geneva Conventions. Yet this example and the broader Israeli-Palestinian situation are marked by ambiguity and complexity. As Hugo Slim notes, many people find the idea of protected civilians to be meaningless in militarized societies.[12]

Are there innocent civilians in democracies? One justification for the 9/11 attacks on the World Trade Center (but not the Pentagon, which was a military target) was that there are no innocent civilians in the United States. Because the United States is a democracy, citizens are responsible for the actions of the government. Thus, Americans can be held accountable for the foreign policy actions of their government, particularly those acts that involve doing harm to civilians elsewhere. This idea blurs the distinctions between individual Americans, the U.S. government, and the entire United States. In a similar way, the detaining of all young Palestinian men from targeted neighborhoods or refugee camps because they are potentially terrorists also blurs the distinctions between individual Palestinians and armed groups that use violence in the name of Palestinians and for the cause of Palestinian statehood.

As much as this might offend one's sense of individualism and justice for the individual, this "blurring" of identity is conceptually easy to do in war:

> The blurring is perceived to come from the "civilian" person's moral, political or material relationship with the enemy war effort, whether as munitions worker, food grower, voter, ideological sympathizer or loyal parent of a fighter. In this view, although such enemy individuals may be unarmed, they may still be harmful in other ways. Many people argue that these relationships

blur civilian identity sufficiently to justify attacking them either as legitimate targets in themselves or as a reasonable means to the wider end of destroying the enemy capacity and morale and forcing enemy capitulation.[13]

And, even when civilians can be distinguished from enemies and combatants, "protecting civilians is often neither possible nor desirable in the urgent pursuit of legitimate war aims."[14]

In many cases, civilians and combatants *are* distinguishable from one another, and claims of "military necessity" for harmful acts against civilians cannot be justified. In such cases, what happens? Who holds parties accountable? Would there have been any way to stop the harm to civilians or prevent it in the first place? I will consider these questions in later discussions of the International Criminal Court and the *Responsibility to Protect*. For now, I will stay with the notion that the idea of protecting human beings from the harmful impact of war is an old one that does not stand up well in the face of a system designed to privilege national security. In this state-centric system, human beings are either assets of or liabilities to states, not entities with intrinsic value that must be secured.

The Post–Cold War Human Security Agenda

There is obvious moral value in attempting to protect civilians from the impact of war and violence. But this might not go far enough. The best way to protect civilians in wartime would be to establish a system that privileges the security of all human beings in peace or war. This would require a shift in perspective that emphasizes human security as the primary purpose of states and the international community. The Preamble to the UN Charter as well as documents such as the 1948 Universal Declaration of Human Rights[15] suggest such a shift, although these documents still start with the centuries-old assumption that human security is derivative of national security.

The *Human Development Report 1994* (*HDR 1994*) of the UN Development Program (UNDP) is credited with creating the momentum for post–Cold War discussions designed to shift the emphasis from national security to human security. The *HDR 1994* begins with a simple, evocative statement: "The world can never be at peace unless people have security in their daily lives."[16] The UNDP's mission is to promote sustainable human development, and in 1994 the UNDP boldly linked development with human security. Human development is about the "process of widening the range of people's choices," and human security concerns whether "people can exercise these choices safely and freely" with relative confidence in the future; thus, these are presented as complementary goals.[17] Human development involves what the founders of the United

Nations called the "freedom from want," while human security involves the "freedom from fear."

The political context in which the UNDP reengaged the issue of human security in the 1990s has been discussed at length throughout this book. A few events might be recalled here to understand why the UNDP linked human development with security in 1994. The Cold War had ended five years before the report, and this initiated a period of optimism regarding international cooperation. The 1991 Gulf War and the follow-on humanitarian intervention in northern Iraq demonstrated how force could be used in common purpose and how broad agreement on the management of international conflict could be achieved. Then the United Nations conducted a largely unsuccessful and in some ways disastrous humanitarian intervention in Somalia and dispatched peacekeepers to Bosnia, facilitating the disintegration of Yugoslavia and a larger war. As the *HDR 1994* went to press with its assertion that human development must be linked to human security, the international community had decided to abandon Somalia, was doing little to stop ethnic cleansing in the former Yugoslav republics, and was about to pass on doing anything about genocide in Rwanda.

Stressing points that would remain part of international discussions a decade later, the *HDR 1994* argued that the concept of security needed to be broadened from its previous anchor in state-state conflict. Post–Cold War threats affected rich and poor states differently in the immediate term, but because of global interdependence and interconnections, threats anywhere ultimately were threats everywhere. The UNDP identified seven broad categories of threats to human security: economic, food, health, environmental, personal, community, and political. The UNDP sought to establish clear sets of human security indicators that might serve as an early-warning system for the international community to know when to intervene to help prevent crises. Prevention was critical because, in the UNDP's words, "it is less costly and more humane to meet these threats upstream rather than downstream, early rather than late."[18] Moreover, alarms were going off all over the globe.

The UNDP set forth a comprehensive framework for security but one that was "awkward as a policy framework"[19] in the words of a key human security proponent. Lloyd Axworthy served as Canada's minister of foreign affairs from 1996 to 2000. He was instrumental in establishing Canada's human security foreign policy. Axworthy's view was that the UNDP's broad framework "tended to distract from the central realization that underdevelopment cannot be addressed in the presence of war and its attendant insecurity."[20] Thus, Axworthy proposed that the human security agenda should be focused on personal security from violence as the first and necessary step to achieving broader, longer-term goals.

The first and noteworthy accomplishment of human security advocates was the Ottawa Treaty to ban the use of antipersonnel land mines. The Ottawa Treaty is formally known as the Convention on the Prohibition of the Use, Stockpiling, Production and Transfer of Anti-Personnel Mines and on Their Destruction. The treaty signatories agreed never to use, develop, produce, stockpile, retain, or transfer antipersonnel mines; to destroy all mines held; and to clear all mine areas within their territories within ten years of signing the treaty.[21]

The land-mine ban was initially encouraged by the International Committee of the Red Cross in the 1970s. Later, the issue was taken up by Bobby Muller, the head of the Vietnam Veterans of America, and U.S. Senator Patrick Leahy (D-Vt.). Ultimately, an organized, coherent International Campaign to Ban Landmines (ICBL) resulted from the efforts of nongovernmental organizations (NGOs), some governments, and what Axworthy called "citizen-diplomats."[22] As Canadian foreign minister, Axworthy pushed the campaign onto a fast track: only a little over a year passed from the day Axworthy called on the international community to devise a land-mine ban and the signing of the treaty in Ottawa in December 1997.[23] Within fifteen months, the treaty entered into force. By April 2006, 151 states had ratified or acceded to the treaty and three states had signed but not yet ratified it. Forty countries did not sign the treaty. The ICBL remained an international force in 2006 with 1,400 NGOs working in ninety countries in support of the treaty's mandate and the ultimate goal of a global land-mine ban.

Mark Gwozdecky and Jill Sinclair conclude that "the ban was possible because its proponents were able to superimpose a human security framework over what had traditionally been treated as an arms control and disarmament issue."[24] This might have been facilitated by widespread acknowledgment of the devastating human toll of land mines, which in the aggregate was economically disastrous to countries attempting to rebuild after conflict. On the individual level, land mines are indiscriminate—they kill or injure whoever (soldiers, children, farmers, peacekeepers) or whatever (livestock, wild animals) triggers their detonating mechanism. Land mines are more likely to injure rather than kill, but the injuries are devastating. Victims often require amputations (and an amputation rarely consists of just one surgical procedure), hospitalizations, and long-term rehabilitation. Land-mine injuries may compromise victims socially—rendering amputees unmarriageable, for instance—and economically for the rest of their lives. In the aggregate, the costs of medical care for so many victims and the loss of the income they would have generated are staggering for countries. Moreover, the presence or the fear of the presence of mines makes large tracts of land and miles of roads unusable for people and their countries. Thus, the campaign to ban land mines found an issue with resonance for citizens and countries alike, success-fully linking human and national security concerns.

But the land-mine issue did not and does not have the same impact on all states. It is useful here to recall why states seeking their own national security would bind themselves to international security arrangements or in this case to a human security cause. The answer turns on the difficulty of unilaterally securing one's state. The nature of security threats in a globalized world makes unilateralism a difficult choice (although not an impossible choice). Self-interest and self-protection therefore prompt international cooperation. However, the land-mine issue is very much ter-ritory bound rather than without boundaries and one that overwhelms the abilities of the impacted states much more than other states. To put forward the fact that some eighty states continue to suffer the impact of land mines is also to suggest that a slight majority of the world's states *do not.* The land-mine ban campaign was successful not only because it linked national and human security concerns but also because it managed to bind states that do not suffer from land mines with those that do in a united front against these weapons. The treaty, then, was a momentous achievement for human security advocates.

Not all states are members of the Ottawa Treaty, of course. Some of the countries that did join—states with no land-mine problems on their own territory—were initially opposed to it. Great Britain and France eventu-ally were pressured or shamed into joining the treaty by domestic con-stituents represented by NGOs.[25] British participation in the treaty came at cross-purposes with some British companies that were manufacturers of antipersonnel mines. But critical civil society groups—who were joined in their mission by Diana, Princess of Wales—were more motivated than status quo business interests to influence official British policy, and the British government finally agreed to join the treaty process.

The U.S. Clinton administration had supported the ban when it was being negotiated under the auspices of the UN Convention on Certain Conventional Weapons (CCW), which dealt in part with mines. The CCW process was deliberately slow, narrow, and limited, perhaps because it was dominated by military negotiators representing state interests. Then "a series of backroom meetings between NGOs and government officials aimed at widening and strengthening the ban took place."[26] Such meet-ings between NGOs and state officials are known as track 2 diplomacy. The track 2 efforts resulted in the moving of the land-mine negotiations outside the CCW framework and into an ad hoc and more creative frame-work supported by the Canadian government. The United States did not want to lose control of the negotiations and so opposed this move. Yet the negotiations did move, so the United States stopped participating in them until the final stages.[27] When the United States came back to the table, it

wanted the treaty to permit the use of "smart" land mines, allow the continued use of land mines in Korea, allow a nine-year delay for countries
to meet their treaty obligations, and allow an opt-out clause for countries
to withdraw from the treaty on short notice.[28] The U.S. demands fit a narrow, military-framed definition of the land-mine problem. The United
States did drop some of its demands, but ultimately it had little impact on
the final document.

Under the Bush administration, the U.S. position on land mines became
less friendly to the purposes of the treaty. The Clinton administration had
pledged to stop all use of land mines by 2006, although it would not sign
the Ottawa Treaty. In March 2004, the Bush administration revoked this
pledge, reserving the right to use land mines where it deemed necessary.
The United States was said to possess the third-largest stockpile of land
mines in the world (11.2 million) after China and Russia, which also
refused to sign the treaty.[29] Despite not signing the treaty, the United
States became "one of the main financial contributors to the global campaign"[30] leading the way in researching better de-mining technologies.

Most of the other nonsignatories are countries with "issues," we might
say. Chechnya in Russia, according to the ICBL, is one of the most heavily mined places on earth. Nuclear rivals and old foes Pakistan and India
have not signed the treaty, nor have North and South Korea. Both sets of
countries have deployed mines along their disputed borders. And, finally,
the Middle East is a region in which the ban has been rejected by all but
one country (Jordan). The nonsignatories in the Middle East are Bahrain,
Egypt, Iran, Iraq (pre- and postinvasion), Israel, Kuwait, Lebanon, Saudi
Arabia, Syria, and the United Arab Emirates. Nearby Libya also has not
signed the treaty.

The land-mine ban was a significant event—significant in terms of who
backed it, who was allowed to "sit at the table" during the negotiations,
and what it accomplished. For the countries that signed and ratified it, the
treaty merged national and human security agendas into a convincing
whole. But the countries that did not sign on to it include three of the permanent Security Council members and important holdouts in some of the
most dangerous neighborhoods in the world. National security and interstate competition issues remained paramount.

The same three Security Council permanent members that refused to
joint the land-mine ban treaty also refused to participate in another
important human security accomplishment—the International Criminal
Court (ICC).[31] The ICC came into being in July 2002 on the ratification of
the Rome Statute[32] by sixty countries. By mid-2006, 139 countries had
signed the Rome Statute, and one hundred countries had ratified it.[33]
Nongovernmental organizations, including again the International Committee of the Red Cross, were critical to building the ICC coalition.[34]

The ICC has jurisdiction over crimes of genocide, crimes against humanity, and war crimes (as enumerated in the Geneva Conventions). The Rome Statute also included the "crime of aggression" in ICC jurisdiction, but the court came into being without agreement on the definition of "aggression." In the earliest negotiations over the Rome Statute, the United States had pushed for the ICC to have jurisdiction over persons involved in drug trafficking and terrorism, although the U.S. position on this changed before the final treaty was approved.[35]

The primary purpose of the ICC was to hold heads of state accountable for the planning, instigating, ordering, or otherwise aiding and abetting of the execution of the covered crimes.[36] Previously, "violence carried out in the name of the state was shielded from accountability by the fiction of corporate responsibility."[37] National leaders could commit acts of mass violence with impunity behind the shield of *raison d'état*. A fully functional ICC would represent "a powerful change in the rules of state sovereignty because [the court's establishment] creates a supranational authority with the power to rule whether or not particular uses of force by state officials are criminal and sanctionable violations of international law."[38]

There are some important limitations on the ICC, limitations that reflected "power politics" among the state representatives who negotiated the Rome Statute.[39] First, although the ICC is said to be "complementary" to national criminal courts, in practical terms national prosecution bars ICC action. Second, the court has jurisdiction only over states party to the Rome Statute or over states that choose to allow ICC jurisdiction in particular cases. Third, the Security Council retains control over the ICC by holding the power to enact renewable suspensions of ICC investigations and prosecutions.[40] Further, Article 98 of the Rome Statute forbids the court to request the surrender of a foreign national for prosecution when the requested state has a treaty obligation with the government of the foreign national that bars surrender of its citizens and personnel.

The power of the Security Council permanent members over the ICC was demonstrated as it came into existence in the summer of 2002. The United States was an early supporter of a standing international criminal court,[41] but by the time the Rome Statute was signed, American support had been withdrawn. The U.S. Clinton administration signed the Rome Statute without intending to ask for its ratification; the U.S. Bush administration went further and "unsigned" the Rome Statute. The U.S. position was that the ICC would be used for frivolous and politically motivated prosecutions. As the court came into existence on July 1, 2002, the Bush administration linked it to a veto threat regarding the unrelated matter of renewing the mandate for UN peacekeeping in Bosnia. The United States insisted that the Security Council bar the ICC from investigating and prosecuting any "current or former officials or personnel from a contributing State not a Party to the Rome Statute over acts or omissions relating to a United Nations established or authorized operation." The Security Council approved such a limitation on the ICC for a year in Resolution 1422 (July 12, 2002), and indicated its intention to renew the suspension each July for another twelve months. The suspension was renewed the following year in Resolution 1487 (June 12, 2003). Another suspension was not taken up by the Council in 2004, but by this time the U.S.-led war in Iraq was in its second year, and few Americans were involved in UN-led or UN-endorsed peacekeeping operations anywhere. Further, the Bush administration, backed by a 2002 law, had been busy coercing other states into Article 98 agreements on the threat of being cut off from military and financial assistance.[42]

Like the United States, Russia signed the Rome Statute but had not ratified it by 2006. China never signed the statute in the first place. Among the ranks of states without the veto on the Security Council, important UN contributors India and Japan did not sign the statute. Israel, a country that figured into an example explored earlier in this chapter, signed the Rome Statute but never ratified it.

The land-mine ban was considered the first major accomplishment of the human security agenda and the ICC a second. The lack of other major successes aimed at preventing and stopping harm to human beings might be explained in part by the lack of convergence between other so-called human security agenda items and national security issues in a way that provokes an "internationalization of conscience."[43] Drug trafficking, human trafficking, organized crime, the use of child soldiers, the trade in small arms, and other items on the human security agenda have provoked as yet uneven concern around the globe. The key to provoking such an internationalization of conscience seems to be a successful "coalition of the willing" between a large number of multilaterally minded states and powerful NGOs.[44] In both the land-mine ban campaign and the ICC, NGOs were critical in shaping the agenda for international discussion, helping to educate states on how their security needs were tied into the problems at hand, and shaming states into ratifying the treaties.[45]

One self-limiting aspect of the human security campaign is that some of its proponents still attempt to cast a very wide net. Consider the report of the Independent Commission on Human Security, *Human Security Now*. This commission was founded at the initiative of the government of Japan, a state, that is, like Canada, devoted to a human security foreign policy. In 2003, the commission released *Human Security Now*, a far-reaching human security agenda that sought to "protect the vital core of all human lives in ways that enhance human freedoms and human fulfilment."[46] The issues at the "vital core of all human lives" include violent conflict, extreme impoverishment, pollution, ill health, illiteracy and "other maladies," and "catastrophic accident and illness."[47] The commission offered this intentionally broad list in order to distinguish human security from narrowly conceived national security.

Yet, to borrow an idea from Axworthy, the Commission on Human Security's agenda would be an awkward policy framework. If states cannot agree about which party to a conflict constitutes the aggressor or cannot agree that they have an obligation to stop genocide from occurring, how will they agree on what enhances human fulfillment? Without any agreement on the nature of the problem (a land-mine ban is easier to frame and promote than is "ill health"), how will states, citizen-diplomats, and NGOs ever begin to forge a common cause that successfully blends human problems with state interests? The land-mine ban campaign demonstrates that the human security agenda is promoted best when it is *linked to* rather than distinguished from national security. The proponents of a responsibility to protect seemed to have understood this important linkage between human and national security, as I discuss next.

Protecting People from Large-Scale Violence

To the extent that any agreement emerged on the issue of international security after the turbulent 1990s, the agreement was that the international community was ill prepared to deal realistically and effectively with massive human disasters. In so many cases in the 1990s, states seemed unable or unwilling to stop violence being done to their own people, and often states were the perpetrators of the abuse. And the community of states seemed unwilling at some times and unable at others to mount effective international humanitarian interventions.

As earlier chapters in this book attest, critical obstacles need to be overcome. Even if there were some agreement that human beings should be protected from large-scale violence, states would need to be pushed out of their unwillingness to act, budged out of their absolute insistence on respecting the principle of nonintervention in the affairs of sovereign states, and presented with an effective and practical strategy for intervention that would avoid selective application. The history of the state system does not offer much hope here.

Continuing its human security focus, the government of Canada— again under the leadership of Lloyd Axworthy—sponsored yet another ambitious international effort "to find tactics and strategies of military intervention that [could] fill the current gulf between outdated concepts of peacekeeping and full-scale military operations that may have deleterious impacts on civilians."[48] The effort became the independent

International Commission on Intervention and State Sovereignty (ICISS). The "policy challenge" before the ICISS was summed up in this way:

> External military intervention for human protection purposes has been controversial both when it has happened—as in Somalia, Bosnia and Kosovo—and when it has failed to happen, as in Rwanda. For some the new activism has been a long overdue internationalization of the human conscience; for others it has been an alarming breach of an international state order dependent on the sovereignty of states and the inviolability of their territory. For some, again, the only real issue is ensuring that coercive interventions are effective; for others, questions about legality, process and the possible misuse of precedent loom much larger.[49]

Before the commission finished its report, the 9/11 terrorist attacks on the United States occurred. Responding to this event, the commission noted that "human security is indeed indivisible"—both in the sense that human insecurity anywhere was a threat to human security everywhere *and* in the sense that human insecurity in a "faraway country" could facilitate a successful attack on the national security of the world's most powerful state. The events of 9/11 demonstrated that "in an interdependent world, in which security depends on a framework of stable sovereign entities, the existence of fragile states, failing states, states who through weakness or ill-will harbour those dangerous to others, or states that can only maintain internal order by means of gross human rights violations, can constitute a risk to people everywhere."[50]

The ICISS proposed that sovereignty as it developed and was understood over time entails more than absolute rights; it also entails two levels of responsibilities. "The primary responsibility for the protection of its people lies with the state itself." But "where a population is suffering serious harm, as a result of internal war, insurgency, repression or state failure, and the state in question is unwilling or unable to halt or avert it, the principle of non-intervention yields to the international responsibility to protect."[51]

How did the ICISS arrive at this responsibility to protect? Sovereignty, as understood since the Treaty of Westphalia, is located in the state rather than in any extraregional authority. In democratic systems, sovereignty resides in the people—popular sovereignty—and the state is granted only that authority necessary to protect the interests of the people—the sovereigns. When a state fails to protect the sovereigns, the state loses its legitimacy. Dislodging that illegitimate government would fall to the people acting alone in the absence of an international community. But states exist in international system. Because the international system is organized to protect the interests of sovereign states, the system also must protect the *source* of the legitimacy of those states—the people. When large-scale loss of life or ethnic cleansing occurs or is likely to occur in the immediate term, someone must protect the sovereigns. If the state cannot or will not, the community must step up to the task.

This may sound like a monumental shift of authority or a monumental interruption or suspension of state authority, but the ICISS made great efforts to indicate that state sovereignty was still critical and that the first line of defense for human protection remained the state. The ICISS also made it clear that the responsibility to protect required more than military intervention. The responsibility was envisioned in three parts: a responsibility to prevent crises, a responsibility to react in "situations of compelling human need with appropriate measures," and a responsibility to rebuild.[52]

[Military intervention, if it occurred, should be guided by "just war" principles.] First, the intervention must be for the right purpose—to prevent large-scale loss of life and/or genocide—which would be ensured by its multilateral nature. The appropriate authority for determining right purpose was the Security Council, then the General Assembly, then regional organizations, and then, only if all else fails, individual states.[53] The Security Council would authorize such an intervention as a Chapter VII civilian protection mandate. Interventions aimed at stopping systematic political repression, racial discrimination and similar human rights abuses,[54] thwarting a military coup (even a coup against a democratic government),[55] regime change,[56] or "in response to a terrorist attack on a state's territory and citizens"[57] were *not* envisioned under this proposal. The UN Charter already provided methods for dealing with these problems.

Further, military intervention would be an act of last resort unless impending large-scale loss of life or genocide required immediate reaction. When it occurred, military intervention would employ proportional force rather than engage in tactics that amount to traditional war fighting (that is, the objective is to save lives, not defeat or destroy an enemy).[58] The intervention force would be given appropriate rules of engagement and plentiful resources to complete the task at hand. Additionally, the mission must have a reasonable prospect for military success and not create greater human insecurity than it seeks to stop. In the words of the ICISS, "It will be the case that some human beings simply cannot be rescued except at unacceptable cost—perhaps of a larger regional conflagration involving major military powers. In such cases, however painful the reality, coercive military action is no longer justified."[59] Because of this, military intervention against any of the permanent members of the Security Council or the other major powers was not envisioned on utilitarian grounds; the prospects for success against a major power would be small to none, and the chances of a greater war would be far too large. Despite the appearance of double standards, political reality and feasibility should govern the responsibility to protect in order to avoid promising more than can or will be delivered to a population in distress. Finally, the inability to mount an intervention in one case should not preclude intervention in any other case.[60]

The *Responsibility to Protect* was designed to offer a practical and effective method for determining when and how the United Nations should intervene to protect human beings. The effort made by the ICISS to respect the political realities of the international system—that is, to accommodate states and their interests—while still promoting human security was admirable. In this respect, the effort approximated the campaign to ban land mines. Unfortunately, the idea that there is a *responsibility* to prevent, react, and rebuild still fails today in the face of many states' unwillingness to accept international responsibilities. The idea has not yet been supported by any sort of international campaign to win the hearts and minds of citizen-diplomats, NGOs, and states outside the UN framework. If such a campaign were mounted, it would have to leap the huge obstacles presented by the Bush doctrine, other states' unilateralist claims, the war on terror (as defined in ways that serve different states' interests), and two major international wars launched since 2001.

The invasion of Iraq in March 2003 by a coalition led and dominated by the United States created discord within the UN Security Council and among UN member states. The Bush administration argued after the invasion that the intervention was required to stop massive human rights abuses. The administration claimed that it acted to uphold the principles of the United Nations when other states were not inclined to do so. These assertions might have fit into a *Responsibility to Protect* framework—as long as the *Responsibility* was not examined too closely.

The secretary-general of the United Nations opposed the U.S.-led war in Iraq. In a speech opening the September 2004 General Assembly session and again in a contemporaneous interview with the BBC, Kofi Annan declared the U.S. invasion of Iraq "illegal" because it had proceeded without Security Council authorization.[61] "Those who seek to bestow legitimacy must themselves embody it, and those who would invoke international law must themselves submit to it," Annan told the General Assembly.[62] Members of the U.S. president's party in Congress called for Annan's ouster in protest. Meanwhile, Annan assembled the High-level Panel on Threats, Challenges and Change to consider the war, terrorism, and other security issues confronting the United Nations. The panel's report, *A More Secure World: Our Shared Responsibility*, was issued in December 2004.[63] It embraced the *Responsibility to Protect* and attempted to refocus collective security on issues of human security and on the borderless security threats challenging all states. It also repudiated Bush administration justifications for the war in Iraq.

The high-level panel affirmed the ICISS emphasis on prevention, intervention, and rebuilding as keys to a more secure world. The panel also reached back to the *Human Development Report 1994* in its assertion that six broad clusters of threats existed in the world: (1) economic and social threats, including poverty, infectious disease, and environmental degradation; (2) interstate conflict; (3) internal conflict, including civil war, genocide, and other large-scale atrocities; (4) nuclear, radiological, chemical, and biological weapons; (5) terrorism; and (6) transnational organized crime.[64]

The report did more than try to breathe new life into the human security ethic; it also rejected the practicality of unilateralism in defense of state security. The panel reaffirmed the primacy of sovereign states but argued that in the twenty-first century "no State can stand wholly alone." What was needed was recognition that collective security—the protection of sovereign states—required a new consensus on rights and responsibilities. The panel proffered that collective security in the new century rested on three "pillars":

> Today's threats recognize no national boundaries, are connected, and must be addressed at the global and regional as well as the national levels. No State, no matter how powerful, can by its own efforts alone make itself invulnerable to today's threats. And it cannot be assumed that every State will always be able, or willing, to meet its responsibility to protect its own people and not to harm its neighbors.[65]

The panel included, among other international dignitaries, a cochair of the ICISS and a cochair of the Human Security Commission—these suggested the intellectual lineage of the report—and the former national security adviser to the first President Bush, Brent Scowcroft, who had opposed publicly the U.S. invasion of Iraq by the second President Bush.

Reality Check

In March 2005, the UN secretary-general issued a report titled *In Larger Freedom: Towards Development, Security and Human Rights for All.*[66] This report was devoted primarily to suggesting measures that the UN member states should take to reduce extreme poverty or the "freedom from want." Attention was paid as well to the "freedom from fear" or issues of collective security, the "freedom to live in dignity" concerning human rights, the rule of law and democracy, and UN reform, including democratizing the Security Council, reconstituting and empowering the UN Human Rights Commission, and strengthening the capacity of the United Nations for postconflict peace building. The title of the report, *In Larger Freedom*, derives from a line in the Preamble to the UN Charter that reads in part that the purpose of the United Nations is "to promote social progress and better standards of life in larger freedom."

This report formed the agenda for discussions at a World Summit held in the days before the opening of the sixtieth UN General Assembly session. When the General Assembly opens its new session each year in September, every head of state has the opportunity to address the gathered member states. Prior to the September 2005 opening of the General Assembly session, a World Summit of national leaders was held to consider Annan's *In Larger Freedom* and perhaps celebrate the sixtieth anniversary of the United Nations by agreeing to its wide-reaching goals and reforms.

The Outcome Document approved by the World Summit was a reality check. It contained few initiatives, goals, or reforms. Security Council expansion and reform were not mentioned, and other structural reforms were ignored or watered down. Aid, trade, and debt issues were left without substance or commitment, and matters of weapons proliferation and disarmament were dropped.[67] Why was there no progress on any front? Perhaps the Australian prime minister spoke for other national leaders when he told reporters, "I am a believer in global institutions and their relevance but I am not somebody who thinks the fate of the world should be placed in them. . . . There are still many things that can only be done by nation states."[68]

As if to confirm this last statement, the Outcome Document rejected the idea that a new collective security ethic required a sense of shared international responsibility to meet the threats of the twenty-first century because "no State can stand wholly alone."[69] The document asserted instead that "no State can best protect itself by acting entirely alone,"[70] a qualification reassuring to those states inclined to unilateralism or to acting in non–UN-approved coalitions of the willing.

The words "responsibility to protect" were included in the Outcome Document but not in association with an expectation about state responsibility that is backed by an international responsibility to prevent, react, and rebuild. The document instead declared that "each individual State has the responsibility to protect its populations from genocide, war crimes, ethnic cleansing and crimes against humanity," but the international community had a limited role to play in this, encouraging and helping states "as appropriate" using "appropriate diplomatic, humanitarian and other peaceful means" in accordance with the UN Charter. Collective action through Chapter VII should be taken in a "timely and decisive manner" on a case-by-case basis.[71] Nowhere did the document endorse the idea that Chapter VII allowed for civilian protection mandates.

Finally, the concept of human security appeared in the Outcome Document in a single stand-alone paragraph. In that paragraph, the summit acknowledged that "all individuals, in particular vulnerable people, are entitled to freedom from fear and freedom from want."[72] Then the document suggested that the General Assembly discuss and define human security at some unspecified point in the future. Since the General Assembly lacks enforcement authority, one might conclude that this was designed to put human security into a lesser, secondary category to the collective (which is to say state) security work of the Security Council. The Outcome Document served only to reaffirm the state-first status quo.

To some supporters of a human security ethic, the World Summit might be seen less as a failure than superfluous. According to a 2005 report by the Human Security Centre, the world has become *less* violent since the end of the Cold War, and the "single best explanation" for this has been the "surge of international activism" through the United Nations that started in the 1990s.[73] The Human Security Centre is a research institute based at the University of British Columbia in Canada and funded by the governments of Canada, the United Kingdom, Norway, Sweden, and Switzerland and by the Rockefeller Foundation. Its mission is to disseminate human security research to multiple communities. The *Human Security Report 2005* was released in the summer of 2005 with good and counterintuitive news. Looking at both more established and newer data sets on human security, the center reported stunning findings. First, since the early 1990s and continuing through 2005, the number of civil wars fell dramatically. Second, the numbers of genocides and mass killings also declined in the same period. Third, international or interstate wars had become less frequent.

The report was focused primarily on conflict involving at least one state/government as a primary actor/disputant. Such conflicts have decreased, according to the report, because of three factors: the end of the colonial period and wars for liberation, the end of the Cold War and related proxy wars or local wars inflamed by Cold War politics, and the "international activism" that began at the end of the Cold War.[74] The evidence in favor of the first two factors is presented in the report and makes sense even with a superficial reading of world history since World War II (the beginning of the end for colonialism). The evidence in support of the third factor—international activism—is missing from the report.

According to the Human Security Centre, the international activism begun in the 1990s resulted from the end of Cold War restraints, growing economic interdependencies and international institutions, and a strong aversion to war shared by more and more people of the world. Writing in 2005, the center claimed that "ideologies that glorify violence and war as a noble and virtuous endeavor are today notable mostly by their absence."[75] These factors—but especially global aversion to war—created a common purpose among states to create lasting peace. This common purpose was manifested in the dramatic increase in UN peacemaking activities since 1989. Thus, UN preventive diplomacy activities increased from one mission in 1990 to six in 2002. Peacekeeping doubled from 1988 through 2004, and peacekeeping mandates were given more punch because the Security Council increasingly was willing to authorize the use of force. The Security Council was more willing to use sanctions to stop conflict, and an assault was launched on the "culture of impunity" by the start of several war crimes tribunals.[76] The center offered these (modest) increases as proof of impact.

The readers of this book might be inclined to respond that an increase in the number of peace missions in the post–Cold War period did not translate into *effective* peace missions. More missions resulted in more broken promises made to peoples in distress. Authorizing peacekeepers to use more liberal rules of engagement did not mean that they were given the requisite resources, personnel, and training. More blanket sanctions generally did more harm than good for the people trapped in a conflict zone, and war crimes tribunals suffered from a lack of resources, states' unwillingness to make arrests, overloaded dockets, and so on. The rhetoric and actions of the Bush administration's war on terror as well as the rhetoric and actions of terrorist groups suggested that "ideologies that glorify violence and war" were not so absent after all.

The optimism embodied in the *Human Security Report 2005* is not warranted by the data the center provided. Increased international activity, as we have seen, did not do more good than harm in the 1990s and through to 2006. The international community stood down in the face of genocides in Rwanda, Bosnia, and Darfur. Some of the UN peace operations in the 1990s ended not because the local conflicts themselves ended but because the international community had had enough. For example, the UN operations in Somalia ended because the United States had suffered casualties. Stop-and-go UN operations in Haiti have had little impact on the continued insecurity there.

There are even more problems for those who would celebrate the counterintuitive findings of the *Human Security Report 2005*. If the presence of UN missions equates to positive movement toward peace and the settlement of conflicts, how would one explain the fact that so many ongoing UN peacekeeping and UN-approved peace enforcement operations are in states that appear on the verge of failure in 2006? In 2005 and again in 2006, the Fund for Peace and *Foreign Policy* magazine constructed a failed states index using twelve social, economic, political, and military indicators. These indicators taken together were used as a measure of a state's "vulnerability to internal conflict"[77] and potential collapse. This vulnerability could be manifested in the inability of a state to "make collective decisions," deliver public services, or enforce tax laws as well as in the loss of government control of some of its territory to competing armed authorities.[78]

Using this index, the Fund for Peace concluded that *2 billion* people lived in insecure states in 2005 and 2006. Six of the top ten and eight of the top twenty countries on the failed states index for 2006 had current UN

Table 10.1 Failing States and the International Response, 2006

Country	Rank Failed States Index*	Current UN Peace Operation**	Current Non-UN Military Presence	UN or Non-UN Peace Operation in 1990s
Sudan	1	Yes	Yes	No
Democratic Republic of the Congo	2	Yes	No	No
Côte d'Ivoire	3	Yes	Yes	No
Iraq	4	No	Yes	No
Zimbabwe	5	No	No	No
Chad	6	No	No	No
Somalia	6	No	No	Yes
Haiti	8	Yes	No	Yes
Pakistan	9	No	No	No
Afghanistan	10	No	Yes	No
Guinea	11	No	No	No
Liberia	11	Yes	No	Yes
Central African Republic	13	No	No	Yes
North Korea	14	No	No	No
Burundi	15	Yes	No	No
Sierra Leone	16	No	No	Yes
Yemen	16	No	No	No
Burma	18	No	No	No
Bangladesh	19	No	No	No
Nepal	20	No	No	No

* *Source:* "The Failed States Index," *Foreign Policy*, May–June 2006, 53.
** Conducted by the UN Department of Peacekeeping Operations.

peacekeeping or enforcement operations and/or current UN-approved, non-UN military interventions. Five of the top twenty failing states— Somalia, Haiti, Liberia, the Central African Republic, and Sierra Leone— also had UN interventions in the 1990s. For a complete list of the top twenty states on the *Foreign Policy* list, see table 10.1.

The top twenty states on the failed states index were considered "critical" in terms of the likelihood of state collapse. Foreign military presence had had no apparent positive impact on the problems that combined to make these states in danger of failing. Included in these were Iraq (no. 4) and Afghanistan (no. 10), states with significant U.S. military occupation forces. Finally, eleven of the top twenty critical countries had no UN or UN-approved peace operations in 2006, and *none was being contemplated*.

Efforts to promote a state and international responsibility to protect people from large-scale violence have not yet made headway in this state-dominated world. This is not to suggest that human security efforts cannot in the future make a real improvement in the lives of human beings, but the window of opportunity that might have opened with the end of the Cold War did not stay open for long. Perhaps another window will open again sometime and national leaders, international organizations, NGOs, and citizen-diplomats will move toward it with deliberate speed. Perhaps, too, this speed will be informed by the lessons of what has and has not been accomplished in terms of making this a safer, more secure world for individuals, states, and the global community.

Conclusion

Reimagining Our Choices

State security has been the primary focus of security discussions and policies for centuries. Yet this state-first focus and its attendant dynamics do not secure individual states, much less secure the community of states or human beings. There is no such thing as state security in this state-first world, much less international and human security, only more or less tolerable and more or less intolerable degrees of insecurity. State-first security is both elusive and illusive.

This situation in which states continually pursue insecurity comes to absurdity in the twentieth-century creation and deployment of nuclear weapons. "Stable" or "mature" nuclear deterrence is achieved between two rivals when both acknowledge that they cannot protect their people from the nuclear threat levied by the other. Some analysts see this as a desirable end point. Extended globally, a world of nuclear armed states would be stable and mature because every state can play the role of the grim reaper for itself and every other state, and with this knowledge each state holds back. But this reasoning is difficult to accept; why would states go to great lengths to achieve such weapons and then never use them? Why even start down that path in the first place?

Further, the state-first logic tells us that states *will not* be content with *any* given weapons capability. Consider this: Keir Lieber and Daryl Press conclude that the American nuclear arsenal had become so enhanced by an accuracy revolution and the next-nearest competitor's arsenal (Russia) so degraded that the era of mutual assured destruction likely was over by

2006.[1] Lieber and Press ran a computer model "of a hypothetical U.S. attack on Russia's nuclear arsenal using the standard unclassified formulas that defense analysts have used for decades." Their model showed that "a simplified surprise attack would have a good chance of destroying every Russian bomber base, submarine, and ICBM."[2] America's nuclear primacy will, of course, threaten others, causing them to attempt to bandage their hemorrhaging national security positions. This, in turn, increases the likelihood of preemptive attacks by potential rivals, a likelihood the United States must be prepared to *pre*-preempt.[3] And so it goes.

All the more terrible, the logic of state-first security requires *more* than the acquisition of destructive power. As the realists tell us, threats must be backed with capability *and* credibility; thus, states *must use their power* from time to time to demonstrate that they will carry through with their threats. As Thomas Schelling explains, "It is the expectation of *more* violence that gets the wanted behavior, if the power to hurt can get it at all."[4]

Jonathan Schell offers an eloquent summary of what has obtained from this self-defeating drive to secure the state:

> The terrible violence of the twentieth century . . . holds a lesson for the twenty-first. It is that in a steadily and irreversibly widening sphere, violence, always a mark of human failure and a bringer of sorrow, has now also become dysfunctional as a political instrument. Increasingly it destroys the ends for which it is employed, killing the user as well as his victim. It has become the path to hell on earth and the end of the earth. This is the lesson of the Somme and Verdun, of Auschwitz and Bergen-Belsen, of Vorkuta and Kolyma; and it is the lesson, beyond a shadow of a doubt, of Hiroshima and Nagasaki.[5]

A state-first security focus remains trapped in the security dilemma. To defenders of the current system, this is the inevitable albeit unfortunate result of the reality of international anarchy and the nonstop competition between self-interested actors. But *what* about this system is inevitable? Is international anarchy reality, or is it the way people have come to imagine the international system? Are states the "natural" unit of analysis and naturally privileged over others or just a human construction? Are there better ways to organize ourselves locally and globally in order to imagine—or reimagine—our future on earth?

This situation is not working. The pursuit of national security brings no national security; the pursuit of international security based on a state-centric ethic also brings no security. Human security, as we have seen, is the afterthought in all of this even though most everyday people would agree that human beings should be the natural starting point in any security discussion. To achieve real security and to put the focus on human beings, we must reimagine politics.

Practically speaking, we cannot "destate" the world; we must work with what is and be more realistic about how the present reality provides little security to states and people. History offers alternatives to the state system—empires, caliphates, and other supranational authorities have operated previously. These historical alternatives would not be able to address the problems, threats, and challenges contained in the present globalized era. Indeed, the state was preferable to the empires of the past in terms of its ability to respond to local interests, needs, and desires. The birth of the modern state in the mid-seventeenth century was part of a process of human advancement. A hundred years or so later, further human advancement in the form of democratic rule and citizenship rights would occur.

History provides us with examples of human organizations that were not well suited to ensuring individual human security needs (and in too many ways we are still mired in that history), but history also provides us with evidence of the ability to achieve real human progress. Democratic states were an improvement on the absolutist national security states that arose in the mid-seventeenth century. Are the present-day democratic states better than present-day nondemocratic states in terms of respecting the rights of the sovereigns, the people? I would answer emphatically yes. Could present-day democratic states themselves be improved on? There is undeniably room for vast improvements in both the domestic and the foreign policies of democratic states. But democracy itself maintains the public space for imagining such improvements.

The mid-seventeenth century seems a long time ago. The self-defeating security practices arising at that moment in history *are* entrenched but not inevitable; they are not indelible reality. The development of democracy was a step away from a state-first ethic. We just need to keep taking steps down that alternative path. Indeed, for the sake of human beings every where, we need to pick up the pace.

In the current international system, there are workable alternatives to a state-first ethic. The land-mine ban treaty, the International Criminal Court, and even aspects of the European Union in its commitment to the political, social, and economic rights of its citizenry all offer workable alternatives that both reassure states and put the emphasis back on the human being as the proper unit of analysis, discussion, and security. International agreements and limited supranational authorities can help maintain and strengthen democratic governments while holding all governments accountable to a human-first ethic. Truly democratic states are not threatened by but strengthened through human empowerment.

There is human progress marked by the enactment of treaties and the creation of organizations designed to promote human security. As I have discussed in this book, the movement sometimes is painfully slow and sometimes horribly inadequate for stopping genocide, war, and other forms of violence. But the movement cannot be denied. Indeed, we need to acknowledge the failures of the present system and the promises of the human security movement in order to hasten human progress. In doing this, we might start to change our expectations about what "is" and what is possible.

What I am suggesting does not require radical change in human practice; revolution is already embedded in human existence. This revolution, importantly, does *not* involve deploying violence to counter the violence of the state-first system. Jonathan Schell's inspiring work *The Unconquerable World* gives example on example from the violent twentieth century of the power of *nonviolent* human campaigns to construct better, more humane political systems at the local and national levels. Pondering the victory of Mohandas K. Gandhi's nonviolent campaign for South Asian independence and many other such movements, Schell concludes that "nonviolent action can serve effectively in the place of violence at *every level* of political affairs."[6] For all those who have led and will lead nonviolent movements in support of human security, the recipe for success lies not in emulating the accepted, violent paths to power but in rejecting those paths.

Rejecting the given accepted paths to power requires seeing with eyes wide open what has been and what is and then imagining a better way of being in the world. Here, the ideas of Susan Griffin are useful:

> Imagination is as necessary to a social order as any legal agreement. That in America we imagine ourselves to be a democracy is crucial, even when democracy is failing . . .
> Such a moment does not require less but rather more imagination. For to imagine is not simply to see what does not yet exist or what one wants to exist. It is also a profound act of creativity to see what is.[7]

This has been one goal of the present book—to see what is and to suggest why and how at many different points the state-first security ethic does not secure states or human beings. Another less tangible but equally important goal has been to facilitate change in how the readers see this world and the security *problématique*. As Griffin writes, "The act of seeing changes those who see."[8]

> Perception is not simply a reflection of reality but a powerful element of reality. Anyone who meditates has had this experience: Observing the activities of the mind changes the mind until, bit by bit, observation creates great changes in the soul. And the effect is the same when the act of perception is collective. A change in public perception will change the public. This is why acts of imagination are so important.[9]

Can we reimagine the situation of the Afghan boat people to allow a resolution that would serve multiple, *noncompeting* security interests? The elements of a different story are already present in this story.[10] The Afghans did not drown as their first vessel sank but instead were rescued by the crew of the Norwegian tanker. When food and water were running short on the *Tampa*, the Australian navy moved the people to a troopship where their basic needs were better met. Meanwhile, human rights groups gave voice to the Afghans by appealing to the Australian legal system. Early in the crisis, the human security needs of the boat people were being championed in different ways by different actors.

We might imagine one small change in the record of this case. Let's imagine that the Australian judge, sensitive to the worries of a vigilant government yet also sensitive to the human security needs of the Afghans, invited the federal authorities and human rights groups to devise a plan that would take into account the multiple interests in the case while attending to the basic human rights of the boat people. Is this an unreasonable turn of events? Not at all—it is common practice in many countries for judges to invite parties to a dispute to engage in mutual problem solving. In the international arena, it is increasingly common for states, international organizations, nongovernmental organizations (NGOs), and expert communities to work together, pooling their resources and expertise, matching their coinciding interests, and reconciling their competing interests in order to achieve a common solution to a problem, sometimes with a judge or arbiter, sometimes without. Such activity, of course, has been rare on *security* issues but not impossible or unimaginable.

Or let's imagine that the Australian navy transported the boat people to Nauru along with a delegation of Australian caseworkers and security agents whose task was to expedite the processing of refugee claims. In this scenario, the United Nations and/or neighboring countries also might lend a hand. Are these unlikely turns of events? Not really—keep in mind that the Australian government took primary responsibility for the well-being of the Afghans early in the crisis. There was already in this case a strong commitment to human security.

As discussed in earlier chapters, Australia's response to the larger problem of boat people was linked to the choices of other states. If there is inevitability in international politics, it is that we cannot escape the consequences of our actions on other peoples or of their actions on us. Australia was unable to impose a 1,000-nautical-mile security zone around itself but instead started cooperating with other states on the mutual problem of boat people. We could inject other interested actors into this. Human rights and refugee NGOs as well as law enforcement agencies could be brought into the discussion. A mutually devised plan could be institutionalized through agreements and administered by an international organization. The reasons to cooperate are apparent, as is the general desire to cooperate and share the burdens of providing security in this present age.

In the first chapter of this book, I wrote that in these pages the definition of security would remain a persistent problem. I stated that the definitional problem drives an operational problem: without a clear understanding of what we are securing and what we are securing against, how do we know when we have found the right policy, doctrine, weapon, or alliance that will in fact secure us? Definitional and operational problems ultimately are political problems. Political problems turn on value judgments, and the ultimate value judgment is determining what must be secured at what expense. In this world, we proceed as if some of the ultimate value judgments were cast in stone centuries ago and cannot be recast. But people have been recasting, remaking, and reshaping their political institutions before and after the birth of the modern state. We can insist that our institutions protect what we most value—human beings, ourselves, our parents, our children, and their children.

"What we seek to protect reflects what we value."[11] States—or more precisely national leaders—can be required to put human beings first in security matters through democratic accountability. Dire human needs and seemingly pervasive insecurities on the one hand and spreading democracy and the irreversible growth of international society on the other will combine to compel states to reassess their old (in)security methods. In one sense, we have no choice—the old methods create greater insecurity. In another sense, we have many choices—we can look at the turn of human events and say that it *went* this way, not that it *was* this way.

Notes

Chapter 1: Elusive Security

1. David Blair, "Revenge Turned Woman Lawyer into a Suicide Bomber," *Daily Telegraph* (London), October 5, 2003, 12; Mia Bloom, "Mother, Daughter, Sister, Bomber," *Bulletin of the Atomic Scientists*, November/December 2005, 57.

2. Blair, "Revenge Turned Woman Lawyer into a Suicide Bomber."

3. Chris McGreal, "Middle East Crisis: Rare Haven of Coexistence Rocked by Blast," *Guardian* (London), October 6, 2003, 15.

4. International Commission on Intervention and State Sovereignty, *The Responsibility to Protect* (Ottawa: International Development Research Centre, 2001), 5.

5. Graham Evans and Jeffrey Newnham, *Penguin Dictionary of International Relations* (New York: Penguin, 1998), 490.

6. Arnold Wolfers, *Discord and Collaboration* (Baltimore: The Johns Hopkins University Press, 1962), 150.

7. David Baldwin, "The Concept of Security," *Review of International Studies* 23, no. 1 (1997): 13.

8. High-Level Panel on Threats, Challenges and Change, *A More Secure World: Our Shared Responsibility* (New York: United Nations, 2004), 17, http://www.un.org/secureworld/ (accessed November 14, 2005).

9. Laura Barnett, "Global Governance and the Evolution of the International Refugee Regime," Working Paper No. 54, UN High Commissioner for Refugees, February 2002, 8–9.

10. Michael Flynn, "Searching for Safe Haven," *Bulletin of the Atomic Scientists*, November/December 2002, 24.

11. Barnett, "Global Governance and the Evolution of the International Refugee Regime," 7.

12. Barnett, "Global Governance and the Evolution of the International Refugee Regime," 2.

Chapter 2: National Security

1. Friedrich Meinecke, *"Raison d'État,"* in *Basic Texts in International Relations,* ed. Evan Luard (New York: St. Martin's Press, 1992), 170.

2. Peter Chalk and William Rosenau, *Confronting the "Enemy Within": Security Intelligence, the Police, and Counterterrorism in Four Democracies,* RAND Corporation, 2004, 35, 38, http://www.rand.org/publications/RB/RB9047/RB9047.pdf (accessed November 1, 2005).

3. Mohammed Ayoob, *The Third World Security Predicament* (Boulder, Colo.: Lynne Rienner, 1995), 7.

4. Ayoob, *The Third World Security Predicament,* 7.

5. Arnold Wolfers, *Discord and Collaboration* (Baltimore: The Johns Hopkins University Press, 1962), 150.

6. David Baldwin suggests that an "absence of threats" is difficult to gauge or judge. He suggests instead the useful rephrasing that security entails "a low probability of damage to acquired core values." David Baldwin, "The Concept of Security," *Review of International Studies* 23, no. 1 (1997): 13.

7. Wolfers, *Discord and Collaboration,* 149.

8. R. B. J. Walker, "Security, Sovereignty, and the Challenge of World Politics," *Alternatives* 15 (1990): 5–6.

9. Barry Buzan, *People, States and Fear,* 2nd ed. (Boulder, Colo.: Lynne Rienner, 1991), 18–19.

10. Graham Evans and Jeffrey Newnham, *Penguin Dictionary of International Relations* (New York: Penguin, 1998), 504.

11. Charles W. Kegley Jr. and Gregory A. Raymond, *Exorcising the Ghost of Westphalia* (Upper Saddle River, N.J.: Prentice Hall, 2002), 190.

12. Kegley and Raymond, *Exorcising the Ghost of Westphalia,* 190.

13. Kegley and Raymond, *Exorcising the Ghost of Westphalia,* 190.

14. Evans and Newnham, *Penguin Dictionary of International Relations,* 504.

15. Walker, "Security, Sovereignty, and the Challenge of World Politics," 9.

16. Walker, "Security, Sovereignty, and the Challenge of World Politics," 9.

17. Kegley and Raymond, *Exorcising the Ghost of Westphalia,* 89.

18. Kegley and Raymond, *Exorcising the Ghost of Westphalia,* 90.

19. Kegley and Raymond, *Exorcising the Ghost of Westphalia,* 90.

20. Kegley and Raymond, *Exorcising the Ghost of Westphalia,* 93.

21. Kegley and Raymond, *Exorcising the Ghost of Westphalia,* 95.

22. Kegley and Raymond, *Exorcising the Ghost of Westphalia,* 93.

23. Kegley and Raymond, *Exorcising the Ghost of Westphalia,* 97.

24. Kegley and Raymond, *Exorcising the Ghost of Westphalia,* 94.

25. Kegley and Raymond, *Exorcising the Ghost of Westphalia,* 97.

26. Kegley and Raymond, *Exorcising the Ghost of Westphalia,* 4.

27. Karen Mingst, *Essentials of International Relations,* 2nd ed. (New York: Norton, 2003), 218.

28. Meinecke, "*Raison d'État*," 166–67.
29. Meinecke, "*Raison d'État*," 167.
30. Meinecke, "*Raison d'État*," 168.
31. Meinecke, "*Raison d'État*," 168.
32. Meinecke, "*Raison d'État*," 169.
33. Meinecke, "*Raison d'État*," 170.
34. Meinecke, "*Raison d'État*," 171.
35. Buzan, *People, States and Fear*, 19.
36. Sheila Croucher, *Globalization and Belonging: The Politics of Identity in a Changing World* (Lanham, Md.: Rowman & Littlefield, 2004), 91. Croucher's intention is to offer the many ways scholars try to pin down "state" and "nation" as well as "state building" and "nation building" and how these efforts often contradict or double back on themselves.
37. Buzan, *People, States and Fear*, 65.
38. The League of Nations was dedicated to preserving the sovereignty of its members, but its membership was limited to a relatively small number of independent states. Moreover and more important, the League was not committed to the liberation of colonial possessions.
39. Steve A. Yetiv, *Explaining Foreign Policy: US Decision-Making and the Persian Gulf War* (Baltimore: The Johns Hopkins University Press, 2004), 23.
40. Buzan, *People, States and Fear*, 69–70.
41. Buzan, *People, States and Fear*, 72–73.
42. Buzan, *People, States and Fear*, 73.
43. Buzan, *People, States and Fear*, 75.
44. Buzan, *People, States and Fear*, 75.
45. Buzan, *People, States and Fear*, 76.
46. Buzan, *People, States and Fear*, 77–78.
47. Buzan, *People, States and Fear*, 106.
48. The controversy over the abuse of prisoners of war in Iraq and Afghanistan by American soldiers and military subcontractors demonstrates the lack of clarity on what is and is not appropriate behavior on behalf of a state.
49. Charles Tilly, "War Making and State Making as Organized Crime," in *Bringing the State Back In*, ed. Peter B. Evans, Dietrich Rueschemeyer, and Theda Skocpol (New York: Cambridge University Press, 1985).
50. Tilly, "War Making and State Making as Organized Crime," 181.
51. For more on this argument, see Ian S. Lustick, "The Absence of Middle Eastern Great Powers: Political 'Backwardness' in Historical Perspective," *International Organization* 51, no. 4 (1997): 653–83.
52. For more on this argument, see Robert H. Jackson, "Juridical Statehood in Sub-Saharan Africa," *Journal of International Affairs* 46, no. 1 (1992): 1–16.
53. Ayoob, *The Third World Security Predicament*, 32–33.
54. Bruce Hoffman, "Defining Terrorism," in *Inside Terrorism* (Columbia University Press, 1993), as reprinted in *Terrorism and Counterterrorism*, ed. Russell D. Howard and Reid L. Sawyer (Guilford, Conn.: McGraw-Hill/Dushkin, 2003), 4.
55. Hoffman, "Defining Terrorism," 5.
56. Jessica Stern, *The Ultimate Terrorists* (Cambridge, Mass.: Harvard University Press, 1999), 78.
57. Hoffman, "Defining Terrorism," 5.

58. Hoffman, "Defining Terrorism," 10. The inclusion of the Stalinist Soviet Union here might be contested by Russians. As reported on National Public Radio, public opinion polls show that a majority of Russians view Stalin's legacy as more positive than negative, even when considering the mass graves of political opponents and other well-known, widespread human rights abuses. National Public Radio, "Group Wants Stalin-Era Mass Graves Recognized," *NPR Weekend Edition Sunday*, September 19, 2004.

59. Chalk and Rosenau, *Confronting the "Enemy Within,"* 13–14.

60. Hoffman, "Defining Terrorism," 10–13.

Chapter 3: Terrorism

1. James Risen, "Evolving Nature of Al Qaeda Is Misunderstood, Critic Says," *New York Times*, November 8, 2004, A18.

2. Bruce Hoffman, "A Nasty Business," *Atlantic Monthly*, January 2002, 49.

3. Bruce Hoffman, "Defining Terrorism," in *Inside Terrorism* (New York: Columbia University Press, 1993), as reprinted in *Terrorism and Counterterrorism*, Howard and Sawyer, 19, 20.

4. Hoffman, "Defining Terrorism," 4.

5. Hoffman, "Defining Terrorism," 23.

6. Hoffman, "Defining Terrorism," 15.

7. Eqbal Ahmad, "Terrorism: Theirs and Ours," in Howard and Sawyer, *Terrorism and Counterterrorism*, 48.

8. Jessica Stern, *Ultimate Terrorists* (Cambridge, Mass.: Harvard University Press, 1999), 11, emphasis added.

9. Stern, *Ultimate Terrorists*, 13-14.

10. Stern, *Ultimate Terrorists*, 11.

11. Stern, *Ultimate Terrorists*, 14.

12. Stern, *Ultimate Terrorists*, 14.

13. International Institute for Strategic Studies, "Combating Transnational Terrorism: Interim Results," *IISS Strategic Comments* 10, no. 10 (December 2004), http://www.iiss.org/stratcom (accessed November 1, 2005). See also National Intelligence Council, *Mapping the Global Future: Report of the National Intelligence Council's 2020 Project*, Washington, D.C., December 2004, http://www.foia.cia.gov/2020/2020.pdf (accessed November 1, 2005).

14. National Intelligence Council, *Mapping the Global Future*, 15.

15. National Intelligence Council, *Mapping the Global Future*, 93.

16. National Intelligence Council, *Mapping the Global Future*, 15.

17. National Intelligence Council, *Mapping the Global Future*, 15.

18. Craig S. Smith and Don Van Natta Jr., "Officials Fear Iraq's Lure for Muslims in Europe," *New York Times*, October 23, 2004, A1.

19. International Institute for Strategic Studies, "Combating Transnational Terrorism."

20. National Intelligence Council, *Mapping the Global Future*, 94.

21. Peter Chalk and William Rosenau, *Confronting the "Enemy Within": Security Intelligence, the Police, and Counterterrorism in Four Democracies*, RAND Corporation, 2004, 33, http://www.rand.org/publications/RB/RB9047/RB9047.pdf (accessed November 1, 2005).

22. Laura Neack, *The New Foreign Policy* (Lanham, Md.: Rowman & Littlefield, 2003), 174.

23. David Fickling, "Jakarta Bombing: Australia Seen as 'America's Deputy Sheriff,'" *Guardian* (London), September 10, 2004, 15.

24. Chalk and Rosenau, *Confronting the "Enemy Within,"* 25.

25. Chalk and Rosenau, *Confronting the "Enemy Within,"* 26.

26. *Securing an Open Society: Canada's National Security Policy*, April 2004, http://www.pcobcp.gc.ca/default.asp?Language=E&Page=publications&Sub=natsecurnat&Doc=natsecurnat_e.htm (accessed December 1, 2005).

27. Laura K. Donohue, "Fear Itself: Counterterrorism, Individual Rights, and US Foreign Relations Post 9/11," in Howard and Sawyer, *Terrorism and Counterterrorism*, 278.

28. Chalk and Rosenau, *Confronting the "Enemy Within,"* 26.

29. David Carr, "The Futility of 'Homeland Defense,'" *Atlantic Monthly*, January 2002, 53.

30. As the public record now clearly shows, the Bush administration came to the realization that terrorism was a national security problem after the 9/11 terrorist attacks despite warnings made by members of the former Clinton administration (including a discussion between Bill Clinton and George W. Bush) and warnings made by Bush administration counterterrorism specialists. See the *9/11 Commission Report: Final Report of the National Commission on Terrorist Attacks upon the United States* (New York: Norton, 2004). See also Richard A. Clarke, *Against All Enemies: Inside America's War on Terror* (New York: Free Press, 2004).

31. Andrea Felsted, "OECD Warns of Unbearable Losses from 'Mega-Terrorism,'" *Financial Times*, July 5, 2005, 19.

32. Robert J. Art, *A Grand Strategy for America* (Ithaca, N.Y.: Cornell University Press, 2003), 16.

33. Stern, *Ultimate Terrorists*, 8.

34. Art, *A Grand Strategy for America*, 17.

35. Martha Crenshaw, "The Logic of Terrorism: Terrorist Behavior as a Product of Strategic Choice," in Howard and Sawyer, *Terrorism and Counterterrorism*, 57.

36. Crenshaw, "The Logic of Terrorism," 57.

37. Stern, *Ultimate Terrorists*, 74–75.

38. Stern, *Ultimate Terrorists*, 74.

39. Stern, *Ultimate Terrorists*, 77–82.

40. Stern, *Ultimate Terrorists*, 80.

41. Stern, *Ultimate Terrorists*, 78.

42. Karen Armstrong, *The Battle for God: A History of Fundamentalism* (New York: Ballantine, 2001), x.

43. Armstrong, *The Battle for God*, vii.

44. Karen Armstrong, *The Battle for God*, ix.

45. Armstrong, The *Battle for God*, viii.

46. Donohue, "Fear Itself," 283.

47. Donohue, "Fear Itself," 276.

48. Donohue, "Fear Itself," 275.

49. Donohue, "Fear Itself," 277, 278.

50. Donohue, "Fear Itself," 278.

51. Jim McGee, "An Intelligence Giant in the Making," *Washington Post*, November 4, 2001, A4.

52. Department of Homeland Security website, http://www.dhs.gov/dhspublic/faq.jsp (accessed November 1, 2005).

53. Criticism of Homeland Security was particularly sharp in the summer of 2004, when terrorist threat alerts were intensified at the conclusion of the Democratic National Convention (DNC), thus siphoning media attention away from the newly nominated Democratic challenger, John Kerry. The basis of the heightened terror alert for financial interests in Washington, D.C., and New York City at the conclusion of the DNC turned out to be two-year-old information. See James Harding, "Bush Administration Defends Latest Warning on Terrorist Threat," *Financial Times*, August 4, 2004, 6.

54. Richard Rainey, "Lack of Single Terror Suspect 'Watch List' Criticized," *Los Angeles Times*, October 2, 2004, A13.

55. Chalk and Rosenau, *Confronting the "Enemy Within,"* xii.

56. Chalk and Rosenau, *Confronting the "Enemy Within,"* xi.

57. Chalk and Rosenau, *Confronting the "Enemy Within,"* 18.

58. Chalk and Rosenau, *Confronting the "Enemy Within,"* 18–19.

59. Chalk and Rosenau, *Confronting the "Enemy Within,"* 21.

60. Chalk and Rosenau, *Confronting the "Enemy Within,"* 27.

61. Chalk and Rosenau, *Confronting the "Enemy Within,"* 28, 18.

Chapter 4: Identifying External Security Threats

1. National Security Strategy of the United States of America, September 2002, 5, 6, http://www.whitehouse.gov/nsc/nss.html (accessed November 1, 2005).

2. Democratic People's Republic of Korea, "Politics," http://www.korea-dpr.com/politics2.htm (accessed November 1, 2005).

3. Vladimir Putin, "An Inhuman Crime, but We Must Not Yield to Panic," *Australian*, September 6, 2004, 14.

4. Rory Carroll, "Rwanda Announces Invasion of Congo," *Guardian* (London), December 1, 2004, 15.

5. Charter of the United Nations, Chapter VII, "Action with Respect to Threats to the Peace, Breaches of the Peace, and Acts of Aggression," Article 51, http://www.un.org/aboutun/charter/index.html (accessed November 1, 2005).

6. Charter of the United Nations, "Preamble," http://www.un.org/aboutun/charter/index.html (accessed November 1, 2005).

7. Charles W. Kegley Jr. and Gregory A. Raymond, *Exorcising the Ghost of Westphalia* (Upper Saddle River, N.J.: Prentice Hall, 2002), 109.

8. Kegley and Raymond, *Exorcising the Ghost of Westphalia*, 104.

9. Kegley and Raymond, *Exorcising the Ghost of Westphalia*, 106.

10. James E. Dougherty and Robert L. Pfaltzgraff Jr., *Contending Theories of International Relations*, 5th ed. (New York: Longman, 2001), 286.

11. Graham Evans and Jeffrey Newnham, *Penguin Dictionary of International Relations* (New York: Penguin, 1998), 41.

12. John J. Mearsheimer, *The Tragedy of Great Power Politics* (New York: Norton, 2001), 21.

13. Nicholas J. Spykman, *American Strategy and World Politics* (New York: Harcourt Brace, 1942), 21–22, as quoted in Dougherty and Pfaltzgraff, *Contending Theories of International Relations*, 43.

14. Glenn H. Snyder, "The Security Dilemma in Alliance Politics," *World Politics* 36, no. 4 (July 1984): 461.

15. As quoted in Klaus Knorr, "Threat Perception," in *Historical Dimensions of National Security Problems*, ed. Klaus Knorr (Lawrence: University Press of Kansas, 1976), 79.

16. Dennis Shanahan, "New Attack on Coastal Terror—Ships to Be Monitored within 1000 Nautical Mile Security Zone," *Australian*, December 15, 2004, 1.

17. "Australia Clarifies Regional Confusion over Maritime Security Zone," *Global News Wire—BBC Monitoring International Reports*, December 16, 2004; Roger Maynard, "Storm Brewing over Aussie Maritime Security Zone Plan; Scheme Will Likely Anger Neighbours and Breach International Law," *Straits Times* (Singapore), December 17, 2004; Chok Suat Ling, "PM Slams Aussie Maritime Security Zone Plan," *New Straits Times* (Malaysia), December 18, 2004.

18. Laura Neack, *The New Foreign Policy* (Lanham, Md.: Rowman & Littlefield, 2003), 172–75.

19. Shawn Donnan and Virginia Marsh, "Jakarta Angry at Canberra Sea Plan Maritime Security Zone," *Financial Times*, December 19, 2004, 3.

20. Jane Perlez, "Indonesia Orders Foreign Troops Providing Aid to Leave by March 26," *New York Times*, January 13, 2005, 8.

21. Perlez, "Indonesia Orders Foreign Troops Providing Aid to Leave by March 26."

22. Knorr, "Threat Perception," 79.

23. See, for example, Christopher Layne, "The Unipolar Illusion: Why New Great Powers Will Rise," *International Security* 17, no. 4 (1993): 5–15. See also the opposite view, that multipolarity is not inevitable, expressed in Robert Jervis, "International Primacy: Is the Game Worth the Candle?" *International Security* 17, no. 4 (1993): 52–67.

24. Josef Joffe, "How America Does It," *Foreign Affairs* 74, no. 5 (1997): 16.

25. Joseph S. Nye Jr., "Soft Power," *Foreign Policy* 80 (autumn 1990): 153–71; see also Joseph S. Nye Jr., *Soft Power: The Means to Success in World Politics* (New York: Public Affairs, 2005).

26. Joffe, "How America Does It," 24.

27. Guy Dinmore, "Bush Has Mandate to Continue Pursuing 'Aggressive' Foreign Policy, Says Powell," *Financial Times*, November 9, 2004, 1.

28. Claire Bigg, "Russia Joins China in First War Games," *Guardian* (London), December 28, 2004, 13.

29. Guy Dinmore, "US Starts to Accommodate the Emerging Influence of China," *Financial Times*, December 23, 2004, 3.

30. C. J. Chivers, "Central Asians Call on US to Set a Timetable for Closing Bases," *New York Times*, July 6, 2005, 3. No doubt Uzbekistan was motivated as well by its unhappiness over U.S. demands that it allow in international inspectors to investigate the killing of antigovernment protesters in May 2005.

31. Michael T. Klare, *Resource Wars* (New York: Owl Books, 2001), 1–10.

32. Jungmin Kang, Peter Hayes, Li Bin, Tatsujiro Suzuki, and Richard Tanter, "South Korea's Nuclear Surprise," *Bulletin of the Atomic Scientists*, January/February 2005, 40–41.

33. Kang et al., "South Korea's Nuclear Surprise," 40.

34. Stephen M. Walt, *The Origins of Alliances* (Ithaca, N.Y.: Cornell University Press, 1987).

35. Knorr, "Threat Perception," 84.

36. "Interview with Condoleezza Rice," *CNN Late Edition with Wolf Blitzer*, September 7, 2002.

37. Knorr, "Threat Perception," 97–98.

38. Knorr, "Threat Perception," 88.

39. Knorr, "Threat Perception," 89.

40. *Comprehensive Report of the Special Advisor to the Director of Central Intelligence on Iraq's WMD*, September 30, 2004, Addenda March 2005, also known as the Duelfer Report, http://www.odci.gov/cia/reports/iraq_wmd_2004/index.html (accessed November 13, 2005).

41. Knorr, "Threat Perception," 97–98.

42. Knorr, "Threat Perception," 94.

43. Knorr, "Threat Perception," 108.

44. Knorr, "Threat Perception," 112.

45. Evans and Newnham, *Penguin Dictionary of International Relations*, 2.

46. Peter Karsten, "Response to Threat Perception: Accommodation as a Special Case," in Knorr, *Historical Dimensions of National Security Problems*, 123.

47. Karsten, "Response to Threat Perception," 136.

48. Karsten, "Response to Threat Perception," 136.

49. Robert S. Norris, Hans M. Kristensen, and Joshua Handler, "North Korea's Nuclear Program, 2003," *Bulletin of the Atomic Scientists*, March/April 2003, 74–77.

50. Peter Slevin and Walter Pincus, "US Will Refer N. Korea Nuclear Effort to UN," *Washington Post*, December 28, 2002, A1.

51. Guy Dinmore and Peter Spiegel, "Washington Pulls Its Punches as a Rogue State Thumbs Its Nose," *Financial Times*, January 11, 2003, 8.

52. David E. Sanger, "When a Virtual Bomb May Be Better Than the Real Thing," *New York Times*, December 5, 2004, sec. 4, p. 5.

53. Karsten, "Response to Threat Perception," 152.

54. Karsten, "Response to Threat Perception," 159.

55. Randall L. Schweller, "Bandwagoning for Profit: Bringing the Revisionist State Back In," *International Security* 19, no. 1 (summer 1994): 105.

56. Schweller, "Bandwagoning for Profit," 74.

57. Schweller, "Bandwagoning for Profit," 94.

58. Schweller, "Bandwagoning for Profit," 95.

59. Schweller, "Bandwagoning for Profit," 79.

60. Glenn H. Snyder, "Alliance Theory: A Neorealist First Cut," *Journal of International Affairs* 44, no. 1 (spring–summer 1990): 104.

61. Snyder, "Alliance Theory," 105.

62. Michael O'Regan, "State Is Not in 'Coalition'—Ahern," *Irish Times*, March 26, 2003, 6.

63. Snyder, "Alliance Theory," 461.

64. Snyder, "Alliance Theory," 467.

65. Snyder, "Alliance Theory," 467.

66. Snyder, "Alliance Theory," 468.

67. Snyder, "Alliance Theory," 483–84.

68. Snyder, "Alliance Theory," 485.

69. Laura Neack, "Peacekeeping, Bloody Peacekeeping," *Bulletin of the Atomic Scientists*, July/August 2004, 44.

70. Donald Rumsfeld, "A New Kind of War," *New York Times*, September 27, 2001, 21, as quoted in Neack, *The New Foreign Policy*, 151.

71. National Security Strategy of the United States of America, September 2002, 6, http://www.whitehouse.gov/nsc/nss.html (accessed November 1, 2005).

72. National Security Strategy of the United States of America, March 2006, 37, http://www.whitehouse.gov/nsc/nss/2006/nss2006.pdf (accessed June 21, 2006).

Chapter 5: Defending against External Security Threats

1. Barry Buzan, *People, States and Fear*, 2nd ed. (Boulder, Colo.: Lynne Rienner, 1991), 277.

2. Buzan, *People, States and Fear*, 277.

3. J. Bryan Hehir, "Military Intervention and National Sovereignty: Recasting the Relationship," in *Hard Choices: Moral Dilemmas in Humanitarian Intervention*, ed. Jonathan Moore (Lanham, Md.: Rowman & Littlefield, 1999), 33.

4. Buzan, *People, States and Fear*, 270.

5. Buzan, *People, States and Fear*, chap. 8.

6. Lizette Alvarez, "British Court Says Detentions Violate Rights," *New York Times*, December 17, 2004, 1.

7. Buzan, *People, States and Fear*, 272.

8. Alvarez, "British Court Says Detentions Violate Rights."

9. Sophie Goodchild et al., "How Chaos in the Commons Descended into a Dangerous Farce," *Independent on Sunday* (London), March 13, 2005, 6, 7; "Blair's Anti-Terrorism Law Passed after Bitter Two-Day Debate," *Agence France-Presse*, March 11, 2005.

10. Jaswant Singh, "Against Nuclear Apartheid," *Foreign Affairs* 77, no. 5 (1998): 41.

11. Singh, "Against Nuclear Apartheid," 52.

12. See Kenneth Waltz's side of the debate presented in Scott D. Sagan and Kenneth N. Waltz, *The Spread of Nuclear Weapons: A Debate Renewed*, 2nd ed. (New York: Norton, 2002).

13. Thomas C. Schelling, "The Diplomacy of Violence," excerpted in *Essential Readings in World Politics*, ed. Karen A. Mingst and Jack L. Snyder (New York: Norton, 2004), 307.

14. Schelling, "The Diplomacy of Violence," 302.

15. Richard K. Betts, "The Concept of Deterrence in the Postwar Era," *Security Studies* 1, no. 1 (1991): 161–62.

16. Walter Pincus, "Nuclear Strike on Bunkers Assessed; Congress Receives Pentagon Study," *Washington Post*, December 20, 2001, A29.

17. "New Nuclear-Weapons Push Invites a Dangerous Backlash," *USA Today*, August 13, 2003, 10A.

18. Matthew L. Wald, "Nuclear Weapons Money Is Cut from Spending Bill," *New York Times*, November 23, 2004, A22.

19. "Conventional Wisdom: Rep. Hobson's Decision to Scrap Nuclear 'Bunker-Busters' Was Right for the Country and Right for the World," *Plain Dealer* (Cleveland, Ohio), November 29, 2004, B6.

20. John Lewis Gaddis, *The Long Peace: Inquiries into the History of the Cold War* (New York: Oxford University Press, 1987).

21. Singh, "Against Nuclear Apartheid," 41.

22. Upendra Choudhury, "Too Close for Comfort," *Bulletin of the Atomic Scientists*, March/April 2003, 23–24.

23. Suzanne Goldenberg, "Seeds of Showdown Lie in Kashmir Conflict," *Irish Times*, October 13, 1999, 12.

24. Peter Popham, "Pakistan Coup: How Betrayal in the Mountains Led to Army's Revenge," *Independent* (London), October 13, 1999, 12.

25. Choudhury, "Too Close for Comfort," 24.

26. Choudhury, "Too Close for Comfort," 24.

27. Robert S. Norris, Hans M. Kristensen, and Joshua Handler, "Pakistan's Nuclear Forces, 2001," *Bulletin of the Atomic Scientists*, January/February 2002, 70–71.

28. Robert S. Norris, William Arkin, Hans M. Kristensen, and Joshua Handler, "India's Nuclear Forces, 2002," *Bulletin of the Atomic Scientists*, March/April 2002, 70–72.

29. Norris et al., "India's Nuclear Forces," 70–72.

30. Norris et al., "Pakistan's Nuclear Forces," 70–71.

31. Peter Baker, "Bush: US to Sell F-16s to Pakistan," *Washington Post*, March 26, 2005, A1.

32. Farhan Bokhari, "Pakistan Changes F-16 Plan," *Jane's Defence Weekly*, May 10, 2006, sec. 1, 18.

33. George F. Kennan, "The Sources of Soviet Conduct," *Foreign Affairs* 25, no. 4 (1947): 566–82, http://www.foreignaffairs.org/19470701faessay25403/x/the-sources-of-soviet-conduct.html (accessed December 16, 2005).

34. Samuel P. Huntington, "After Containment: The Functions of the Military Establishment," *Annals of the American Academy of Political and Social Science* 406, The Military and American Society (March 1973): 5.

35. Huntington, "After Containment," 3.

36. Benjamin Schwarz, "Why America Thinks It Has to Run the World," *Atlantic Monthly*, June 1996, 100.

37. Quoted in D. F. Fleming, "Is Containment Moral?" *Annals of the American Academy of Political and Social Science* 362, Nonalignment in Foreign Affairs (November 1965): 19.

38. Quoted in Fleming, "Is Containment Moral?" 20.

39. Speech of September 20, 2001, quoted in Laura Neack, *The New Foreign Policy* (Lanham, Md.: Rowman & Littlefield, 2003), 150.

40. Chalmers Johnson, *The Sorrows of Empire: Militarism, Secrecy, and the End of the Republic* (New York: Metropolitan/Owl Books, 2004), 4.

41. Johnson, *The Sorrows of Empire*, 191.

42. Thomas G. Weiss, *Military-Civilian Interactions: Humanitarian Crises and the Responsibility to Protect*, 2nd ed. (Lanham, Md.: Rowman & Littlefield, 2005), 43–44.

43. Weiss, *Military-Civilian Interactions*, 45.

44. Weiss, *Military-Civilian Interactions*, 44.

45. Weiss, *Military-Civilian Interactions*, 46.

46. Weiss, *Military-Civilian Interactions*, 47.

47. For example, see Barbara Crossette, "Russia and France Balk at US Plan to Punish Iraq Even More," *New York Times*, October 22, 1997, 13, and Stephen C. Fehr, "Protestors Deride UN Sanctions," *Washington Post*, August 7, 2000, B3.

48. Condoleezza Rice, "Promoting the National Interest," *Foreign Affairs* 79, no. 1 (2000): 61.

49. John Gittings and Oliver Burkeman, "Bush Plans Sanctions on North Korea," *Guardian* (London), December 30, 2002, 11.

50. Bruno Tertrais, "Nuclear Policy, France Stands Alone," *Bulletin of the Atomic Scientists*, July/August 2004, 48.

51. Tertrais, "Nuclear Policy, France Stands Alone," 53.

52. Tertrais, "Nuclear Policy, France Stands Alone," 52.

53. Geoffrey Wiseman, *Concepts of Non-Provocative Defense* (New York: Palgrave, 2002), 4.

54. Wiseman, *Concepts of Non-Provocative Defense*, 4.

55. Evert Jordaan and Abel Esterhuyse, "South African Defence since 1994: The Influence of Non-Offensive Defence," *African Security Review* 13, no. 1 (2004): 59.

56. Johan Galtung, "Transarmament: From Offensive to Defensive Defense," *Journal of Peace Research* 21, no. 2, Special Issue on Alternative Defense (June 1984): 128.

57. Wiseman, *Concepts of Non-Provocative Defense*, 5.

58. Wiseman, *Concepts of Non-Provocative Defense*, 5.

59. Wiseman, *Concepts of Non-Provocative Defense*, 17.

60. Jordaan and Esterhuyse, "South African Defence since 1994," 59.

61. See, for example, Bjørn Møller, *Resolving the Security Dilemma in Europe: The German Debate on Non-Offensive Defence* (London: Brassey's, 1991).

62. See Radmila Nakarada and Jan Oberg, eds., *Surviving Together: The Olof Palme Lectures on Common Security 1988* (Brookfield, Vt.: Dartmouth Publishing, 1989).

63. Wiseman, *Concepts of Non-Provocative Defense*, 26.

64. Galtung, "Transarmament," 128, esp. fig. II.

65. Wiseman, *Concepts of Non-Provocative Defense*, 5; Jordaan and Esterhuyse, "South African Defence since 1994," 61.

66. Wiseman, *Concepts of Non-Provocative Defense*, 58.

67. Wiseman, *Concepts of Non-Provocative Defense*, 57–58, emphasis added.

68. Galtung, "Transarmament," 136.

69. Jordaan and Esterhuyse, "South African Defence since 1994," 60.

70. Galtung, "Transarmament," 135.

71. Galtung, "Transarmament," 135.

Chapter 6: Going on the Offensive

1. Charles Tilly, "War Making and State Making as Organized Crime," in *Bringing the State Back In*, ed. Peter B. Evans, Dietrich Rueschemeyer, and Theda Skocpol (New York: Cambridge University Press, 1985), 181.

2. Heinrich von Treitschke, "War as the Foundation of the State," in *Basic Texts in International Relations*, ed. Evan Luard (New York: St. Martin's Press, 1992), 206.

3. Charles Tilly, "War and State Power," *Middle East Report*, July–August 1991, 38.

4. Herbert Spencer, "War Secures the Survival of the Fittest," in Luard, *Basic Texts in International Relations*, 66–67.

5. Treitschke, "War as the Foundation of the State," 207.

6. Treitschke, "War as the Foundation of the State," 209.

7. Treitschke, "War as the Foundation of the State," 207.

8. Edward N. Luttwak, "Give War a Chance," *Foreign Affairs* 78, no. 4 (1999): 36.

9. Luttwak, "Give War a Chance," 38.

10. Luttwak, "Give War a Chance," 44.

11. Samuel P. Huntington, "The Clash of Civilizations?" *Foreign Affairs* 72, no. 3 (1993): 22–48; Samuel P. Huntington, *The Clash of Civilizations and the Remaking of World Order* (New York: Simon & Schuster, 1996).

12. Donald Rumsfeld remarks from October 28, 2001, quoted in Neta C. Crawford, "The Slippery Slope to Preventive War," *Ethics and International Affairs* 17, no. 1 (2003): 30.

13. George W. Bush, "Remarks by the President at 2002 Graduation Exercise of the United States Military Academy," West Point, New York, June 1, 2002, http://www.whitehouse.gov/news/releases/2002/06/20020601-3.html (accessed November 1, 2005).

14. The National Security Strategy of the United States of America, September 2002, 15, http://www.whitehouse.gov/nsc/nss.html (accessed November 1, 2005).

15. George W. Bush, "Inaugural Address by President George W. Bush," January 20, 2005, http://www.whitehouse.gov/news/releases/2005/01/20050120-3 .html (accessed November 1, 2005).

16 "US Releases Ship Carrying Missiles from N. Korea to Yemen," *Deutsche Presse-Agentur*, December 11, 2002.

17. William Safire, "Bush's Stumble: The So San Affair," *New York Times*, December 19, 2002, 39.

18. Michael Dobbs, "Waylaid at Sea: Launch of Policy," *Washington Post*, December 13, 2002, A51.

19. For more dissection of the Bush doctrine, see Robin Wright, "Iraq Occupation Erodes Bush Doctrine," *Washington Post*, June 28, 2004, A1; Steven R. Weisman, "Bush Aides Divided on Confronting Iran over A-Bomb," *New York Times*,

September 21, 2004, 3; Tyler Marshall, "Heady US Goals for Iraq Fall by Wayside," *Los Angeles Times*, September 27, 2004; and Hans Blix, "Will President Bush Apply the Lessons from Iraq to Iran, Libya and North Korea?," *Independent* (London), October 10, 2004, 29.

20. Richard K. Betts, "Striking First: A History of Thankfully Lost Opportunities," *Ethics and International Law* 17, no. 1 (2003): 23.

21. "Iraq: Prime Minister's Meeting, 23 July," Secret Downing Street memo written to David Manning from Matthew Rycroft, July 23, 2002, printed in *TimesOnline* (*Sunday Times* [London]), May 1, 2005, emphasis added. The memo can be found online in its entirety at http://www.downingstreetmemo.com/docs/memotext.pdf (accessed November 1, 2005). See also John Daniszewski, "Indignation Grows in US over British Prewar Documents," *Los Angeles Times*, May 12, 2005.

22. International Commission on Intervention and State Sovereignty, *The Responsibility to Protect: Research, Bibliography, Background*, Supplemental Volume to the Report of the International Commission on Intervention and State Sovereignty (Ottawa: International Development Research Centre, 2001), 64.

23. Michael J. Glennon, "The Fog of Law: Self-Defense, Inherence, and Incoherence in Article 51 of the United Nations Charter," *Harvard Journal of Law and Public Policy* 25, no. 2 (2002): 557.

24. Betts, "Striking First," 18.

25. Betts, "Striking First," 18.

26. Crawford, "The Slippery Slope to Preventive War," 31.

27. Chris Brown, "Self-Defense in an Imperfect World," *Ethics and International Affairs* 17, no. 1 (2003): 2.

28. Glennon, "The Fog of Law," 541–42.

29. Glennon, "The Fog of Law," 543–44.

30. Betts, "Striking First," 19.

31. Randall L. Schweller, "Domestic Structure and Preventive War: Are Democracies More Pacific?" *World Politics* 44 (January 1992): 236.

32. Charles W. Kegley Jr. and Gregory A. Raymond, "Preventive War and Permissive Normative Order," *International Studies Perspectives* 4 (2003): 388.

33. Betts, "Striking First," 18.

34. Brown, "Self-Defense in an Imperfect World," 4.

35. Brown, "Self-Defense in an Imperfect World," 5.

36. Charles W. Kegley Jr. and Gregory A. Raymond, *Exorcising the Ghost of Westphalia* (Upper Saddle River, N.J.: Prentice Hall, 2002), 134. See also Bruce W. Jentleson and Ariel E. Levite, "The Analysis of Protracted Foreign Military Intervention," in *Foreign Military Intervention: The Dynamics of Protracted Conflict*, ed. Ariel E. Levite, Bruce W. Jentleson, and Larry Berman (New York: Columbia University Press, 1992).

37. Edmund Burke, "The Right to Intervene against a Public Menace," in Luard, *Basic Texts in International Relations*, 178–79.

38. Burke, "The Right to Intervene against a Public Menace," 179.

39. Luard, *Basic Texts in International Relations*, 173.

40. Lord Palmerston, "The Right to Intervene to Secure Justice for a National," in Luard, *Basic Texts in International Relations*, 186.

41. International Commission on Intervention and State Sovereignty, *The Responsibility to Protect: Research, Bibliography, Background*, 50.

42. Dorothy Jones, *Code of Peace: Ethics and Security in the World of the Warlord States* (Chicago: University of Chicago Press, 1991).

43. International Commission on Intervention and State Sovereignty, *The Responsibility to Protect: Research, Bibliography, Background*, 51. The pre-1990 interventions were Belgium in Congo, 1960; Belgium and the United States in Stanleyville, Congo, 1964; the United States in the Dominican Republic, 1965; India in East Pakistan, 1971; France and Belgium in Shaba province, Zaire, 1978; Vietnam in Cambodia, 1978; Tanzania in Uganda, 1979; France in Central Africa, 1979; the United States in Grenada, 1989; and the United States in Panama, 1989.

44. International Commission on Intervention and State Sovereignty, *The Responsibility to Protect: Research, Bibliography, Background*, 52.

45. International Commission on Intervention and State Sovereignty, *The Responsibility to Protect: Research, Bibliography, Background*, 67.

46. International Commission on Intervention and State Sovereignty, *The Responsibility to Protect: Research, Bibliography, Background*, 55.

47. International Commission on Intervention and State Sovereignty, *The Responsibility to Protect: Research, Bibliography, Background*, 56.

48. International Commission on Intervention and State Sovereignty, *The Responsibility to Protect: Research, Bibliography, Background*, 58.

49. International Commission on Intervention and State Sovereignty, *The Responsibility to Protect: Research, Bibliography, Background*, 62.

50. Jentleson and Levite, "The Analysis of Protracted Foreign Military Intervention," 3.

51. Charles A. Kupchan, "Getting In: The Initial Stage of Military Intervention," in Levite et al., *Foreign Military Intervention*.

52. Kupchan, "Getting In," 256, emphasis added.

53. Kupchan, "Getting In," 252–53.

54. Kupchan, "Getting In," 257.

55. "Estimates for Iraq Occupation Skyrocket 'Hundreds of Thousands' of Troops, Billions Needed," *Seattle Times*, February 26, 2003, A1.

56. Kupchan, "Getting In," 249–50.

57. Office of the Press Secretary, "President Meets with Defense and Foreign Policy Teams," August 11, 2005, http://www.whitehouse.gov/news/releases/2005/08/20050811-1.html (accessed December 6, 2005).

58. John Burns, "It's Still a Mystery," *New York Times*, November 20, 2005, sec. 4, pp. 1, 5.

59. Burns, "It's Still a Mystery," 5.

60. Martin van Crevald, "The Future of War," in *Security in a Post-Cold War World*, ed. R. G. Patman (New York: St. Martin's Press, 1999), 23.

61. Crevald, "The Future of War," 24.

62. Crevald, "The Future of War," 25.

63. Crevald, "The Future of War," 26.

64. Crevald, "The Future of War," 27.

65. Crevald, "The Future of War," 28.

66. Crevald, "The Future of War," 36.

67. John Mueller, "Policing the Remnants of War," *Journal of Peace Research* 40, no. 5 (2003): 507.

68. Mueller, "Policing the Remnants of War," 510.

69. Brigadier General (P) Hank Stratman, "Adaptive Dominance," *Armed Forces Journal (International)*, February 2002, 64–65.

70. Stratman, "Adaptive Dominance, 68.

71. Major E. J. R. Chamberlain, British Army, "Asymmetry: What Is It and What Does It Mean for the British Armed Forces?" *Defence Studies* 3, no. 1 (2003): 24.

72. Stratman, "Adaptive Dominance," 68.

73. Chamberlain, "Asymmetry," 25.

74. Chamberlain, "Asymmetry," 26.

75. Colin McInnes, "Spectator Sport Warfare," in *Critical Reflections on Security and Change*, ed. Stuart Croft and Terry Terriff (London: Frank Cass, 2000), 154–55.

76. McInnes, "Spectator Sport Warfare," 155.

77. McInnes, "Spectator Sport Warfare," 144.

78. McInnes, "Spectator Sport Warfare," 157.

79. Donald H. Rumsfeld, "Transforming the Military," *Foreign Affairs* 81, no. 3 (2002): 20–21.

80. Stratman, "Adaptive Dominance," 68.

81. Chamberlain, "Asymmetry," 32.

Chapter 7: International Security

1. High-level Panel on Threats, Challenges and Change, *A More Secure World: Our Shared Responsibility* (New York, December 2004), 16, http://www.un.org/secureworld (accessed November 1, 2005).

2. United Nations Division for Ocean Affairs and the Law of the Sea, "Key Provisions of the Convention," http://www.un.org/Depts/los/convention_agreements/convention_historical_perspective.htm#Setting%20Limits (accessed November 1, 2005).

3. United Nations Division for Ocean Affairs and the Law of the Sea, "Suspension of Innocent Passage," http://www.un.org/Depts/los/convention_agreements/innocent_passages_suspension.htm (accessed November 1, 2005).

4. Michelle Wiese Bockman, "Maritime Zone Plans Scrapped," *Australian*, July 11, 2005, 2.

5. Graham Evans and Jeffrey Newnham, *Penguin Dictionary of International Relations* (New York: Penguin, 1998), 269.

6. Dorothy V. Jones, *Code of Peace: Ethics and Security in the World of the Warlord States* (Chicago: University of Chicago Press, 1991), 6–7.

7. Jones, *Code of Peace*, 8.

8. Abbé de Saint-Pierre, "A European Union," in *Basic Texts in International Relations*, ed. Evan Luard (New York: St. Martin's Press, 1992), 412.

9. John G. Stoessinger, *The Might of Nations*, 10th ed. (New York: McGraw-Hill, 1993), 4.

10. Ian S. Lustick, "The Absence of Middle Eastern Great Powers: Political 'Backwardness' in Historical Perspective," *International Organization* 51, no. 4 (1997): 657.

11. Lustick, "The Absence of Middle Eastern Great Powers," 663.

12. Woodrow Wilson, "The Fourteen Points," in *Classics of International Relations*, 3rd ed., ed. John A. Vasquez (Englewood Cliffs, N.J.: Prentice Hall, 1996), 38–39.

13. Wilson, "The Fourteen Points," 40.

14. Wilson, "The Fourteen Points," 40.

15. Both quotes from the UN Charter, "Preamble," http://www.un.org/aboutun/charter/preamble.htm (accessed November 1, 2005).

16. Karen Mingst, *Essentials of International Relations* (New York: Norton, 2005), glossary entry.

17. Jones, *Code of Peace*, 50.

18. Jones, *Code of Peace*, 23.

19. Leonard Woolf, "The Need for an International Organisation to Prevent War," in Luard, *Basic Texts in International Relations*, 465.

20. Woolf, "The Need for an International Organisation to Prevent War," 463.

21. J. A. Hobson, "The Need for a New League of States," in Luard, *Basic Texts in International Relations*, 461.

22. Hobson, "The Need for a New League of States," 461.

23. Inis L. Claude Jr., *Power and International Relations* (New York: Random House, 1964, 3rd printing), 111.

24. Claude, *Power and International Relations*, 126.

25. Claude, *Power and International Relations*, 113.

26. Claude, *Power and International Relations*, 123.

27. Claude, *Power and International Relations*, 272–74.

28. Barry Buzan, *People, States and Fear*, 2nd ed. (Boulder, Colo.: Lynne Rienner, 1991), 334.

29. Buzan, *People, States and Fear*, 334.

30. Claude, *Power and International Relations*, 5.

31. Buzan, *People, States and Fear*, 334.

32. Buzan, *People, States and Fear*, 334.

Chapter 8: The United Nations and International Security

1. "The Declaration at St. James's Palace," History of the United Nations Charter, http://www.un.org/aboutun/charter/history/index.html (accessed November 14, 2005).

2. "The Atlantic Charter," History of the United Nations Charter, http://www.un.org/aboutun/charter/history/atlantic.html (accessed November 14, 2005).

3. "The United Nations Declaration," History of the United Nations Charter, http://www.un.org/aboutun/charter/history/declaration.html (accessed November 14, 2005).

4. Inis L. Claude Jr., *Power and International Relations* (New York: Random House, 1964), 278–79.

5. In 1964, Cambodia protested cross-border incursions by the South Vietnamese army. The Council requested that South Vietnam make compensation and then sent a delegation composed of representatives of Brazil, Ivory Coast (Côte d'Ivoire), and Morocco to investigate the incidents and report back to the Council (UN Security Council Resolution 189, June 4, 1964). No mention was made of the United States in the resolution.

6. There was some effort to move the discussion of the impending invasion to the General Assembly under the Uniting for Peace Resolution. This resolution will be discussed in more detail shortly. The effort to move the discussion to the General Assembly would have involved a resolution condemning the United States, Great Britain, and other members of the coalition of the willing for threatening to breach international peace and security by allying and preparing to use force against Iraq.

7. Claude, *Power and International Relations*, 283–84.

8. Karen A. Mingst and Margaret P. Karns, *The United Nations in the Post-Cold War Era*, 2nd ed. (Boulder, Colo.: Westview Press, 2000), 28.

9. "60th Anniversary of the San Francisco Conference," History of the United Nations Charter, http://www.un.org/aboutun/sanfrancisco/history.html (accessed November 14, 2005).

10. Michael J. Glennon, "The Fog of Law: Self-Defense, Inherence, and Incoherence in Article 51 of the United Nations Charter," *Harvard Journal of Law and Public Policy* 25, no. 2 (2002): 553.

11. Jonathan Soffer, "All for One or All for All: The UN Military Staff Committee and the Contradictions within American Internationalism," *Diplomatic History* 21, no. 1 (1997): 57.

12. Soffer, "All for One or All for All," 62.

13. Glennon, "The Fog of Law," 545.

14. Soffer, "All for One or All for All," 61.

15. Soffer, "All for One or All for All," 61.

16. Richard C. Longworth, "Phantom Forces, Diminished Dreams," *Bulletin of the Atomic Scientists*, March/April 1995, 26.

17. Roméo Dallaire, *Shake Hands with the Devil: The Failure of Humanity in Rwanda* (New York: Carroll & Graf, 2005), 124.

18. Soffer, "All for One or All for All," 48.

19. Soffer, "All for One or All for All," 52.

20. Soffer, "All for One or All for All," 54.

21. Soffer, "All for One or All for All," 58.

22. Soffer, "All for One or All for All," 66.

23. Jim Wurst, "UN Command of Gulf Action Unlikely," *Bulletin of the Atomic Scientists*, January/February 1991, 4.

24. "2005 World Summit Outcome," United Nations General Assembly, Sixtieth Session, A/60/L.1, October 24, 2005, 38, paragraph 178. The working draft of the Outcome Document recommended elimination; the approved document recommended reconsideration of the "composition, mandate and working methods" of the MSC.

25. For a longer discussion of this movement, see the Center for Constitutional Rights, "There Is a Way to Stop the War," http://www.ccr-ny.org/v2/reports/report.asp?ObjID=0hZHHegENn&Content=186 (accessed November 14, 2005).

26. Steve A. Yetiv, *Explaining Foreign Policy: US Decision-Making and the Persian Gulf War* (Baltimore: The Johns Hopkins University Press, 2004), 42.

27. Thomas L. Friedman, "How the US Won Support to Use Mideast Forces," *New York Times*, December 2, 1990, 1.

28. Peter Ellingsen, "UN Gulf Vote Returns China to World Stage," *Financial Times*, November 30, 1990, 4.

29. Friedman, "How the US Won Support to Use Mideast Forces"; Ellingsen, "UN Gulf Vote Returns China to World Stage"; Robert Pear, "Bush, Meeting Foreign Minister, Lauds Beijing Stand against Iraq," *New York Times*, December 1, 1990, 8.

30. Ellingsen, "UN Gulf Vote Returns China to World Stage."

31. Pear, "Bush, Meeting Foreign Minister, Lauds Beijing Stand against Iraq."

32. Graham E. Fuller, "Moscow and the Gulf War," *Foreign Affairs* 70, no. 3 (1991): 60.

33. Friedman, "How the US Won Support to Use Mideast Forces."

34. Paul Quinn-Judge, "Lithuania Leaders Urge Calm, Soviet Assault Leaves 13 Dead," *Boston Globe*, January 14, 1991, 1; Annika Savill, "The Soviet Crackdown: Iraq Crisis Stifles US Action on Baltic," *Independent* (London), January 14, 1991, 1.

35. Quinn-Judge, "Lithuania Leaders Urge Calm."

36. Marc Fischer, "Some Europeans States More Open to Negotiated Settlement in Gulf," *Washington Post*, January 4, 1991, A19.

37. Claude, *Power and International Relations*, 283–84.

38. Claude, *Power and International Relations*, 284.

Chapter 9: Keeping the Peace

1. UNTSO continues to operate. In April 2006, it numbered 154 military observers supported by 99 UN and 120 local civilian staff. United Nations Department of Peacekeeping Operations (UNDPO), Middle East—UNTSO, "Facts and Figures," http://www.un.org/Depts/dpko/missions/untso/facts.html (accessed June 23, 2006).

2. UNMOGIP continues its work, numbering forty-three military observers and twenty-two UN and forty-five local civilian staff in April 2006. UNDPO, India and Pakistan—UNMOGIP, "Facts and Figures," http://www.un.org/Depts/dpko/missions/unmogip/facts.html (accessed June 23, 2006).

3. For more on potential linkages, see Gustáv Kecskés, "The Suez Crisis and the 1956 Hungarian Revolution," *East European Quarterly* 35, no. 1 (2001): 47–57, and William R. Keylor, *The Twentieth Century World: An International History*, 3rd ed. (New York: Oxford University Press, 1996), 294–95.

4. UNDPO, First United Nations Emergency Force (UNEF I), "Background," http://www.un.org/Depts/dpko/dpko/co_mission/unef1backgr2.html (accessed November 14, 2005).

5. UNDPO, First United Nations Emergency Force (UNEF I), "Background."

6. UNDPO, First United Nations Emergency Force (UNEF I), "Background."

7. UNDPO, First United Nations Emergency Force (UNEF I), "Background."

8. UNDPO, First United Nations Emergency Force (UNEF I), "Background."

9. Barry Buzan, *People, States and Fear*, 2nd ed. (Boulder, Colo.: Lynne Rienner, 1991), 219–21.

10. Laura Neack, "UN Peace-keeping: In the Interests of Community or Self?" *Journal of Peace Research* 32, no. 2 (1995): 186, table 11.

11. Laura Neack, "The Abdication of Leadership: Major Powers and UN Peace Operations" (paper presented at the First Global International Studies Conference, Istanbul, Turkey, August 2005).

12. Thomas G. Weiss, *Military-Civilian Interactions: Humanitarian Crises and the Responsibility to Protect*, 2nd ed. (Lanham, Md.: Rowman & Littlefield, 2005), 44.

13. Weiss, *Military-Civilian Interactions*, 44.

14. Charter of the United Nations, Chapter I, "Purposes and Principles," http://www.un.org/aboutun/charter/index.html (accessed November 14, 2005).

15. Weiss, *Military-Civilian Interactions*, 47.

16. Sheri Prasso, "Cambodia: A $3 Billion Boondoggle," *Bulletin of the Atomic Scientists*, March/April 1995, 37.

17. Ramesh Thakur, "Cambodia, East Timor and the Brahimi Report," *International Peacekeeping* 8, no. 3 (2001): 119.

18. UNDPO, United Nations Transitional Authority in Cambodia, "Facts and Figures," http://www.un.org/Depts/dpko/dpko/co_mission/untacfacts.html (accessed November 14, 2005).

19. David Roberts, "Finishing What UNTAC Started: The Political Economy of Peace in Cambodia," *Peacekeeping and International Relations* 28, no. 1 (1999): 17.

20. Prasso, "Cambodia," 37.

21. Much of this section is extracted from Laura Neack, "Peacekeeping, Bloody Peacekeeping," *Bulletin of the Atomic Scientists*, July/August 2004, 42–43.

22. Weiss, *Military-Civilian Interactions*, 61.

23. Donald C. F. Daniel and Bradd C. Hayes with Chantal de Jonge Oudraat, *Coercive Inducement and the Containment of International Crises* (Washington, D.C.: United States Institute of Peace Press, 1999), 90.

24. Daniel and Hayes, *Coercive Inducement and the Containment of International Crises*, 161.

25. Daniel and Hayes, *Coercive Inducement and the Containment of International Crises*, 102.

26. Weiss, *Military-Civilian Interactions*, 68.

27. Walter Clarke and Jeffrey Herbst, "Somalia and the Future of Humanitarian Intervention," *Foreign Affairs* 75, no. 2 (1996): 70.

28. Weiss, *Military-Civilian Interactions*, 85.

29. Weiss, *Military-Civilian Interactions*, 85.

30. Daniel and Hayes, *Coercive Inducement and the Containment of International Crises*, 120. See also Roméo Dallaire, *Shake Hands with the Devil: The Failure of Humanity in Rwanda* (New York: Carroll & Graf, 2005).

31. Dallaire, *Shake Hands with the Devil*.

32. Weiss, *Military-Civilian Interactions*, 102.

33. Weiss, *Military-Civilian Interactions*, 102.

34. Dallaire, *Shake Hands with the Devil*, 145.

35. International Commission on Intervention and State Sovereignty, *The Responsibility to Protect* (Ottawa: International Development Research Centre, 2001), vii.

36. Report of the Panel on United Nations Peace Operations, A/55/305, S/2000/809, August 21, 2000, Executive Summary, http://www.un.org/peace/reports/peace_operations/ (accessed November 14, 2005).

37. Report of the Panel on United Nations Peace Operations, Executive Summary, viii.

38. Report of the Panel on United Nations Peace Operations, Executive Summary, viii.

39. Report of the Panel on United Nations Peace Operations, Executive Summary, x.

40. United Nations, "Present-Day Peacekeeping Demands Exceed Capacity of Any Single Organization," press release, GA/SPD/297, Fifty-Ninth General Assembly, October 25, 2004.

41. UNDPO, First United Nations Emergency Force (UNEF I), "Background."

42. Report of the Panel on United Nations Peace Operations, Executive Summary, ix.

43. Dallaire, *Shake Hands with the Devil*.

44. Laura Neack and Roger M. Knudson, "The Multiple Meanings and Purposes of Peacekeeping in Cyprus," *International Politics* 36, no. 4 (1999): 473–510.

45. Richard K. Betts, "The Delusion of Impartial Intervention," *Foreign Affairs* 73, no. 6 (1994): 21.

46. Christopher Clapham, "Peacekeeping and the Peacekept: Developing Mandates for Potential Intervenors," in *Peacekeeping and Peace Enforcement in Africa*, ed. Robert I. Rotberg et al. (Washington, D.C.: Brookings Institution Press, 2000), 54.

47. Edward N. Luttwak, "Give War a Chance," *Foreign Affairs* 78, no. 4 (1999): 38.

48. Betts, "The Delusion of Impartial Intervention," 28–29.

49. Betts, "The Delusion of Impartial Intervention," 30–31.

50. Clapham, "Peacekeeping and the Peacekept," 54.

Chapter 10: Human Security

1. Nick Squires, "UN in Plea for Failed Asylum Seekers," *South China Morning Post*, April 19, 2005, 11.

2. Mia Bloom, "Mother, Daughter, Sister, Bomber," *Bulletin of the Atomic Scientists*, November/December 2005, 57.

3. Michael Struett, "The Meaning of the International Criminal Court," *Peace Review* 16, no. 3 (September 2004): 318.

4. The term "warlord states" is derived from Dorothy Jones, *Code of Peace: Ethics and Security in the World of Warlord States* (Chicago: University of Chicago Press, 1991). The idea that civilians came last in the drafting of the Geneva Conventions comes from Hugo Slim, "Why Protect Civilians? Innocence, Immunity and Enmity in War," *International Affairs* 79, no. 3 (2003): 495.

5. International Committee of the Red Cross (ICRC), "The Battle of Solferino," http://www.icrc.org/Web/Eng/siteeng0.nsf/html/57JNVR (accessed December 14, 2005).

6. ICRC, "The ICRC and the Geneva Convention (1863–1864)," http://www.icrc.org/Web/Eng/siteeng0.nsf/html/57JNVRT (accessed December 14, 2005).

7. The text of the Geneva Conventions and other key documents on international humanitarian law can be found online at the website of the ICRC at http://www.icrc.org/ihl (accessed December 14, 2005). Resources on the Geneva Conventions can also be found at the website of the Society of Professional Journalists at http://www.genevaconventions.org/ (accessed December 14, 2005).

8. Lt. Col. Mark David "Max" Maxwell, "The Law of War and Civilians on the Battlefield: Are We Undermining Civilian Protections?" *Military Review*, September–October 2004, 19.

9. Maxwell, "The Law of War and Civilians on the Battlefield," 18–19.

10. Society of Professional Journalists, "Reference Guide to the Geneva Conventions," http://www.genevaconventions.org/ (accessed November 21, 2005).

11. Society of Professional Journalists, "Reference Guide to the Geneva Conventions."

12. Slim, "Why Protect Civilians?" 481.

13. Slim, "Why Protect Civilians?" 497.

14. Slim, "Why Protect Civilians?" 498.

15. For the text of the Universal Declaration of Human Rights, see http://www.un.org/Overview/rights.html (accessed December 14, 2005).

16. United Nations Development Program (UNDP), *Human Development Report 1994* (New York: Oxford University Press, 1994), 1.

17. UNDP, *Human Development Report 1994*, 23.

18. UNDP, *Human Development Report 1994*, 3.

19. Lloyd Axworthy, "Introduction," in *Human Security and the New Diplomacy: Protecting People, Promoting Peace*, ed. Rob McRae and Don Hubert (Montreal: McGill-Queen's University Press, 2001), 4.

20. Axworthy, "Introduction," 4.

21. For basic information on the Ottawa Treaty, see the website of the International Campaign to Ban Landmines at http://www.icbl.org/treaty/treatyenglish.html (accessed November 14, 2005).

22. Axworthy, "Introduction," 5.

23. Mark Gwozdecky and Jill Sinclair, "Landmines and Human Security," in McRae and Hubert, *Human Security and the New Diplomacy*, 29.

24. Gwozdecky and Sinclair, "Landmines and Human Security," 28.

25. Fen Osler Hampson, *Madness in the Multitude: Human Security and World Disorder* (Don Mills, Ontario, Canada: Oxford University Press, 2002), 90.

26. Hampson, *Madness in the Multitude*, 85.

27. Hampson, *Madness in the Multitude*, 90.

28. Hampson, *Madness in the Multitude*, 91. A "smart" mine contains a timing mechanism that causes the mine to deactivate after a set amount of time.

29. International Campaign to Ban Landmines, "Landmines and the United States," http://www.icbl.org/problem/country/usa (accessed November 14, 2005).

30. Hampson, *Madness in the Multitude*, 81.

31. For more information on the International Criminal Court, see its official website at http://www.icc-cpi.int (accessed December 14, 2005).

32. For the full text of the Rome Statute of the International Criminal Court, see http://www.un.org/law/icc (accessed December 14, 2005).

33. United Nations Treaty Collection, "Rome Statute of the International Criminal Court," http://untreaty.un.org/ENGLISH/bible/englishinternetbible/partI/chapterXVIII/treaty11.asp (accessed June 24, 2006).

34. Hampson, *Madness in the Multitude*, 71.

35. Hampson, *Madness in the Multitude*, 69, 73.

36. Carla Del Ponte, "Holding Leaders Accountable," *Global Agenda*, January 2005, 74–75.

37. Michael Struett, "The Meaning of the International Criminal Court," *Peace Review* 16, no. 3 (September 2004): 318.

38. Struett, "The Meaning of the International Criminal Court," 319.

39. Hampson, *Madness in the Multitude*, 77.

40. Hampson, *Madness in the Multitude*, 72, table 4.1.

41. The U.S. Congress passed a law in 1988 that instructed the president to begin negotiations for an international court to deal with drug trafficking. Hampson, *Madness in the Multitude*, 69.

42. Although by the close of 2005 the United States had signed Article 98 agreements with over one hundred states, at least thirty states had refused to give in to U.S. threats. Eleven Latin American countries had their military and financial aid cut by the United States over failure to conclude these immunity agreements. By early 2006, the Pentagon and State Department were scrambling to restore assistance to these countries despite the lack of Article 98 agreements. See Elizabeth Sullivan, "US Tactics Work to China's Advantage," *Plain Dealer* (Cleveland), March 30, 2006, D11, and Steven R. Weisman, "US Rethinks Its Cutoff of Military Aid to Latin American Nations," *New York Times*, March 12, 2006, 6.

43. Axworthy, "Introduction," 5.

44. Andrew F. Cooper, *Stretching the Model of "Coalitions of the Willing"* (Waterloo, Ontario, Canada: Centre for International Governance Innovation, Working Paper No. 1, October 2005).

45. Hampson, *Madness in the Multitude*, 75.

46. Commission on Human Security, *Human Security Now* (New York, 2003), 4, http://www.humansecurity-chs.org/finalreport/index.html (accessed November 14, 2005).

47. Commission on Human Security, *Human Security Now*, 6.

48. International Commission on Intervention and State Sovereignty (ICISS), *The Responsibility to Protect* (Ottawa: International Development Research Centre, 2001), vii. There is a website dedicated to the *Responsibility to Protect* located at http://www.responsibilitytoprotect.org (accessed November 14, 2005). This site contains the entire report and related documents such as *A More Secure World* and *In Larger Freedom* (also discussed in this chapter).

49. ICISS, *The Responsibility to Protect*, vii.

50. ICISS, *The Responsibility to Protect*, sec 1, para. 21.

51. ICISS, *The Responsibility to Protect*, xi.

52. ICISS, *The Responsibility to Protect*, xi.

53. ICISS, *The Responsibility to Protect*, sec. 6, paras. 13–40.

54. ICISS, *The Responsibility to Protect*, sec. 4, para. 25.

55. ICISS, *The Responsibility to Protect*, sec. 4, para. 26.

56. ICISS, *The Responsibility to Protect*, sec. 4, para. 33.

57. ICISS, *The Responsibility to Protect*, sec. 4, para. 47.

58. ICISS, *The Responsibility to Protect*, sec. 7, para. 1.

59. ICISS, *The Responsibility to Protect*, sec. 4, para. 41.

60. ICISS, *The Responsibility to Protect*, sec. 4, para. 42.

61. Warren Hoge, "Annan Reiterates His Misgivings about Legality of War in Iraq," *New York Times*, September 22, 2004, 10.

62. Gary Younge, "Annan Rebukes Law-Breaking Nations," *Guardian* (London), September 22, 2004, 4.

63. For an explanation of the panel and process that produced the report, see Horst Rutsch, "*A More Secure World: Our Shared Responsibility*. High-Level Panel Presents New Vision of Collective Security," *UN Chronicle Online Edition*, http://www.un.org/Pubs/chronicle/2004/issue4/0404p77.html (accessed November 14, 2005).

64. High-level Panel on Threats, Challenges and Change, *A More Secure World: Our Shared Responsibility* (New York: United Nations, 2004), 2, http://www.un.org/secureworld/ (accessed November 14, 2005).

65. High-level Panel on Threats, Challenges and Change, *A More Secure World*, 1.

66. Report of the Secretary-General, *In Larger Freedom: Towards Development, Security and Human Rights for All*, UN General Assembly, Fifty-Ninth Session, A/59/2005, March 21, 2005, http://www.un.org/largerfreedom/contents.htm (accessed November 14, 2005).

67. Mark Townsend, "The World: Summit Failure Blamed on US," *The Observer* (London), September 18, 2005, 21.

68. Matthew Franklin, "World Summit: Declaration a Mealy-Mouthed 'Mongrel Dog with Three Legs,'" *The Advertiser* (Adelaide), September 17, 2005, 60.

69. High-level Panel on Threats, Challenges and Change, *A More Secure World*, 1.

70. "2005 World Summit Outcome," UN General Assembly, Sixtieth Session, A/60/L.1, October 24, 2005, 21, para. 72.

71. "2005 World Summit Outcome," 30, paras. 138, 139.

72. "2005 World Summit Outcome," 31, para. 143.

73. Human Security Centre, *Human Security Report 2005*, 155, http://www.humansecurityreport.into/index.php?option=content&task=view&id=28&Itemid=63 (accessed November 14, 2005).

74. Human Security Centre, *Human Security Report 2005*, 147–48.

75. Human Security Centre, *Human Security Report 2005*, 149–50.

76. Human Security Centre, *Human Security Report 2005*, 153.

77. "The Failed States Index," *Foreign Policy*, July–August 2005, 58, and "The Failed States Index," *Foreign Policy*, May–June 2006, 52.

78. "The Failed States Index," July–August 2005, 57.

Conclusion

1. Keir A. Lieber and Daryl G. Press, "The Rise of U.S. Nuclear Primacy," *Foreign Affairs* 85, no. 2 (March/April 2006): 42–54.

2. Lieber and Press, "The Rise of U.S. Nuclear Primacy," 47, 48.

3. Benjamin Schwarz, "The Perils of Primacy," *Atlantic Monthly*, January/February 2006, 33, 36–37.

4. Thomas C. Schelling, "The Diplomacy of Violence," excerpted in *Essential Readings in World Politics*, ed. Karen A. Mingst and Jack L. Snyder (New York: Norton, 2004), 302.

5. Jonathan Schell, *The Unconquerable World* (New York: Metropolitan Books, 2003), 6–7.

6. Schell, *The Unconquerable World*, 8, emphasis added.

7. Susan Griffin, "Can Imagination Save Us?" *Utne Reader*, July–August 1996, 45.

8. Griffin, "Can Imagination Save Us?" 45.

9. Griffin, "Can Imagination Save Us?" 45.

10. I base this argument for reimagining life stories and human history on Susan Griffin, *A Chorus of Stones: The Private Life of War* (New York: Doubleday, 1992). In this work, Griffin asks whether we are fated to live what has been or whether we are free to imagine a different future.

11. High-level Panel on Threats, Challenges and Change, *A More Secure World: Our Shared Responsibility* (New York: United Nations, 2004), 17, http://www.un.org/secureworld/ (accessed November 14, 2005).

Index

About the Author

Laura Neack is Rejai Professor of Political Science at Miami University, Oxford, Ohio. She is the author of *The New Foreign Policy: US and Comparative Foreign Policy in the 21st Century* and coeditor of *Global Society in Transition* and *Foreign Policy Analysis: Continuity and Change in Its Second Generation* as well as numerous book chapters and articles. Dr. Neack is a former editor of the journal *International Politics* and a member of the editorial boards of the *Bulletin of the Atomic Scientists, Foreign Policy Analysis,* and New Millennium Books in International Studies, Rowman & Littlefield. She lives in Kentucky with her husband, son, and an old pup.